Lecture Notes in Computer Science 1602

Edited by G. Goos, J. Hartmanis and J. van Leeuwen

T0223243

Springer

Berlin
Heidelberg
New York
Barcelona
Hong Kong
London
Milan
Paris
Singapore
Tokyo

Anand Sivasubramaniam   Mario Lauria (Eds.)

Network-Based Parallel Computing

Communication, Architecture, and Applications

Third International Workshop, CANPC '99
Orlando, Florida, USA, January 9th, 1999
Proceedings

Springer

Series Editors

Gerhard Goos, Karlsruhe University, Germany
Juris Hartmanis, Cornell University, NY, USA
Jan van Leeuwen, Utrecht University, The Netherlands

Volume Editors

Anand Sivasubramaniam
The Pennsylvania State University
Department of Computer Science and Engineering
University Park, PA 16802, USA
E-mail: anand@cse.psu.edu

Mario Lauria
University of California, San Diego
Department of Computer Science and Engineering
La Jolla, CA 92093-0114, USA
E-mail: mlauria@cs.ucsd.edu

Cataloging-in-Publication data applied for

Die Deutsche Bibliothek - CIP-Einheitsaufnahme

Network based parallel computing : communication, architecture,
and applications ; third international workshop ; proceedings /
CANPC '99, Orlando, Florida, USA, January 9th, 1999. Anand
Sivasubramaniam ; Mario Lauria (ed.). - Berlin ; Heidelberg ; New
York ; Barcelona ; Hong Kong ; London ; Milan ; Paris ; Singapore ;
Tokyo : Springer, 1999
    (Lecture notes in computer science ; Vol. 1602)
    ISBN 3-540-65915-3

CR Subject Classification (1998): C.2, D.1.3, F.1.2, D.4.4

ISSN 0302-9743
ISBN 3-540-65915-3 Springer-Verlag Berlin Heidelberg New York

© Springer-Verlag Berlin Heidelberg 1999
Printed in Germany

Typesetting: Camera-ready by author
SPIN: 10704826   06/3142 – 5 4 3 2 1 0   Printed on acid-free paper

Preface

Clusters of workstations/PCs connected by off-the-shelf networks have become popular as a platform for cost-effective parallel computing. Hardware and software technological advances have made this network-based parallel computing platform feasible. A large number of research groups from academia and industry are working to enhance the capabilities of such a platform, thereby improving its cost-effectiveness and usability. These developments are facilitating the migration of many existing applications as well as the development of new applications on this platform.

Continuing in the tradition of the two previously successful workshops, this 3rd Workshop on Communication, Architecture and Applications for Network-based Parallel Computing (CANPC'99) has brought together researchers and practitioners working in architecture, system software, applications and performance evaluation to discuss state-of-the-art solutions for network-based parallel computing systems. This workshop has become an excellent forum for timely dissemination of ideas and healthy interaction on topics at the cutting edge in cluster computing technology.

Each submitted paper underwent a rigorous review process, and was assigned to at least 3 reviewers, including at least 2 program committee members. Each paper received at least 2 reviews, most received 3 and some even had 4 reviews. We have selected the 15 best papers for this workshop. We evaluated not only the technical content of each submission, but also the potential for stirring debate and bringing about controversial discussions. This CANPC workshop was sponsored by the IEEE Computer Society, and was held in conjunction with the Fifth International Symposium on High Performance Computer Architecture (HPCA-5), Orlando, Florida. The workshop itself took place on January 9, 1999.

Several people deserve credit for the success of this workshop. Dhabaleshwar Panda and Craig Stunkel, the organizers of the previous two CANPC workshops, deserve special mention for guiding us along the way. We would like to thank all the authors who submitted papers and the program committee for doing an excellent job of helping us select the papers with detailed and timely reviews. Thanks are also due to the HPCA-5 organizing committee (D. Agrawal, J-L. Gaudiot, and B. Lecussan in particular) for their support of this workshop. Ajay Hampapur and Shailabh Nagar did a wonderful job of handling the electronic submission and review process at Penn State. Finally, we would like to thank the editorial staff of Springer-Verlag for agreeing to publish a final version of these proceedings.

February 1999
Anand Sivasubramaniam
Mario Lauria

CANPC '99 Program Committee

Anand Sivasubramaniam, *Pennsylvania State University* (co-chair)
Mario Lauria, *University of California at San Diego* (co-chair)

Henri Bal, *Vrije University, The Netherlands*
Ann Chervenak, *Georgia Tech, USA*
Alok Choudhry, *Northwestern University, USA*
Robert Clay, *Sandia Natl. Laboratory, USA*
Jose Duato, *Universidad Politécnica de Valencia, Spain*
Sandhya Dwarkadas, *University of Rochester, USA*
Tom Fahringer, *University of Vienna, Austria*
Babak Falsafi, *Purdue University, USA*
Liviu Iftode, *Rutgers University, USA*
Vijay Karamcheti, *New York University, USA*
Carl Kesselman, *USC/UCI, USA*
Leonidas Kontothanasis, *DEC CRL, USA*
Ken Mackenzie, *Georgia Tech, USA*
Evangelos Markatos, *ICS, FORTH, Greece*
Ashwini Nanda, *IBM T.J. Watson, USA*
Dhabaleswar Panda, *Ohio State University, USA*
Philip Papadopoulos, *Oak Ridge Natl. Laboratory, USA*
Joel Saltz, *University of Maryland, USA*
Klaus Schauser, *Univ. of California at Santa Barbara, USA*
Craig Stunkel, *IBM T.J. Watson, USA*

Table of Contents

A Parallel Implementation of the Everglades Landscape Fire Model in Networks of Workstations *

Fusen He and Jie Wu

Department of Computer Science and Engineering
Florida Atlantic University
Boca Raton, FL 33431
{fhe, jie}@cse.fau.edu

Abstract. This paper presents a low-communication overhead and high-performance data parallelism implementation of the Everglades Landscape Fire Model (ELFM) in a network of workstations (NOWs). Checkpointing and rollback techniques were used to handle the spread of fire which is a dynamic and irregular component of the model. A synchronous checkpointing mechanism was used in the parallel ELFM code using Message Passing Interface (MPI). The speedup and performance of the parallel program were also studied. Results show that the performance of ELFM using MPI is significantly enhanced by using the checkpointing and rollback mechanisms.

1   Introduction

With the advance of the network technology, network computing has entered into the main stream of solving scientific problems. Network computing is a process whereby a set of workstations connected by a network work collectively to solve a single large problem. As more and more organizations have already had high-speed networks/switches interconnecting many general-purpose workstations, the combined computational resources may exceed the power of a single high-performance computer. This trend has gained sufficient popularity to establish a new parallel processing paradigm: *network of workstations* (NOWs) [1].

A NOWs can be organized as a "cooperative cluster" to perform parallel/distributed computation for a single application. Each individual workstation can be assigned a part of a given problem and these parts can be computed concurrently between synchronization points. When the computation reaches these points, the participating workstations pause in their computation stage and enter a communication stage. During the communication stage, these workstations exchange messages containing the intermediate results needed in the

* This work was supported in part by a grant from South Florida Water Management District (SFWMD).

A.Sivasubramaniam, M.Lauria (Eds.): CANPC'99, LNCS 1602, pp. 1–15, 1999.
© Springer-Verlag Berlin Heidelberg 1999

next computation stage. A local area network (LAN) is a widely used network structure in a NOWs. Since LAN technology was not initially developed for parallel processing, communication overheads among workstations are still quite high [1]. This has placed severe constraints on obtaining high performance in a NOWs. The unacceptable performance of the parallel implementation of the Everglades Landscape Fire Model (ELFM) using the network programming environment *Express* is such an example [3].

The Everglades landscape is a vast freshwater marsh in South Florida and is one of the largest subtropical wetlands in the world. The Everglades has changed dramatically during this century with vast areas being converted to urban and farming land use. These changes may significantly affect efforts to restore natural vegetation and hydroperiods in the remaining Everglades. Fire has been an important ecological process in the Everglades and a primary factor shaping the Everglades vegetation patterns. We cannot fully understand the Everglades without understanding the function of fire. Unfortunately, fire is a difficult process to experimentally manipulate, especially at a landscape level. This is because that the spread of fire is dynamic and probabilistic in nature. Recently, an Everglades Landscape Fire Model (ELFM) [8] was developed to understand fire behavior in Water Conservation Area 2A (WCA 2A) in the Everglades.

Computer simulation can be applied to evaluate impacts and understand ecosystem dynamics. In order to speedup the simulation process, ELFM has been parallelized using Express [3] in several platforms such as UNIX workstations, CM-5 supercomputers, and Macintosh transputers. The parallel ELFM code has also been ported from Express to Message Passing Interface (MPI) [4]. The study in [2] showed that the major reason for the poor performance of the parallel ELFM code is the heavy interprocessor communication overhead. It is also shown that the process synchronization consumes a huge portion of CPU time. In parallel ELFM simulation, when a fire occurs in landscape, it spreads. If a fire occurs near a boundary area of a subdomain simulated by a processor, it will spread to an adjacent subdomain that is simulated by a different processor. In this situation, data exchange is needed to simulate the process of fire spreading that acrosses the boundary of one subdomain to another subdomain. It is required that this data exchange be performed at the same simulation time step through process synchronization.

According to the fire behavior in landscape, the probability of fire occurrence is relatively small. Even when a fire occurs in a subdomain which is simulated by a processor, it may not be necessary to synchronize all the processors unless the fire spreads to other subdomains simulated by other processors. The main purpose of this study is to provide an efficient mechanism to support this type of parallel applications. Specifically, we try to enhance the performance of the parallel ELFM code, with MPI as its parallel programming environment, by using the checkpointing and rollback techniques. The traditional checkpointing and rollback are normally used to address fault tolerance issues [5]; however, we use them solely for the performance enhancement purpose in this study. The interval between two adjacent checkpoints (also called checkpoint interval) is adjustable. The heavy interprocessor communication can be reduced by a proper selection of the frequency of process synchronization among processors.

This paper is organized as follows: Section 2 discusses the current status of ELFM. Section 3 overviews several checkpointing and rollback techniques in a NOWs. An approach aiming to reduce the heavy interprocessor communication and synchronization overhead is discussed in Section 4. Section 5 presents the results of this study and shows the improved performance of the parallel ELFM code using MPI. Section 6 concludes this paper.

2   Everglades Landscape Fire Model (ELFM)

The ELFM code was used to simulate fire in the Water Conservation Area 2A (WCA 2A) in the northern Everglades. The WCA 2A landscape, with an area of 43,281 ha, is a mosaic of sawgrass marshes, sloughs, shrub and tree islands, and invasive cattail communities. The ELFM code simulates fire on a large spatial scale with a fine resolution of 20m × 20m which, in terms of grid cell, comes to 1755 × 1634. ELFM is a spatial model with mostly nearest neighbor interactions except *fire spotting* in which a fire jumps from one area to another. *Fire spreading* is a special case in which a fire jumps (spreads) to its adjacent areas only. We assume that each cell in the landscape is homogeneous, i.e., the same computation and communication structure is used. The ELFM code is portable with its ability to compile and run on UNIX workstations, CM-5 supercomputers, and Macintosh Transputers without any significant changes in code.

In the current ELFM code, the simulation time step of fire spreading and spotting is measured in minutes and the fuel level (a static component in the fire model) is updated every hour. Process synchronization is performed on a daily base. Therefore, the simulation on fire spreading and spotting is computational intensive.

The early version of the parallel implementation of the ELFM code uses a pessimistic approach. Process synchronization through interprocessor communication is performed at each simulation step (either in minutes or in hours) even when there is no fire in the landscape. Since interprocessor communication overhead is still quite high in a NOWs, this pessimistic approach results in a poor performance of the parallel ELFM code [2]. By analyzing the ELFM code, we have found that the occurrence of fire spreading and spotting is rare. Even a fire occurs and spreads in the landscape, it usually affects a small portion of the landscape rather than the entire one. If a fire does not spread to another subdomain simulated by another processor, there is no need to exchange data among processors. We can use *checkpointing* (saving a set of local states) combined with *rollback* (processes rolling back to their checkpoints) to enhance the performance. In this approach, data exchange is treated as message passing among processors in a NOWs. No message passing among processors is needed in regular simulation steps. Checkpointing is made at a regular interval. Rollback is needed only when a fire spreads to its neighboring subdomains to keep simulation data consistent.

3   Checkpointing and Rollback

For parallel processing in a NOWs, a global state is defined as a collection of local states, one from each workstation in the NOWs. In the ELFM, the state is a set of numerical data which determines the evolution of the ecosystem in the Everglades. The checkpointing method [6], [7] is usually used to save the global state. During the normal execution, each processor periodically checkpoints its state by storing its execution state into a stable storage such as a hard disk. Checkpointing is normally used to achieve fault tolerance. In such an application, system states are stored regularly as checkpoints. When a failure causes an inconsistent state, it can rollback to a previous consistent state by simply restoring a prior checkpointing state. This rollback process is also known as rollback recovery.

A *strongly consistent set of checkpoints* consists of a set of local checkpoints such that no information flow takes place between any pair of processors during the interval spanned by the checkpoints. Checkpointing can be either synchronous, asynchronous, or a combination of both. Another choice is whether or not to log messages that a processor sends or receives. For parallel applications such as the ELFM, synchronous checkpointing is the best choice since message exchange must be performed at the same physical process evolution time. Clearly, checkpoints produced by synchronous checkpointing form a strongly consistent set.

During the simulation, when a global state becomes inconsistent, as in the case when a fire acrosses boundary of a subdomain, all the processors need to restore a previous state which is stored in the latest checkpoint. This process is referred to as rollback.

In the parallel ELFM code, we use checkpointing combined with rollback to enhance the performance of the program. To simplify our discussion, we consider an example of a NOWs consists of four workstations and the problem domain of the ELFM is partitioned into four subdomains with each subdomain assigned to a distinct workstation. It can be easily extended to a generalized case with n workstations in a NOWs. We refer to each workstation as a processor. Figure 1 shows a typical rollback process. The horizontal parallel lines represent the simulation time space (rather than the physical time space) in each processor. The vertical dashed lines represent synchronous checkpoints. d is the checkpoint interval, which is a constant in our simulation. The black dot on each horizontal line represents the simulation time step of the corresponding subdomain at the current physical time. Since each processor may have different workloads and different processing speed, if there is no process synchronization, the actual simulation time step at different processors may also be different. This means that processors run asynchronously. The $\times$ sign in Figure 1 means that a fire occurs in processor P_2 and it is going to spread across the boundary of the subdomain (re-

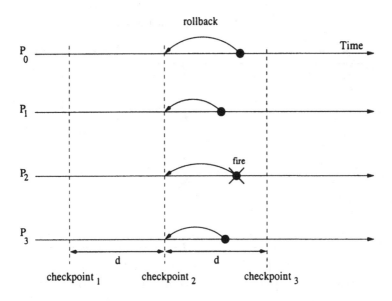

Fig. 1. Rollback process in a 4-workstation NOWs.

ferred to as message exchange). All the processors rollback to their most recent checkpoints. After that, processors resume simulation from that checkpoint but still in the asynchronous mode. When reaching the time that message exchange is needed (the start of fire spreading and spotting simulation), all processors are synchronized and then perform message exchanges. This point is known as the synchronization point. Since a checkpoint is also a synchronization point, if a processor reaches a checkpoint while other processors are still behind this checkpoint, this processor is blocked for other processors to catch up. There exist several optimization methods, like lazy rollback (i.e. rolling back just the subdomains involved). However, they would not improve speedup in our case, since it is based on the completion time of the last processor that finishes its simulation.

The shaded area in Figure 2 represents the period that the processors simulate fire spreading and spotting concurrently in the synchronous mode. After the completion of simulation on fire spreading and spotting, all the processors switch back to the asynchronous mode. The completion point of synchronous computation is logged as an new checkpoint. A checkpoint based on the checkpoint interval d is referred to as a *regular checkpoint*. Checkpoints 1, 2, and 4 in Figure 2 are regular checkpoints. A checkpoint immediately after the completion of synchronous computation is referred to as a *dynamic checkpoint*. Checkpoint 3 in Figure 2 is such an example.

Figure 3 shows the difference between regular and dynamic checkpoints. When multiple message exchanges are needed (because of multiple fires) in a regular checkpoint interval, all the processors rollback to their most recent dynamic checkpoints, restore their consistent states there, and resume simulation

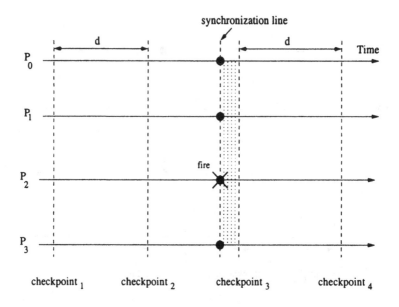

Fig. 2. Synchronize processors before message exchange.

similar to those shown in Figures 1 and 2. If processors rollback to their most recent regular checkpoints, all the processors will enter into an infinite loop between the regular checkpoint 1 and the point of the current fire in Figure 3. By applying dynamic checkpointing, we avoid such infinite loops. Clearly, if there is no fire spreading and spotting during the simulation, only regular checkpoints are used. In the next section, we propose an algorithm based on the checkpointing and rollback mechanisms and show its application in parallelizing the ELFM code using MPI.

4   The Proposed Approach

This section introduces a low-communication overhead model based on checkpointing and rollback mechanisms. We start with a mathematical model for the estimation of simulation time, discuss several relevant collective communication functions provided by MPI, and use checkpointing and rollback to parallelize the ELFM code.

4.1   Mathematical model

The goal of developing a parallel version of a model is to allow a simulation to run in much less time than an equivalent serial version with the same numerical accuracy. By distributing workload over several processors, the amount of time taken to perform computation on an individual processor should be reduced. However, additional interprocessor communication and synchronization

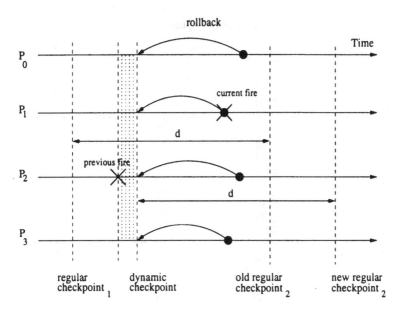

Fig. 3. Rollback with multiple message exchanges between a checkpoint interval.

overheads make the program spend more time on simulation. Whether a parallel algorithm is successful or not depends on a balance between these two factors.

For parallel simulation in a NOWs, each workstation is assigned part of the workload and works independently. We can name this kind of computation as *asynchronous computation*. However, when a neighbor interaction (such as fire spreading and spotting) occurs near the boundary of the subdomain simulated by a workstation, data exchange between workstations must be performed in order to make the result consistent. The corresponding workstations exchange data using the message passing mechanism, and data exchanges always occur at the same simulation time. Therefore, process synchronization is needed. This type of computation can be viewed as *synchronous computation*. The length of synchronous computation varies with time, based on the duration of fire spreading and spotting. Figure 4 illustrates this type of application in a NOWs with four workstations.

Suppose that the probability of message passing among processors is p, the cost for message passing is c, the cost for process synchronization is s, the process synchronization interval (also called checkpoint interval) is d, the number of steps needed for the simulation is N, the total workload of the parallel program is W, the number of processors in the NOWs is n, and the processor processing speed is v_p which is the amount of workload the processor can process per unit time, then the execution time of parallel program can generally be expressed as,

$$T = T_e + T_c + T_s + T_r = max\{\frac{W}{n \times v_p}\} + p \times N \times c + \frac{N \times s}{d} + T_r(p, d, v_p, N)$$

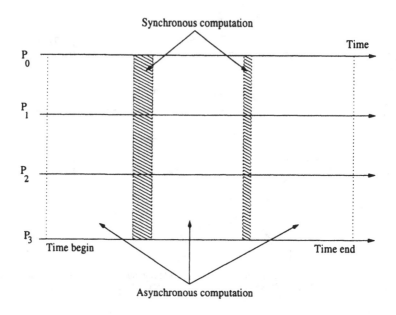

Fig. 4. Synchronous and asynchronous computations of an application in a NOWs with four workstations.

here, T_e is the execution time for effective workload, T_c is the execution time for interprocessor communication, T_s is the execution time for process synchronization, and T_r is the execution time for rollback and is a function of p, d, v_p, and N. If the workload is uniformly distributed, then $W = Nw$. w is the workload for each simulation step. $\frac{w}{n}$ is the workload on each processor per simulation step. Normally, c and s are much larger than $\frac{w}{n}$. When $\frac{w}{n}$ is small, it is obvious that if process synchronization is performed at every simulation step, that is $d = 1$, the interprocessor communication overhead will be large. The longer the checkpoint interval, the less the simulation time. However, if a fire spreads to adjacent subdomains simulated by other processors during the interval, the simulation time will increase. This is because the rollback process will force the system to return to an early state that has already been simulated. Therefore, more simulation time is needed. If we reduce the process synchronization interval, synchronization time will be wasted if there is no fire spreading and spotting to other subdomains at each checkpoint interval. The purpose of this paper is to study how to choose the checkpoint interval to gain a maximum possible speedup.

In the parallel ELFM, in order to keep consistent data, each processor needs to know the maximum number of simulation steps for each burning fire in the entire landscape, not just in the subdomain simulated by the local processor. MPI collective communication functions such as *MPI_Allgather* and *MPI_Allreduce* are used to collect the maximum number of simulation steps in the NOWs. Since the interprocessor communication in the current MPI implementation is sender/receiver based, the above mentioned collective communication functions synchronize the processors while collecting information. There is no need to use *MPI_Barrier*, a synchronization function in MPI, to perform the process synchronization.

The performance of a parallelized program can be referred to as *speedup*, which is the ratio of the computation time for a sequential computation to that of a parallelized version of the same computation. The ideal speedup of a computation is proportional to the number of processors used in the computation.

Since UNIX is a multiuser/multitask operating system, the execution time varies between individual runs. However, the CPU time dose not change. We use the CPU time to measure the performance of the parallel ELFM program. The speedup of the parallel ELFM program can be expressed as follows,

$$Speedup = \frac{Average\ sequential\ CPU\ time}{Average\ parallel\ CPU\ time}$$

4.2   Application of checkpointing and rollback in parallel ELFM

The previous study [2] of the parallel ELFM code indicated that the synchronous computation is needed only when there are data exchanges between adjacent processors. This occurs when a fire acrosses the boundary to another subdomain simulated by a different processor. Checkpointing with rollback is an ideal choice to improve the performance of the parallel ELFM code. Since data exchange among processors is performed at the same simulation time step, synchronous checkpointing will be the best choice. In our simulation, the synchronous checkpointing interval is measured by days.

The interprocessor communication in the current version of MPI is a two-sided communication. It is invoked at both sender and receiver sides. Regular send-receive communication requires matching operations by sender and receiver. This message-passing communication achieves two goals: communication of data from sender to receiver and synchronization of sender with receiver. However, in the parallel ELFM code, when a fire spreads across the boundary of a subdomain, only the processor holds that subdomain has the information needs to be sent. This means that data to be transferred to other processors are available only on one side. The receiving processors do not know in advance when the relevant information will be sent to them. Regular send-receive commands cannot be placed in respective sending processors and receiving processors. It would be better if we can transfer data to receiving processors asynchronously. That is, sending data whenever it is ready at sending processors and reading data when needed at receiving processors. Even the MPI nonblocking operations cannot meet our requirements. We have to use another way to achieve asynchronous one-sided interprocessor communication.

Sun Microsystems' Network File System (NFS) is a convenient choice. NFS is a remote file access mechanism defined in the UNIX operating system. NFS allows applications on one system to access files on a remote system as if it is a local file. In the parallel ELFM code, data need to be sent out can be stored into files in a hard disk. Processors read these files when needed. By doing so, unnecessary interprocessor communications can be avoided, and therefore, it provides an effective means to implement process synchronization.

During the process of simulation, each processor keeps a set of flags that are referred to as rollback flags. This flag set stores the status information of all the processors in a NOWs. Each flag set is stored as a data file in the hard disk and the size of the flag set is equal to the number of processors in the NOWs. These files are referred to as the rollback files. The number of files is also equal to the number of processors. The position of a rollback flag for a specific processor in the file matches the processor id of that processor. Reading and writing operations on files are performed based on rules described in Figure 5: Each processor reads the complete rollback flag set from the file assigned to it. However, processor P_i only updates rollback flags which store the rollback information of this particular processor. That is, the ith position of all the data files in Figure 5. This kind of operations can be expressed as "reads in row and writes in column". The rollback flag set is checked by a processor on a daily base.

Just before a fire spreads across the boundary to another subdomain simulated by a different processor, the processor executing the current simulation sets its rollback flag to true and updates the data files that store the rollback flag set. This processor also creates a starting time file that stores the time at which the fire begins to spread across the boundary to other subdomains simulated by other processors. Then this processor rollbacks to its most recent checkpoint. It restores the saved state of that processor at the checkpoint and resumes simulation from the checkpoint in the asynchronous mode. However, it switches to the synchronous mode once it reaches the starting time, i.e., the start of a fire crossing the boundary.

The operations for those processors which do not initiate the rollback process are described as follows: Processors read the rollback flags from the rollback flag files. If they find that some of these flags are set to true, these processors reset them back to false. They also select the minimum starting time from the corresponding starting time files. These processors then rollback to their most recent checkpoints, restore their states at the checkpoints, and resume the simulation in the asynchronous mode. However, these processors will switch to the synchronous mode once their simulation time reaches the minimum starting time they read from starting time files. All processors will switch back to the asynchronous mode once the current fire stops. The mechanism that resets rollback flags back to false avoids the infinite loop that may occur in the parallel ELFM. If the flag is not set to false, after the synchronous computation, the processors read the rollback flag set again and get an incorrect conclusion that message exchange is needed. In order to keep the stored data up-to-date, the *fsync* function in UNIX should be called each time when data writing is performed. *fsync* forces the UNIX operating system to flush data in memory buffer to a hard disk.

In the proposed approach, the most recent checkpoint of each processor is stored in the main memory of each processor. The size of the data is $3 \times 1755 \times 1634/n$, where n is the number of processors in the NOWs.

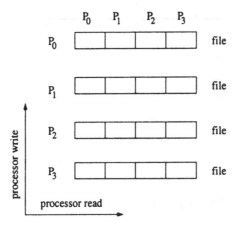

Fig. 5. File operations on rollback information in a 4-workstation NOWs.

5   Results and Discussion

The parallel ELFM using the proposed approach is implemented using MPICH, which is an MPI implementation provided by Argonne National Laboratory. The computing environment is a set of Sun Sparc V workstations running Solaris. These workstations are interconnected by a 10 Mbits Ethernet.

We use speedup to measure the performance of the parallel ELFM using MPI. In order to show the improvements achieved by the proposed approach, we first look at the speedup of the parallel ELFM using Express [3]. The performance analysis in [3] indicated that the four-processor-version of the parallel ELFM was slower than the one processor code by a factor of about four; the four-processor-version took roughly 10 minutes to simulate one day, and the one processor version clocked in at about 2.6 minutes. There is a light variation in these values between individual runs of these models, however, due to network traffic and other factors. The true serial version of the code runs at a rate of roughly 11 years simulation in 90 minutes, or 0.02 minutes per day. Thus, the performance of the parallel ELFM code using Express is unacceptable.

In an early study [2], the parallelized ELFM code using MPI has been run on a NOWs with four workstations. Figure 6 shows the speedup of the parallel ELFM using MPI without using the checkpointing technique. This version of the parallel ELFM code uses a pessimistic approach. That is, processor synchronization is conducted at every simulation time step. The sequential version of the ELFM code also runs on each individual workstation in the NOWs. Compared to the results using Express, the performance of the parallel ELFM code is improved; however, it is still unsatisfactory.

Since workstations are usually used as a multitask and multi-user system, the workload varies from processor to processor and the execution time also varies with different workloads. In order to analyze the performance of the parallel ELFM, we focus on CPU time, rather than elapsed time. A process's CPU time

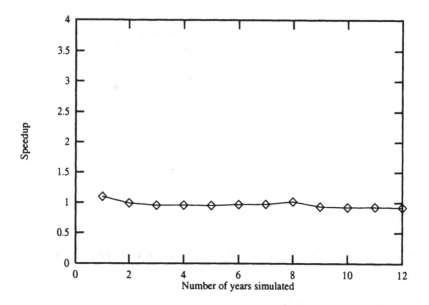

Fig. 6. Speedup of the parallel ELFM using MPI by a pessimistic approach.

is composed of two parts. One is known as *user time*, and the other is *system time*. User time is the CPU time used while executing instructions in the user space of the calling process, and system time is the CPU time used by the system on behalf of the calling process. Most of computational costs are reflected in the user time, almost the entire system time and part of user time are related to interprocessor communication. The processor idle time is the actual elapsed execution time less the user time and the system time. The idle time on each processor is much larger than the user time and the system time.

In order to study the influence of the proposed algorithm on the performance of the parallel ELFM, we first performed a simulation of the parallel ELFM using checkpointing, but without rollback. In this model, processors only synchronize at certain given checkpoints. The parallel ELFM with only checkpointing synchronizes processors at each checkpoint. This is the ideal case of our checkpointing and rollback algorithm. However, if a fire spreads to the adjacent subdomains simulated by other processors in the NOWs, the result will be inaccurate. The numerical accuracy can be enhanced by reducing the checkpoint interval, but it can never reach the level as the one with a rollback process.

The application of checkpointing and rollback techniques in the parallel ELFM significantly reduces the interprocessor communication overhead of the parallel ELFM program. Compared with the execution time of the parallel ELFM without using checkpointing mechanism, the system time is greatly reduced. Figure 7 compares the execution time of the parallel ELFM program with only checkpointing to that with checkpointing and rollback.

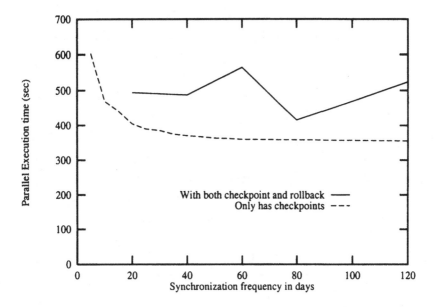

Fig. 7. Program execution time of the parallel ELFM vs. synchronization frequency in a 4-workstation NOWs.

Figure 8 shows the comparison in terms of speedup. A superlinear speedup is obtained for execution only with process synchronization. Compared with the serial ELFM code, the parallel ELFM code uses only a quarter of the memory that the serial version uses. This might be the reason for this superlinear speedup. We can see that the execution time with checkpointing and rollback takes a little longer than the one with only process synchronization. This is because the rollback process takes some extra time. Since the probability of fire spreading and spotting between subdomains is small, the probability of a rollback process invoked is also small. When there is no fire spreading and spotting during the process of simulation, the parallel ELFM with checkpointing and rollback reduces to the parallel ELFM with only process synchronization. When the process synchronization interval varies from 20 to 120 days, the speedup of the parallel ELFM program fluctuates in the range of 2.6 to 3.7. The average speedup is above 3. The performance of the parallel ELFM code is significantly enhanced using the checkpointing and rollback techniques. Figure 9 shows the landscape pattern after a 1-year simulation period. The grey area in the landscape indicates that fires have occurred in that area.

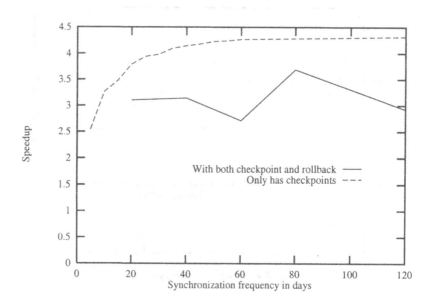

Fig. 8. Speedup of the parallel ELFM vs. synchronization frequency in a 4-workstation NOWs.

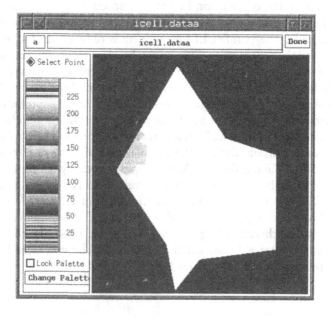

Fig. 9. Landscape pattern of WC2A in the Everglades after a 1-year period simulation by the parallel ELFM code.

6   Conclusion

In this paper, we have reported a study of parallelization of Everglades Landscape Fire Model (ELFM) using Message Passing Interface (MPI). The ELFM code has been successfully ported to MPI. We have studied the checkpointing and rollback techniques and have applied the synchronous checkpointing mechanism combined with the rollback technique to parallelize the ELFM code using MPI. The simulation results show that a better speedup has been obtained compared to the parallel ELFM code without using the checkpointing and rollback techniques. The present study indicates that for certain type of parallel applications such as the ELFM, if the probability of interprocessor communication is small, checkpointing and rollback techniques can enhance their performance.

Our future work will focus on generalization of the parallel computation model with the mixture of a variety of asynchronous and synchronous computations. Parameters that affect the performance of the parallel applications, such as synchronization cost, asynchronous and synchronous computation ratio, load balancing, etc., will be studied both theoretically through numerical analysis and empirically through simulation.

References

1. D. K. Panda, and L. M. Ni. Special Issue on Workstation Clusters and Network-Based Computing. *Journal of Parallel and Distributed Computing*, **40**:1 – 3, 1997.
2. F. He, J. Wu, C. Fitz, F. Sklar, and Y. Wu. A Parallel Implementation of the Everglades Landscape Fire Model Using Message Passing Interface. Report to South Florida Water Management Disctrict, Florida Atlantic University, March 1998.
3. L. T. Wille, and P. J. Ulintz. Parallel Simulations of Fire in the Everglades – Performance Analysis of Alogirthm. Report to South Florida Water Management District, Florida Atlantic University, December 1996.
4. Message Passing Interface Forum. MPI: A Message-Passing Interface Standard, version 1.1. Available via anonymous ftp from *ftp.mcs.anl.gov*, June 1995.
5. P. Jalote. *Fault Tolerance in Distributed Systems*. Prentice Hall, Inc., Englewood Cliffs, NJ, 1994.
6. J. Wu. *Distributed System Design*. CRC Press, Boca Raton, FL, 1998.
7. Y.-M. Wang, Y. Huang, K.-P. Vo, P. Y. Chuang, and C. Kintala. Checkpointing and Its Applications. In *Proceedings of the 25th Int'l Symp. on Fault-Tolerant Computing*, pages 22–30, 1995.
8. Y. Wu, F. H. Sklar, K. Gopu, and K. Rutchey. Fire Simulations in the Everglades Landscape Using Parallel Programming. *Ecological Modelling*, **93**:113–124, 1996.

Adaptation Models for
Network-Aware Distributed Computations *

Peter Steenkiste

School of Computer Science, Carnegie Mellon University
Pittsburgh, PA 15213, USA

Abstract. Network-aware applications actively adapt to the level of service they receive from the network. This allows the application to execute well over a diverse set of networks and under a wide range of network conditions. However, network diversity and dynamic network conditions make the development of network-aware applications a difficult task, since the developer has to be an expert in both the application domain and networking. In this paper we look at a number of network-aware applications and identify three adaptation strategies that have proven to be effective. These strategies can be viewed as adapation models that capture the essential structure of the adaptation process. Similar to the use of programming models in parallel and distributed computing, adaptation models can be used to guide the development of other network-aware applications and they can also form the basis for programming support, e.g. middleware, that supports the development of network-aware applications. In this paper we describe the three adaptation models, compare their features and applicability, and briefly discuss how these models impact the design of middleware that supports network-aware applications.

1 Introduction

Clusters of PCs or workstations have become a widely used architecture for compute-intensive applications because of their attractive price-performance ratio. Clusters consist of a collection of high-performance PCs or workstations connected by a commodity network. Clusters can be dedicated, i.e. they sit in a machine room and are used exclusively for high-performance computing, or they can be distributed and shared, i.e. the machines are scattered in offices, labs, and machine rooms and are used for a diverse set of tasks. While both types of clusters may have similar hardware characteristics, distributed clusters are a more challenging environment, both because they typically are more heterogeneous and exhibit a higher degree of resource sharing which results in a continuously changing environment. This is especially true for the network, which is by nature a shared resource, and where different technologies can have very different performance characteristics (e.g. ATM versus 10 Mbs Ethernet). This presents

---

* This research was supported by the Advanced Research Projects Agency/ITO under contract N66001-96-C-8528.

A.Sivasubramaniam, M.Lauria (Eds.): CANPC'99, LNCS 1602, pp. 16–31, 1999.

a challenge to applications since the level of service they can expect from the network is unpredictable. It can easily change by as much as three orders of magnitude from one invocation to the next, and by a smaller factor during a particular invocation. This means that communication operations can take anywhere from milliseconds to seconds depending on the environment and current network conditions.

For some applications, e.g. *telnet*, the only possible response to variable network conditions is to speed up or slow down proportionally with the level of network service [6]. This type of "elastic" application can use protocols such as TCP [11] to adapt to network conditions. However, more complex applications often have a richer set of options for adapting to the network. A simple example is a video streaming application. Changes in available network bandwidth should not result in simply sending the same video data at a slower or faster rate. Instead, the video source can respond by changing the video frame size or the video frame rate. Similarly, in a congested network, a distributed computation may want to reduce the number of nodes it uses instead of seeing its communication time go up significantly. We call applications that *actively* adapt to the level of service they receive from the network network-aware applications.

Developing network-aware applications is difficult because the developer must have expertise in both the application domain and networking. Libraries and middleware could potentially help applications adapt to network conditions, but in the network-aware applications that exist today, the adaptation process is mostly ad hoc and highly application-specific, complicating the design of broadly applicable programming support. As a first step towards developing such middleware, we have to better understand the fundamental adaptation processes. In this paper we argue that, while the details of the adaptation algorithms may differ, existing adaptive applications mostly use one of a small number of "good" adaptation strategies. The main contribution of this paper is that we identify three such "adaptation models" that characterize widely applicable adaptation strategies.

The rest of this paper is organized as follows. We first give some examples of network-aware applications and describe the general structure of such applications (Section 2). In Sections 3 through 5 we present three different adaptation models. We then discuss the relative advantages and disadvantages of the models, and their impact on the design of middleware (Section 6). We conclude with related work and a summary.

2   Network-aware applications

We describe the general structure of network-aware applications using examples.

2.1   Examples

Applications can adapt to network conditions in a variety of ways. A first possibility is that the application changes how much data it sends. Data volume can for example be reduced by reducing the frame size of a video stream [10], or by dropping the pictures from a document (plain text instead of postscript, Web pages with or without images). Other ways of modifying how much data is sent is to apply (lossless) compression; this approach trades compute resources for communication resources. Another possibility is to use domain-specific adaptation methods. For example, when rendering an image on a remote node, the source can transmit the rendered image or rendering commands, depending on how much network bandwidth and computational resources are available.

The options for adaptation for distribution computing applications are typically much more restricted than the above examples may suggest. The reason is that distributed computations typically want reliable data transfers so it is not possible to drop data, while options such as compression are often too expensive. However, adaptation is often still possible. For example, applications can change what nodes or how many nodes they use. Examples are deciding to perform certain tasks locally or remotely [13], or determining the optimal number of nodes to use for a distributed computation [17, 18].

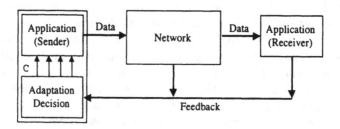

Fig. 1. The adaptation process

2.2   The adaptation process

The goal of network-aware adaptation is to optimize application performance, given a certain level of service from the network. This process is illustrated for a simple point-to-point application in Figure 1:

- A change in the network is observed at a measurement point, e.g. a switch in the network or an application task running on the destination node. The measurement point must measure the disturbance with a certain accuracy, translate it in information that is of use to the application, and send the information to the source or sources.
- The application makes a decision on adaptation, and waits until it can adapt. Depending on the application this may be short, e.g. the next frame of a video transfer, or long, e.g. the application has to reach a synchronization point.
- The application adapts. Depending on the application this can happen quickly, e.g. change a parameter in a device, or it can be an expensive and slow process, e.g. large amounts of state have to be moved between nodes.

Figure 1 shows two different feedback mechanisms. With *implicit* feedback, the application monitors the end-to-end performance of its own traffic, and uses these observations to derive information about the status of the network, e.g. dropped packets can be viewed as a sign of congestion by both protocols (TCP [11]) and applications (vic [10]) or the throughput for a recent data transfer can be used as an estimate for the throughput of future transfers. With *explicit* feedback, the network provides explicit information about the status of the network to endpoints. While explicit feedback is used in some communication protocols [1,5], it is not very common because of concerns that it may add too much complexity to the network. However, there is a growing recognition that explicit feedback can simplify the development of network-aware applications [7,12].

The effectiveness of adaptation will depend on several features of the feedback loop in Figure 1. A first factor is the delay in the feedback loop: the shorter the delay, the better the application will be able to track changes in the network. The second factor is the accuracy of the feedback information. Clearly inaccurate information can degrade performance by having the application adapt needlessly, or by having the application select an incorrect operating point. A final factor is less obvious but quite significant in practice. There often is a cost associated with adaptation, which means that improving efficiency by adapting may not always result in a performance gain. To determine whether adaptation will pay off, applications have to compare the cost of adaptation with the potential benefits. The cost of adaptation and the performance gain can typically be estimated based on information about the current and "optimal" state. The performance benefit is typically proportional to time, so the condition for adaptation becomes

$$AdaptationCost < Benefit = Gain \times Duration$$

Unfortunately, the duration of the benefit is typically unknown since it depends on future conditions, e.g. network conditions could change immediately after the adaptation operation. We conclude that in a best effort environment there is no guarantee that adaptation will pay off.

2.3   Adaptation models

Whether adaptation is effective depends strongly on what adaptation decisions the application makes, i.e. the nature of the application decision module in Figure 1. While the specific adaptation algorithms may be application-specific, we argue that only a small number of mechanisms are used by today's applications. We will call these "adaptation models", similar to the programming models used in parallel and distributed computing. Identifying these models is a first step towards providing programming support for adaptation. We identify three such models in the next three sections.

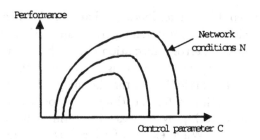

Fig. 2. Adaptation decision process

3 Model-based adaptation

In the first adaptation model, the application has a model of its performance as a function of the various parameters characterizing the runtime environment, e.g. network latency, ... Given information on the runtime environment, the application uses the model to select the settings for the control parameters that will give the best performance. We will call this *model-based adaptation*. We elaborate on the methodology and provide some examples.

3.1 The adaptation decision

In the simplest case, the adaptation decision module has to select a single control parameter (e.g. increasing or decreasing frame rate), and there is a simple relationship both between the control parameter and application performance (e.g. higher rate is better) and between the control parameter and the required network service (e.g. higher frame rates require more bandwidth) (Figure 2). In general, multiple control parameters have to be selected, and the relationship between application performance, control parameters, and network service is complex.

The adaptation decision process can be captured in a few simple formulas. The application performance P is a function p of the network conditions N and the values of a set of control parameters C:

$$P = p(N, C)$$

The challenge is to find the values for C that maximize P, given the network conditions N.

In reality, neither the network conditions nor the dependencies between P, N, and C are known and understood completely accurately. The following formulation of the adaptation problem captures this uncertainty: given a measured set of conditions $N_{measured}$ and a performance model p_{model} of the application, determine the values C_{opt} for the control parameters that maximize performance, i.e. $p_{model}(N_{measured}, C_{opt})$ is maximized. C_{opt} is a function of $N_{measured}$:

$$C_{opt} = c_{model}(N_{measured})$$

where c_{model} is based on p_{model}.

In model-based adaptation, the function p_{model} is an explicit formula that is derived by the application designer. c_{model} is calculated by setting the derivative of p_{model} with respect to C equal to zero, and by solving for C. This formula for C_{opt} is then used by the adaptation decision module at runtime to calculate the "optimal" values for the control parameters, based on the measured network conditions. Information about network conditions can be collected by the application by running a built in set of benchmarks, or from the network by querying a special interface [7, 13].

In reality using C_{opt} will of course not result in optimal performance in any formal sense. The systems involved are too complex to be modeled completely accurately, so p_{model} is only a rough approximation of reality p_{real}. Similarly, noise, delay, and errors will cause $N_{measured}$ to be only an approximation of the real network conditions N_{real}. Ideally, these effects will have little impact on performance, i.e.

$$P = p_{real}(N_{real}, c_{model}(N_{measured}))$$

is high and is not very sensitive to errors in $N_{measured}$ and c_{model} (i.e. p_{model}).

The above equation also shows that adaptation is in general application specific since both c and p are application specific. However, some components of the implementation are application independent, so it may be feasible to develop adaptation libraries that can be customized by the application. Collecting network status information or a callback mechanism that notifies the application of significant changes in network conditions are examples of support that would simplify the task of application developers [7].

3.2   Examples

Most examples of model-based adaptation are in applications that make a simple decision based on a very simple application model. Examples include selecting the best file server or Web server for replicated data (highest bandwidth wins) [4], or a decision on whether a computation should be off-loaded (available bandwidth has to be above some threshold) [14].

A more complex application that uses model-based adaptation is described in [17]. It is a Successive Over Relaxation (SOR) application that has been distributed through pipelining (Figure 3). The input matrix is distributed in block-column fashion across the nodes, with a one-column overlap between adjacent blocks. The computation is pipelined: each node processes G rows before it passes on new values for the shared column to its right neighbor and receives values from its left neighbor. Given a data size and a number of nodes, the performance is primarily determined by the grain size G. G determines how much computation is performed between communication steps and its optimal value depends on the performance of the network: as network performance increases, smaller grain sizes become more effective since they reduce the pipeline startup and drain cost.

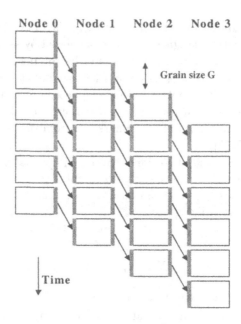

Fig. 3. Pipelined SOR

The application was made network-aware by building a model that represents the execution time as a function of the grain size, the floating point performance of the nodes, and the performance of the network, modeled as a per-messages cost and a per-byte cost (see [17] for details). From this model one can derive the grain size that results in the minimal execution time, as described above. The optimal grain size is a function of the network and host parameters, which are estimated by having the application execute small built-in benchmarks at start up. Figure 4 illustrates how adaptation works. It shows how the efficiency (inverse of the execution time) changes with grain size. The graph includes curves representing measured efficiencies on a workstation cluster, estimated efficiencies based on the application model and measurements of communication parameters, and an upperbound on efficiency (communication cost is zero). The vertical line represents the grain size that is selected by model-based adaptation. We observe that it achieves close to the actual best efficiency. We found similar results for networks with different performance characteristics [17, 16].

Adaptation in SOR has two interesting features that seem to be quite common in distributed computations. First, adaptation is expensive, both because the nodes have to synchronize and because they have to reshuffle a lot of application data. This overhead limits the frequency of adaptation. Second, adaptation tradeoffs are asymmetric. For the SOR application, it is better to underestimate network performance than to overestimate it.

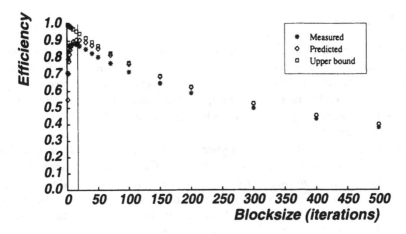

Fig. 4. Model-based adaptation in SOR

3.3 Discussion

Model-based has the advantage that it can potentially quickly zoom in on the right control parameter values. It can be used at startup time or at runtime to periodically reevaluate control parameters during execution. While we have only limited experience, a disadvantage of this approach seems to be its robustness: the performance is very sensitive to both the accuracy of the network status information and the correctness of the application model. Building an accurate model is clearly difficult for complex applications, although one can argue that some form of model will be needed for any method of adaptation. Getting reliable estimates for the system parameters also turned out to be difficult. One of the reasons is that appropriate estimates for system parameters are often application specific, e.g. applications can have widely different floating point performance, and network throughput may depend on features such as message size and protocols used. The SOR application deals with this issue by using segments of the application to estimate the system parameters. While this give more accurate estimates for the system parameters, it complicates application development.

4   Performance-based adaptation

In a second model, the application continuously monitors its own performance and it changes its control parameters based on these observations. The control parameters are typically updated incrementally, because there is not enough information available to explicitly calculate the parameters. While model-based adaptation is based on explicit network information, performance-based adaptation collects and uses information about the network implicitly.

4.1 Examples

Congestion control in the widely used TCP transport protocol can be viewed as an example of performance-based adaptation. It optimizes performance by maximizing the rate at which it can send data reliably. If the receiver reports data loss, the sender reduces its rate, on the assumption that the data loss was due to network congestion, and reducing the rate will thus result in (more) reliable transmission.

The prototypical example of application-level network-aware adaptation is adaptive video streaming [19, 8, 9]. Similar to TCP, the video streaming applications try to maximize their throughput, while trying to eliminate or minimize data loss. As with TCP, the receiver provides feedback to the sender about packet loss, but in this case the sender will changes its transmission rate by changing the frame rate or frame size of the video stream.

4.2 Discussion

The advantage of performance-based adaptation is its simplicity, at least for applications that have a simple definition of "performance" that depends in a straightforward manner on network performance. We are not aware of any complex applications that fit this model. This approach does not need a detailed model or accurate measurements of system parameters, and as a result, it is likely to be fairly robust. A disadvantage is that this method is purely reactive, i.e. the application adapts after performance has degraded. Moreover, changes will typically be incremental because the application only has access to minimal information on network conditions. Incremental adaptation can be expensive if there is a non-trivial cost associated with adaptation. Finally, performance-based adaptation typically supports only "one-way" adaptation: the application can observe that it is overloading the network (observes poor performance) but it cannot easily detect whether the network can support a higher load. A solution is to periodically probe the network by increasing the load (e.g. increasing the frame rate), using the effect on performance (e.g. presence or lack of packet loss) to determine whether the network can handle it. Probing can be difficult to manage and introduces extra overhead.

5 Feature-based adaptation

In a third model, the application monitors some feature of the application and uses that to adapt. This is possible if the feature has a known "good value" that correspond to a good application state, and deviations can be translated into changes of the control parameters. We will call this *feature-based adaptation*. This can be viewed as a generalization of the previous model, in the sense that performance is an application feature. However, by picking the feature carefully, it might be possible to achieve more desirable adaptation behavior. Improvements are possible in two areas. First, it might be possible to adapt before there has been a significant loss in performance, i.e. adaptation may be preventive instead of reactive. Second, adaptation is possibly symmetric, i.e. adaptation can increase and reduce the load on the network without having to periodically probe for additional resources.

5.1 Example

An example of feature-based adaptation in transport protocols is TCP Vegas [3]. TCP Vegas continuously monitors the roundtrip time, and compares it with a roundtrip time estimate that is based on a model of the roundtrip time as a function of throughput. By comparing the measured and estimated roundtrip time, the sender can determine how its rate compares with the available rate on the bottleneck link, so it can adapt without having to wait for packet loss.

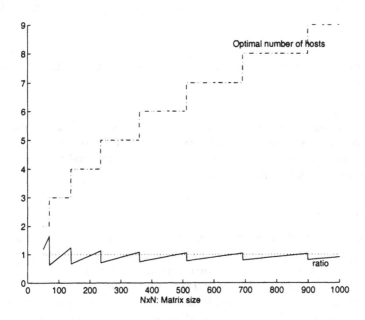

Fig. 5. Optimal communication to computation ratio in MM

An example of application-level feature-based adaptation is described in [18]. The problem addressed is determining the optimal number of nodes for a distributed matrix multiply. A first solution is to use model-based adaptation. While model-based adaptation works, it is very sensitive to the measurements of the system parameters, as we already observed for the SOR application. An alternative is to use feature-based adaptation, using the communication to computation ratio as the feature being monitored. As described in [18], for a certain class of parallel applications, this ratio is a known constant when the optimal number of nodes is used, independent from the network conditions. For the distributed matrix multiply, the communication to computation ratio is one when the optimal number of nodes is used. This is illustrated in Figure 5. So by monitoring this ratio, and increasing (decreasing) the number of nodes if the ratio is higher (lower), one can stay in a good operating point.

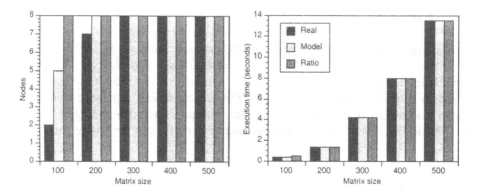

Fig. 6. Performance for the network-aware MM: number of nodes (left) and execution time (right)

Figure 6 compares the performance of both model-based and feature-based adaptation with the experimentally-determined best performance. We observe that both mechanisms do a good job estimating the optimal number of nodes, and the execution times are close to optimal.

5.2 Discussion

Feature-based adaptation shares many of the characteristics of performance-based adaptation. One difference is that it does not require probing. It is however not clear how easily this approach generalizes: it is difficult to identify an application feature that reliably indicates how well the application's current use of the network fits the network conditions. Note also that neither performance-based nor feature-based adaptation work at all for adaptation at startup, since the methods are based on feedback from a running application.

6   Applicability of the adaptation models

We can highlight the differences between the three models by presenting them as simple control loops, as is shown in Figure 7. Performance-based adaptation has the simplest loop (Figure 7(a)): the receiver provides feedback on the observed performance and the adaptation module in the sender uses this information to change the setting of the control parameters. This is only possible if the appropriate control parameters can be derived directly from the observed performance.

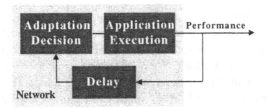

(a) Performance-based adaptation

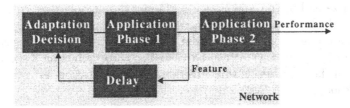

(b) Feature-based adaptation

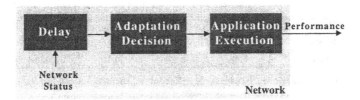

(c) Model-based adaptation based on explicit network information

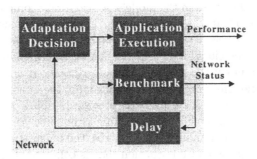

(d) Model-based adaptation based on application benchmark

Fig. 7. Adaptation represented as control loop

Feature-based adaptation has a very similar structure (Figure 7(b)), except that part of the application is outside of the control loop. The main impact of this change is on robustness: if the relationship between the feature that drives adaptation and performance is not correctly understood, the system will adapt to the wrong operating point. However, selecting an appropriate feature may simplify adaptation compared with performance-based adaptation.

Figure 7(c) shows the control loop for model-based adaptation based on information provided by the network. We note that there is no closed-loop feedback: application-level adaptation is done open loop. This means that both the adaptation decision process (based on an application model) and the measurements have to be fairly accurate, otherwise the adaptation process can easily go astray. Figure 7(d) shows model-based adaptation based on information collected by the application. This is still an open loop process: the benchmark typically does not characterize end-to-end application performance but only tries to characterize the network. However, the benchmark can be customized by the application, increasing the level of confidence that appropriate data is being collected.

Figure 7(a), (b), and (d) can be viewed as three points on a spectrum. The variable in the spectrum is what fraction of the application is "covered" by the feedback loop.

	Robustness adaptation	Timeliness information	Nature of adaptation	Locality information
Performance	high	low	incremental	local
Feature	medium	medium	incremental	local
Model	low	high	jump	broader

Table 1. Features of different adaptation models

Based on these differences in the models, we can make some high-level observations about the applicability of the models. Table 1 lists some important features of each of the models. Robustness characterizes what fraction of the application is covered by the closed loop feedback, as we described above. Timeliness characterizes how quickly the application can learn about changes in network conditions. In general, the simpler the feedback loop, the quicker it can respond. This means that benchmarks are likely to provide feedback more quickly than complete applications, although benchmarking is not likely to be a continuous activity. Feedback based on monitoring may give the quickest response. The last two features affect the type of information that is collected. Performance-based and feature-based adaptation provide "relative" information that in general only allows incremental adaptation. Model-based adaptation uses absolute information that in principle should allow the application to move directly into an optimal operating point. The information obtained as part of performance-based and feature-based adaptation is also limited in scope (i.e. whatever network information is observable through the performance or feature) and restricted to the part of the network used by the application. In contrast, model-based adaptation can use a broader set of information.

We conclude that all the models have both desirable and undesirable features, and which model is most appropriate will depend on the application and the environment. The features in Table 1 provides some guidance. Application may benefit from using a combination of models. Model-based adaptation can be used to select an appropriate operating region from a potentially very large space of operating options that cover both network topology and application set up; this can be done at startup and periodically throughout execution. More frequent incremental runtime adaptation can be based on the performance or feature-based models.

7   Middleware support for network-aware applications

We discuss a number of ways in which middleware can support network-aware applications.

7.1   Network information

The simplest way in which middleware can help network-aware applications is to provide information about the network conditions. This is especially true for applications that use model-based adaptation since they rely critically on precise low-level network information. If the application can simply query the network to find out about network properties such as application-level throughput and latency, then it does not have to do its own benchmarking. This should simplify code development significantly, and will also reduce the level of network expertise needed by the application developer since network benchmarking is a difficult task. Applications will often be interested in different types of information, e.g. delay versus bandwidth or behavior on different time scales, so network should provide access to a rich set of information.

Another feature of adaptation that should be considered when developing middleware is that adaptation tradeoffs are often asymmetric, so the application would like to know the accuracy of the information. For example if the network information is highly variable, the SOR application would lower its estimate of the available network bandwidth (more conservative), while it might be more optimistic if the bandwidth estimate is known to be accurate.

The Remos interface [7, 12] developed at CMU is a first attempt at defining the application programming interface for such a middleware layer. It has been implemented and is being evaluated.

7.2   Application structure

Making an application network-aware requires profound changes in the application structure. An interesting approach to simplifying this task [2] is to use frameworks to capture the control flow of the adaptation process. Application can fill in the application-specific components. Figure 7 shows graphically some possible structures for simple point-to-point applications. Clearly, a richer set of options for adaptation exists for multi-party applications with more than two end-points. The middleware layer could for example coordinate the movement of data (state) that has to happen as part of the adaptation, or it can provide the necessary synchronization between the nodes involved in adaptation. Much more work is needed in this area.

7.3 Service selection

An important issue for any network-aware application is the predictability of network conditions. If network conditions are very unpredictable, effective adaptation will be difficult, if not impossible (Section 4). This suggests that we should build networks that have more predictable performance. The networking community is addressing this problem by implementing networks with multiple classes of service [6]. Besides best effort service, which is what today's networks support, networks can for example support guaranteed service [15], which offers highly predictable service, albeit at a higher cost. Another example is controlled load service [20], which maintains a minimum level of service for applications by limiting the number of users in the network. So far, there is little experience in using these service classes.

8 Conclusion

Network-aware applications actively adapt to the level of service they receive from the network. In this paper we take a first step towards providing structured support for network-aware applications by identifying three adaptation models that capture the essential properties of effective adaptation. Model-based adaptation uses a performance model of the application and measurements of the network conditions to determine the optimal operating point for the application. Performance-based adaptation is based on monitoring application performance and adapting if the performance drops. Feature-based adaptation is a generalization of performance-based adaptation: adaptation is based on an application feature other than performance. These adaptation models have very different properties, but they each have some advantages that make them attractive to some applications.

References

1. ATM Forum Traffic Management Specification Version 4.0, October 1995. ATM Forum/95-0013R8.
2. J. Bolliger and Thomas Gross. A Framework-based Approach to the Development of Network-aware Applications. *IEEE Transactions on Software Engineering*, 24(5):376–390, May 1998.
3. L. S. Brakmo, S. W. O'Mally, and L. L. Peterson. TCP Vegas: New Techniques for Congestion Detection and Avoidance. In *Proceedings of ACM SIGCOMM'94*, London, UK, August 1994.
4. Robert Carter and Mark Crovella. Server selection using dynamic path characterization. In *IEEE INFOCOM'97*, volume 3, pages 8C–4, Kobe, Japan, April 1997. IEEE.

5. Prashant Chandra, Allan Fisher, Corey Kosak, and Peter Steenkiste. Experimental evaluation of atm flow control schemes. In *IEEE INFOCOM'97*, pages 1326–1334, Kobe, Japan, April 1996. IEEE.

6. Dave Clark, S. Shenker, and L. Zhang. Supporting real-time applications in an integrated services packet network: Architecture and mechanisms. In *Proceedings of the SIGCOMM '92 Symposium on Communications Architectures and Protocols*, pages 14–26, Baltimore, August 1992. ACM.

7. Tony DeWitt, Thomas Gross, Bruce Lowekamp, Nancy Miller, Peter Steenkiste, and Jaspal Subhlok. ReMoS: A Resource Monitoring System for Network Aware Applications. Technical Report CMU-CS-97-194, Carnegie Mellon University, December 1997.

8. R. Frederick.   Network video (nv), 1993.   Software available via ftp://ftp.parc.xerox.com/net-research.

9. J. Inouye, S. Cen, C. Pu, and J. Walpole. System support for mobile multimedia applications. In *Proceedings of the 7th International Workshop on Network and Operating System Support for Digital Audio and Video*, pages 143–154, St. Louis, May 1997.

10. V. Jacobson and S. McCanne.   Vic, 1995.   Software available via ftp://ftp.ee.lbl.gov/conferencing/vic.

11. Van Jacobson. Congestion Avoidance and Control. In *Proceedings of the SIG-COMM '88 Symposium on Communications Architectures and Protocols*, pages 314–329. ACM, August 1988.

12. Bruce Lowekamp, Nancy Miller, Dean Sutherland, Thomas Gross, Peter Steenkiste, and Jaspal Subhlok. A Resource Query Interface for Network-aware applications. In *7th IEEE Symposium on High-Performance Distributed Computing*. IEEE, July 1997.

13. Brian Noble, M. Price, and M. Satyanarayanan. A Programming Interface for Application-Aware Adaptation in Mobile Computing. *Computing Systems*, 8, Fall 1995.

14. Brian Noble, M. Satyanarayanan, Dushyanth Narayanan, James Tilton, Jason Flinn, and Kevin Walker. Agile application-aware adaptation for mobility. In *Proceedings of the Sixteenth Symposium on Operating System Principles*, pages 276–287, October 1997.

15. S. Shenker, C. Partridge, and R. Guerin. Specification of guaranteed quality of service, September 1997. IETF RFC 2212.

16. Bruce Siegell. *Automatic Generation of Parallel Programs with Dynamic Load Balancing for a Network of Workstations*. PhD thesis, Department of Computer and Electrical Engineering, Carnegie Mellon University, 1995. Also appeared as technical report CMU-CS-95-168.

17. Bruce Siegell and Peter Steenkiste. Automatic selection of load balancing parameters using compile-time and run-time information. *Concurrency - Practice and Experience*, 9(3):275–317, 1996.

18. Hongsuda Tangmunarunkit and Peter Steenkiste. Network-aware distributed computing: A case study. In *Second Workshop on Runtime Systems for Parallel Programming (RTSPP)*, Orlando, March 1998. IEEE. Springer-Verlag.

19. Hideyuki Tokuda, Yoshito Tobe, Stephen Chou, and Jose Moura. Continuous Media Communication with Dynamic QOS Control Using ARTS with an FDDI Network. In *Proceedings of the SIGCOMM '92 Symposium on Communications Architectures and Protocols*, pages 88–98, Baltimore, August 1992. ACM.

20. J. Wroclawski. Specification of the Controlled-Load Network Element Service, September 1997. IETF RFC 2211.

Prototyping Execution Models for HTMT Petaflop Machine in Java

Lilia Yerosheva (Suslov) and Peter M. Kogge

384 Fitzpatrick Hall, CSE, University of Notre Dame
Notre Dame, IN 46556, USA
{lsuslov,kogge}@cse.nd.edu

Abstract. The Hybrid Technology MultiThreaded (HTMT) project is an attempt to design a machine with radically new hardware technologies that will scale to a petaflop by the 2004 time frame. These technologies range from multi-hundred GHz CPUs built from superconductive RSFQ devices through active optical networks and 3D holographic memories to Processing-In-Memory (PIM) for active memories. The resulting architecture resembles a three level hierarchy of "networks of processing nodes" of different technologies and functionality. All this new technology, however, has a huge and unknown effect on software execution models for applications. This paper discusses several potential HTMT models and how they can be prototyped and demonstrated using a combination of multithreaded Java and LAN-connected workstations.

1 Introduction

The ASCI program [1], [2] represents the state of art of high performance computers with several thousand microprocessors where the total performance peaks in the teraflop range (10^{12} flops/sec). The problem with this and similar systems is the latency in memory access and in communication between nodes. As a result, software development for ASCI is challenging. If we look to the next level of performance, petaflops (10^{15} flops/sec), projections of machines using conventional CMOS technology indicate that even by the 2010 era, over a million 1GHz CPUs will be needed in a complex interconnection scheme.

The HTMT project [3] is a solution to the hardware problem in a way that, hopefully, simplifies the software problem. Its focus lies in an attempt to design a machine with radically new hardware technologies that will scale to a petaflop by the 2004 or earlier. Its goal is to have a working machine 5 to 10 years earlier than such performance levels might be possible with conventional CMOS.

In terms of effects on a software model, HTMT introduces multithreading in parallel CPUs, extremely deep memory hierarchies, and active memories to counteract the resulting extreme latencies.

This paper attempts to define several high-level concurrent programming models that match different key points of the HTMT architecture, and develop a framework for constructing reasonable prototypes today that can be used for early software demonstrations, with Java for implementation.

A.Sivasubramaniam, M.Lauria (Eds.): CANPC'99, LNCS 1602, pp. 32–46, 1999.

The rest of this paper is organized as follows. Section 2 provides an overview of the HTMT project. Section 3 discusses software models that potentially may fit the HTMT model. In Section 4 different schemes are suggested for simulated HTMT execution models. Section 5 outlines the opportunities for concurrent programming that can be expressed in Java. Section 6 discusses the HTMT programming prototype. In Section 7 prototype demonstrations are considered and implementation is discussed. In Section 8 we draw some conclusions from the discussion and show extension to this work for the future.

2   HTMT: the ultimate "network" computer

The goals of the current HTMT project [4] are threefold.

First, it will explore and characterize a synthesis of exotic technologies, innovative architecture, and aggressive latency management techniques in a way that could dramatically accelerate availability of near Petaflops scale computing systems. Second, it will develop component, architecture, and design data to minimize future design risk and establish confidence in the approach. Third, it will determine the feasibility and effectiveness of the HTMT strategy for executing real world computations at revolutionary performance level. A successful HTMT program will lay the groundwork for prototypes in the 2004 time frame that achieve near petaflops level performance, with much less than million-way physical parallelism.

2.1   HTMT hardware architecture

HTMT is a shared memory nonuniform memory access (NUMA) architecture. There are multiple levels to the memory hierarchy with the lowest level physically partitioned to individual processors. All the processors share the same address space; however, the time it takes processors to access different memory locations at different levels varies greatly.

The HTMT architecture consists of the following components (Fig. 1):

- 4096 multithreaded CPUs, called SPELLs, constructed from RSFQ (Rapid Single Flux Quantum) superconducting devices with special cache like local memories called Cryo RAM (CRAM), cooled in a cryostat to 4K, and capable of clock rates in excess of 100 GHz. These memories are connected to the next level through an RSFQ-implemented communication network (CNet),
- very high bandwidth optical networks with 10 Gbps channels to interconnect components in the cryostat with external components,
- "smart" SRAM and DRAM memories based on PIM technologies on either side of the optical network,
- 3D holographic memories for extremely dense and fast on-line backing storage that capable of storing Petabytes or more.

The smart memories use the Processing-In-Memory (PIM) technology to combine on a single CMOS memory chip both dense logic and dense memory [3], [5].

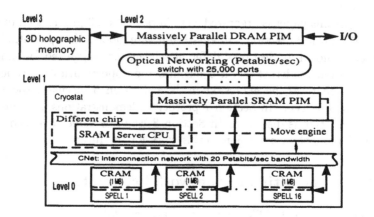

Fig. 1. HTMT architecture

This simple trick has a profound impact on computer architecture: if the logic is used to construct CPU-like devices, these CPUs are much closer electrically to the memory arrays containing instructions and data. Furthermore, the number of bits available from each access can be literally orders of magnitude greater than what one can transfer in a single cycle from today's conventional memory chips to today's conventional (and separate) CPU chip or cache system. Together, this greatly reduces memory latency and greatly increases memory bandwidth - the twin demons of modern computer design. One example of the kind of processing logic that will be implemented in the PIMs are Move engines which allow automatic data transfer between different memory areas over the networks.

As an example of the kind of latencies that show up in HTMT, if the SPELLs run at 100 GHz, the latency to the CRAMs is on the order of 10's of cycles, to SRAM is 100s' of cycles, 10,000 to 100,000 cycles to DRAM, and millions of cycles to 3D memories. Note that having 100 GHz CPUs (vs. 1GHz for CMOS) means that much less parallelism is needed out of applications. This is good, but at the same time memories do not speed up 100 times, leaving more levels of memory hierarchy and huge access latency. The PIM enabled memory hierarchy counteracts this by active pushing data down the hierarchy before SPELLs request it. Our software models and prototypes must mimic this.

When we look at modern conventional designs, we see a variety of common speedup techniques (such as out-of-order execution, register renaming, speculation) most of which were considered and discarded from HTMT because of complexity or lack of focus on the real design challenge - memory latency. Multithreading is a competing approach that exploits parallelism in processor architecture and directly attacks the latency issue. Consequently it forms the basis for much of the HTMT SPELL design. Threads in a SPELL can run concurrently, and can be executed in parallel by separate execution units. Stalling on a thread, because of memory latency, does not stall the entire processor. Other threads utilize the hardware. The same is true of code running locally in the PIMs.

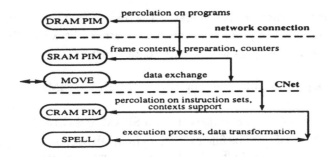

Fig. 2. Data accessibility in HTMT

Memory management The HTMT system will use sophisticated memory management hardware to move data throughout the memory hierarchy and satisfy the latency and bandwidth needs of the SPELLs. This feature is incorporated into the HTMT threading model. Instead of moving individual elements of data within the memory hierarchy, HTMT will manage complete contexts, including data, program instructions, and control state. In the HTMT multithreaded scheme the contexts migrate automatically through the memory hierarchy so that SPELLs always have access to executable contexts with ready data in buffer in the CRAM with minimal latencies. This technique is called percolation. Context percolation from DRAM, through SRAM to CRAM will be controlled by processors in the PIM chip. Within this percolation model, the processors in the SRAM and DRAM PIMs take on different rules, as pictured in (Fig. 2) and (Fig. 3).

The functions performed by programs in the DRAM PIMs include:

- transferring complete data sets between DRAM memory, disks, and 3D memory (employing compression and decompression in the process),
- transferring selected subsets of data objects to different SRAM contexts,

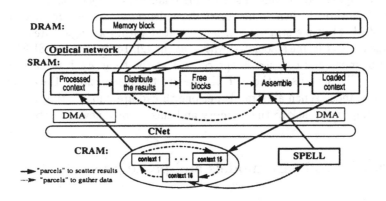

Fig. 3. HTMT execution model

- performing synchronization operations to recognize when all intermediate results from a set of processed context have arrived back in DRAM,
- performing simple operations on large data structures.

The functions performed by the programs in the SRAM PIMs include:

- keeping track of usage of buffers in both SRAM and CRAM,
- selecting free buffers to be filled with data from DRAM, providing the DRAM the addresses of these buffers, and recognizing when all data has arrived,
- moving full buffers of data into ready queues for each SPELL, initiating DMA transfers from SRAM to CRAM buffers, when a free CRAM buffer has been identified, and then signaling the SPELL that the buffer is ready,
- recognizing when a SPELL has declared a CRAM buffer processed and starting a DMA transfer of the results from that CRAM to a free SRAM buffer,
- when a DMA has completed, to start scattering the results in a SRAM buffer back into DRAM, or to other SRAM buffer,
- when all results has been scanned from a SRAM buffer, to move it to free areas, so this can be refilled, and process restarted.

SPELL processor We consider two different types of SPELL level processes: threads and strands [6]. A *thread* is associated with a separate context, buffer or a frame, of function parameters and local variables. Threads can run in parallel on a single SPELL, can be created and destroyed at runtime, and can create new threads. A *frame* is a block of memory with a collection of registers for holding intermediate data. The frame is used as a storage (like stack within a thread) of local variables. Each thread is associated with its own context that can be activated simultaneously. The frames are dynamic, and linked to one another in a non-linear structure. A *strand* is a block of instructions grouped together by the user (or compiler) to become a scheduling quantum of execution. It is enable at runtime by a thread when all necessary dependence, data and control, constraint are satisfied. Multiple strands can be activated within a single thread, and all share the register frame associated with that thread. 16 threads in a SPELL share CRAM memory and can access one context at the time. Each thread supports 8 strands. The strands in the SPELL execute the instructions. Data is divided between strands. When all strands per one thread are "done", the thread sends the resulting data back to the memory and checks for a new available thread.

3   Parallel software models and paradigms

Many parallel programming models and paradigms have been introduced in the last three decades, virtually all of which resemble some level in the HTMT system. The following paragraphs briefly describe several of these.

3.1 Multithreading

Modern multithreaded architecture models support the potential of simultaneous exploitation of parallelism at all levels (e.g. fine, medium, and coarse-grain), and an efficient and smooth integration of interprocessor communication/synchronization with computation. Multithreading has been proposed as a promising processor execution model to overcome latencies in parallel machines. The basic unit, a thread, is a unit of control for parallel execution. It has its own registers, may have its own stack, but typically shares address space with other threads. A thread may be created at any point of the program where an independent stream of control is needed and all data required by the thread is available. When one thread is suspended because of a long latency access to memory, another thread may be executed by the hardware at the next machine cycle. During the execution, the threads in a sequential code cooperate to solve a given problem; they are dynamically created, asynchronously scheduled according to data and control dependences, and concurrently executed. From the programmer's view, the threads can run simultaneously, and even on a single processor they can increase efficiency (and thus, throughput) during execution, such as in case of a shared data model when one thread is waiting for some event (input/output, task completion by other threads, etc.) and another is ready to compute.

Looking at HTMT, multithreading is explicitly part of the SPELL architectures [7]. In fact, each SPELL has two such levels of multithreading - threads and strands. It also may play an important role in the PIMs, especially DRAM, where access to data for multiple threads from RSFQ will need to be concurrent.

3.2 Client-server model

The idea behind this model is to structure the system as a group of cooperating processes, called servers, that provide services to the user processes, called clients. The machine may run a single process, or it may run multiple processes on multiple clients or multiple servers, or a mixture of the two.

To avoid the considerable communication overhead, the client-server model is usually based on a simple, connectionless request/reply protocol. The client sends a request message to the server asking for some service. The server does the work and returns the data requested or an error code indicating why the work could not be performed.

In HTMT the PIMs, especially the DRAM-based PIMs, are so far away from the SPELLs (latencies are huge) and will have so much internal processing capability that HTMT programming models may wish to view them as some sort of servers with the programs running in the SPELLs as clients.

3.3 Message-passing

A communication network provides a means to send raw bit streams of data between nodes in distributed memory parallel system. The message-passing model provides two basic primitives over such a network: send and receive. Send has two parameters, a message and its destination. Receive has two parameters, the source of a message and a buffer for storing the message. The message-passing model provides a highly flexible communication capability, and involves the following functionality: pairing of responses with request messages, data representation mechanism, resolving the addresses of clients and servers, and also taking care of communication and system failures.

In the HTMT model, variations of messages are being designed, including parcels. A parcel is an active message [8], [9], [10]. It is a logically complete grouping of the information that initiates work on the HTMT units and can result in creation of new parcels. Message-passing can occur in different places: between CPUs, as a part of client-server model over the optical network, or inside PIMs, as message-passing between nodes in the memory.

3.4   Remote Method Invocation

Remote Procedure Call (RPC) and Remote Method Invocation (RMI) [11] allow programs to call procedures located on other machines. When a process on machine A calls a procedure on machine B, the calling process on A is suspended, and the execution of the called procedure takes place on B. Information can be transported from the caller to the callee in the parameters, and can come back in the procedure result. No message passing or I/O at all is visible to the programmer.

In HTMT, for reasons similar to that for the client-server model, it may be appropriate for RMI-like calls to be made by the SPELLs to be executed in the DRAM PIMs. This is especially relevant for operations which require multiple data accesses, but little processing per access, such as object construction and initialization, pointer-chasing, garbage collection, or even simple matrix operations such as scaling rows, columns, or subarrays.

3.5   Object-based distributed shared memory LINDA paradigm

Linda is a parallel programming paradigm based on an abstract "tuple space" that functions as a kind of data base. The tuples can be of two types: data and patterns. Data tuples consist of multiple fields much like a conventional data base. Pattern tuples consist of conditions to match (like a query in a database system) and the name of the process that created the pattern. The tuple space is global to the entire system, and processes on any machine can insert/remove or search for either type of tuple without regard to how or where they are stored. To the user, the tuple space looks like a big, global shared memory, but the implementation may involve multiple servers. This memory is accessed through a small set of primitive operations that can be added to existing languages [12].

The HTMT is a distributed shared memory model with significant processing in the memory. Thus, the search and memory management functions of LINDA could be done in parallel in the PIM memories of either SRAM or DRAM levels. A prototype of such a PIM system has been constructed [13] and demonstrated.

4   Prototyping HTMT models

An HTMT machine with a huge number of embedded multilevel PIMs and multithreaded SPELLs, running in parallel and interconnecting through a network is a new architectural model. The HTMT hardware is being designed to minimize the effects of latency, but as a result, it needs an alternative software support. Depending on the physical form of communication between processes running on different SPELLs, two subclasses of HTMT software models might be distinguished: 1) shared memory where the SPELLs all "see" the same memory directly, and 2) communicating process architectures (distributed multi processors) where the processors are logically connected through a communication network, and access to different objects may require intermediate communication. Searching for programming models that will match the HTMT architecture and the best possible performance, and yet still allow "non-heroic" programming of real applications led us to consider a list of "real world" problems, to create a library of possible models, and to consider how to demonstrate those models in Java on a cluster of workstations.

4.1   "Client-server like" models

Let us first consider the following scheme for simulating real life applications on HTMT. The interaction between any two levels in the HTMT hierarchy (DRAM and SRAM PIMs, or SRAM PIM and CRAM SPELLs) is treated as a client-server relationship. In this scheme each client signs on a server, which assigns jobs and returns necessary data. Then, clients execute their portion of the original task (via processing in the SPELLs) and transfer results to the server for further manipulations. The server can execute some tasks itself at the same time using its own concurrent threads. Depending on what level of memory we choose, two special cases of this model are possible.

In the first scheme server and multiple clients do not share memory. In this case, each client sees data that were sent from server and executes only a task which is assigned by the server. The server provides all service to the multiple clients, and distributes data between them. The server is implemented as a multithreaded system with multiple threads to handle sending and receiving messages for each client during the data exchange process, and also to control the execution process.

Relating the HTMT model to the above scheme, we have to consider the architecture along with the structure of the new computer. The portion of the HTMT design that fits into this scheme consists of multiple multithreaded DRAM servers that provide the necessary data to the multiple multithreaded SRAM PIM clients, which, in turn, manage and control the execution process for the next level of HTMT system. The DRAM servers provide the initial support for thread percolation and to guarantee reliable service for multiple clients [7], especially in terms of synchronization. Organizing multithreaded models in such a way will allow us better control of execution and will simplify the scheduling

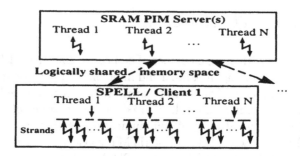

Fig. 4. Prototyping the SRAM-CRAM level of HTMT

mechanism. Fast datagrams over the optical network are suggested as a communication mechanism in this scheme, and the communication process will be the main topic in consideration. Similarly, the SRAM PIM - SPELL relationship for this scheme can be viewed as a socket communication relation through assigned SRAM PIM ports for SPELLs.

In the second scheme server and multiple clients share the memory. For this case, server and client see the same data in the memory. This model provides a virtual address space that is logically shared among physically distributed server(s) and client(s), and mirror the SRAM/ SPELLs interaction (via simple LOADs and STOREs operations and parcels) in realistic ways (Fig. 4).

In this scheme each multithreaded server in the DRAM PIMs can explicitly exchange data over the optical network with the SRAM memory in the SRAM PIMs, without a datagram protocol. The same may be true for the SRAM PIM clients and DRAM memory. The major client-server interchange here is for synchronization, supporting RMI calls, exchange of acceptable buffer addresses for the transfer, and completion signaling. This model does not require the extra communication threads for sending and receiving messages (especially data) across network, but it still needs mechanisms to distinguish between processes on clients and servers in order to provide the correct data exchange and a control for reliable scheme of interaction.

5   Using Java and its packages as a basis for concurrent prototypes

We chose Java as a programming framework for exploring HTMT programming models, especially those derived from the PIM-enhanced memory hierarchy, because of its unique features to support different kinds of concurrency and its growing use in the distributed and parallel programming environment [14], [15]. This section briefly describes some of them.

5.1   Threads

Java provides easy-to-use features for synchronization that make programming easier. Java threads are usually mapped onto real operating system threads if the underlying operating system supports this action. On a computer with only one processor, threads aren't actually processed in parallel. Rather, at regular intervals or when the thread is waiting for something, the computation will switch from one thread to another. This gives the appearance of parallelism. On computers with multiple processors, such as a modern SMP node, there is potential for real parallelism if the underlying system supports it. Thus applications written in Java are MP-hot, which means they will run concurrently if they are executed on multi-processor machine.

5.2 Datagrams

The Uniform (User) Datagram Protocol (UDP) protocol provides a mode of network communication whereby applications send packets of data, called datagrams to one another. The DatagramPacket and DatagramSocket classes in the java.net package implement system-independent datagram communication using UDP. Sockets for Clients can be used to connect Java's I/O system to other programs that may reside either on the local machine or any other machine on the Internet. Socket classes are used to represent the connection between a client program and a server program. The java.net package provides two classes Socket and ServerSocket that implement the client side of the connection and the server side of the connection, respectively. A ServerSocket will wait for a client to connect to it, whereas a Socket will treat the unavailability of a ServerSocket to connect to as an error condition. Sockets for Servers will wait at known addresses and published ports listening for either local or remote client programs.

5.3 RMI - Remote Method Invocation

RMI in Java enables programmers to create distributed Java-to-Java applications, in which the methods of remote Java objects can be invoked from other Java virtual machines, possibly on different hosts. A Java program can make a call on a remote object once it obtains a reference to the remote object, either by looking up the remote object in the bootstrap naming service provided by RMI or by receiving the reference as an argument or a return value. A client can call a remote object on a server, and that server can also be a client of other remote objects.

Object Serialization extends the core Java Input/Output classes with support for objects, and is used to save, send and restore object instances. Object Serialization supports the encoding of objects and the objects reachable from them into a stream of bytes, and the matching reconstruction of the object graph from the stream on the decoding end. Serialization is used for lightweight persistence and for communication via sockets or RMI [16]. The default encoding of objects protects private and transient data, and supports the evolution of the classes. A class may implement its own external encoding and is then solely responsible for the external format.

5.4   Java wrapper for MPI

The Java wrapper for MPI consists of a small set of classes with a lightweight functional interface to a native MPI implementation. The classes are based upon the fundamental MPI object types (e.g. communicator, group, etc.). There is a one-to-one mapping between MPI functions and their Java wrapper bindings. The Java wrapper for MPI functions are method functions of MPI classes.

6   The HTMT programming prototype

There are four reasons for building a prototyping model. First, it can show that we can built "correct" code for complex hierarchical concurrent systems like HTMT. Second, we can estimate how much computing resources are needed to simulate even small HTMT programs in a reasonable period of time. Then, we can derive statistics about concurrency and data distribution process in the system that could be useful to the HTMT design community. Forth, creating this prototype model helps to identify and to build a generalized tool set that allows a variety of other HTMT algorithms to be modeled.

In our demonstration prototype we model five units which represent the HTMT modules: DRAM, SRAM, MOVE engine, CRAM, and SPELLs.

Initially, a daemon thread in a SPELL signs to a server (SRAM PIM). In the HTMT execution model this thread may access the register set and CRAM, and supports thread creation, synchronization, communication, and termination. This thread can address CRAM explicitly and directly. It is up to the programmer or compiler control to support those functions. In our programming model this thread also supports the availability of the contexts through the check of values of counters (registers in the SRAM PIMs that count down as data arrives in contexts). If the value is equal to zero, then all data is available and the context is ready to be executed. This scheme needs to support a lot of synchronization mechanisms for strands and thread memory accesses. It is very close to the architecture execution flow and can be considered as a model to study the flow in HTMT system for parallel algorithms.

6.1   The present model

The current structure of the HTMT model consists of the following software components, each represented by a Java object with multiple methods:

- DRAM level models the storage of contexts and context percolation.
- Optical Network models datagram transfer between DRAM - SRAM PIMs.
- SRAM level object models the frame of context storage, "simulates" the data transfer process to and from CRAM through CNet using sockets, and sends data back to DRAM using datagrams.
- CNET: implementation of client - server model to support SRAM PIM - SPELL communication.

- CRAM level models the data storage and communication between SRAM and SPELLs via IN and OUT queues.
- SPELL level: assigns jobs to threads, distributes work between strands at thread level, and sends results back to SRAM via OUT queue.

6.2 Hardware environment

Three UltraSparc Sun workstations provide the engines to run prototype interconnect communication and socket interface between different levels of the HTMT. Two workstations were used as hosts for SPELL processors. The third machine was used to simulate the SRAM PIM as a server for SPELLs, and provided the interface for data transfers. This configuration can be easily expanded to more machines to simulate the larger set of SPELL processors in the model, and modeling even larger problems increasing the number of SRAMs and DRAMs.

7 Prototype demonstrations

As a demonstration platform for prototyping these models, we are writing a variety of multithreaded, multiple level client-server models in Java. The relative performance numbers of the setup being used is in approximately the same ratio as the HTMT will have, although 1000 times slower in actual numbers, and nowhere near the parallelism present at any level of a full HTMT. Using a 150 MHz SMP to simulate a single 100 GHz multithreaded RSFQ node gives about the same ratio as our 10 Mbps switched Ethernet is to the 10 Gbps optical channel. Servers and other PIM functions are simulated as programs for the SMP nodes.

We considered several Java applications for demonstration of the HTMT parallelization mechanisms using the two schemes that were described in the previous section. First, we considered Fox's proposed set of petaflops kernels [7], [17], [18], [19]. For each problem we considered the parallelization algorithms that will match the suggested schemes for client-server model and found the ease of implementation with the Java object-oriented language. Those examples were directly mapped to the multithreaded programming model.

Matrix Multiplication was also implemented in Java as a candidate for an "ideal" model for comparing the performance of a new architecture with existing machines that fit the considered scheme.

In all examples, the clients and server first shared data consisting of initial matrices, and clients requested data. Multiple threads on server and clients were responsible for different data elements of the given matrix and for control of data flow. Each client executed its portion of multiplication (row and column) and the server printed the result.

In the other case, the clients and server did not share memory, and all sending-receiving mechanisms involved the intercommunication mechanism (datagrams). Java provides the necessary interface to implement this fairly simply, giving

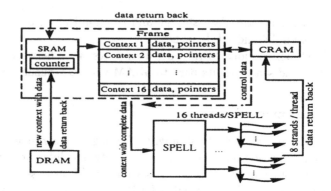

Fig. 5. Matrix multiplication data flow

difficulties only in distribution of data between clients and in the synchronization of execution process.

7.1 Matrix multiplication example algorithm

Let us consider the simple matrix multiplication data flow during execution process in our HTMT programming prototype (Fig. 5).

Each context contains the following information: the program code multiplies one row by a single element, the data consists of a row of numbers and an element of the column, plus a pointer to where the result should go, and control information including of context number, time stamp, etc.

Each strand multiplies one element in the row by one element in the column. (A trivial extension replaces the single element by single element multiply by a small submatrix by submatrix product that fits in registers). The last strand puts the sum of the products in the output queue for CRAM with the completion code ("done", "intermediate",...). This data can be used for further calculations or can be stored in SRAM / DRAM. The SRAM / DRAM servers create these contexts and percolate them up and down the simulated memory hierarchy (Fig. 6).

7.2 The implementation and results

A Java program simulates execution of contexts with Java multithreading modeling the strands. This code is currently running, and we are in the process of adding implementation to it to allow some actual statistics to be fed back into the HTMT hardware and architecture design process.

Analysis of our programming model had shown that the number of messages in the system grows linearly. For matrix size 1000x1000 in our model with estimate a message size of 164 bytes (one context per message), the number of messages only through DRAM-SRAM level will be close to one million. It shows the necessity of very high speed network and well balanced algorithms for this HTMT system. Our design also shows that multiple level interleaving in the

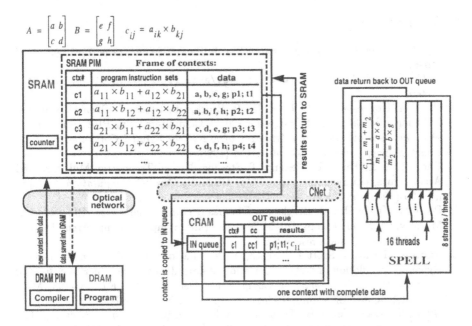

Fig. 6. Matrix multiplication operation in HTMT

HTMT system makes it very difficult to estimate time spent during execution in the system. Studying dynamics of other algorithms for the HTMT machine will help us to understand the nature of this system and develop an approach to quantitative analysis of the HTMT.

8   Conclusions and future work

In this paper we introduced the HTMT computer architecture and developed a combination of existing parallel protocol paradigms that neatly match this new design. The implementation of these paradigms in Java allows early insight into how real algorithms need to be structured for such a machine, and the kinds of support functions that need to be built into the hardware, especially the PIMs.

Our future work will involve the consideration of new, more elaborate models, especially to mirror low level runtime functions. We will add new algorithms to our set that will also fit to the suggested models, will develop timing instrumentation for those algorithms to allow studies of performance statistics for our models, and will run the simulations on larger collections of workstations. In defining the SRAM and CRAM execution time, it could be useful to see how balanced their work is. If the execution time in SPELLs is much less than the data preparation in SRAM or if data transfer time through the network is more than computation time in SPELLs, then we will need to reconsider our algorithms and communication interface. The results should directly impact both the hardware and system software designs of the next phase.

References

1. ASCI. Accelerated Strategic Computing Initiative, http://www.llnl.gov/asci (1996)
2. ASCI Blue RFP, http://www.llnl.gov/asci_rfp/cover.html, ~/late.html (1996)
3. Peter M. Kogge, Steven C. Bass, Jay B. Brockman, Danny Z. Chen, Edwin Sha: Pursuing a Petaflop: Point Designs for 100 TF Computers Using PIM Technologies, *Frontiers '96. 6th Symp. on Frontiers of Massively Parallel Computation*, IEEE Comp. Society Press, Los Alamitos, CA (1996)
4. Gao, G., K. Likharev, P. Messina, T. Sterling: Hybrid Technology Multithreaded Architecture, *6th Symp. on Frontiers of Massively Parallel Computation*, Annapolis, MD (1996), 98-105
5. Peter M. Kogge, Jay B. Brockman, Thomas Sterling, Guang Gao: Processing In Memory: Chip to Petaflops, IRAM Workshop, Int. Symp. on Comp. Arch., Denver, CO (1997), paper and presentation
6. Andreas Moshovos, Scott E. Breach, T. N. Vijaykumar, and Gurindar S. Sohi: Dynamic speculation and synchronization of data dependences, In *Proceedings of the 24th Annual Int. Symp. on Comp. Arch.*, Denver, CO (1997) 181-193, ACM SIGARCH and IEEE Comp. Society, Comp. Arch. News (1997)
7. Guang R. Gao, Kevin B. Theobald, Andres Marquez. Thomas Strerling: The HTMT Program Execution Model, *CAPSL Technical Memo 09* (1997)
8. Steven S. Lumetta, David E. Culler: Managing Concurrent Access for Shared Memory Active Messages, Comp. Science Division, Univ. of California at Berkeley
9. Lewis W. Tucker, Alan Mainwaring: CMMD: Active Messages on the CM-5, Thinking Machines Corporation (1993)
10. Thorsten von Eiken, David Culler, Seth Copen Goldstein, Klaus Erik Schauser: Active Messages: a Mechanism for Integrated Communication and Computation, 19th ISCA (1992)
11. Birrel, A., and B.J. Nelson: Implementing Remote Procedure Calls, *ACM Transactions on Comp. Systems*, vol. 2, no. 1 (1984) 39-59
12. George S. Almasi, Allan Gottlieb: *Highly Parallel Computing*, 2nd ed. (1994) 253-255
13. Kogge, Peter M., T. Giambra, H. Sasnowitz: RTAIS: An Embedded Parallel Processor for Real-time Decision Aiding, *1995 NAECON*, Dayton, OH (1995)
14. Denis Caromel and Julien Vayssiere: A Java Framework for Seamless Sequential, Multi-threaded, and Distributed Programming, Workshop on Java for High-Perf. Network Computing, Stanford University, Palo Alto, CA (1998)
15. Satoshi Hirano, Yoshiji Yasu, and Hirotaka Igarashi: Performance Evaluation of Popular Distributed Object Technologies for Java, Workshop on Java for High-Perf Network Computing, Stanford University, Palo Alto, CA (1998)
16. George K. Thiruvathukal, Lovely S. Thomas, and Andy T. Korczynski: Reflective Remote Method Invocation, Workshop on Java for High-Perf. Network Computing, Stanford University, Palo Alto, CA (1998)
17. Thomas Sterling: Proceeding of the 1996 Petaflops Architecture Workshop, The Petaflops Systems Workshops, Caltech/JPL (1996)
18. J. Dongarra, J. Bunch, C. Moler, and G.W. Stewart: *LINPACK User's Guide*, SIAM Publications, Philadelphia (1979)
19. Harry A.G. Wijshoff: Implementing Sparse BLAS Primitives on Concurrent/Vector Processors: a Case Study, *Lectures on parallel computation*, ed. by Alan Gibbons, Paul Spirakis, *Cambridge Int. Series on Parallel Computation: 4*, Cambridge university press (1993)

Is It Worth the Flexibility Provided by Irregular Topologies in Networks of Workstations?*

Federico Silla and José Duato

Dpto. Informática de Sistemas y Computadores
Universidad Politécnica de Valencia
Camino de Vera, 14, 46071–Valencia, Spain
{fsilla,jduato}@gap.upv.es

Abstract. Networks of workstations (NOWs) are becoming a cost-effective alternative for small-scale parallel computing. Usually, NOWs present an irregular topology as a consequence of the needs in a local area network. Routing algorithms used in NOWs are inherently different from those used in regular networks, mainly due to the irregular connections between switches. In these algorithms, routing is considerably restricted in order to avoid deadlocks. Recently, a general methodology for the design of adaptive routing algorithms for irregular networks has been proposed by the authors. The resulting algorithms increase the maximum achievable throughput while reducing message latency.

In this paper, we study how much network performance we are losing due to the irregular topology of NOWs. We analyze the performance of the up*/down* routing algorithm in a 2D mesh topology and compare it with the performance achieved by the XY routing scheme in the same network, in order to answer the following two questions: 1) in a 2D mesh, which of the two routing algorithms achieves better performance?, and 2) where does the up*/down* routing algorithm work better, in a 2D mesh or in an irregular network?. Simulation results show that the up*/down* routing strategy performs better in a regular network than in an irregular one. On the other hand, the XY routing algorithm considerably outperforms the up*/down* scheme. However, when the adaptive routing algorithm proposed by the authors is used, differences in performance are much smaller. Thus, the higher performance of a regular topology could not compensate for the loss in wiring flexibility with respect to irregular networks, or their capability of adding a single switch at any moment.

1 Introduction

Networks of workstations (NOWs) are being considered as a cost-effective alternative for small-scale parallel computing. In order to achieve a high efficiency, the interconnects used in NOWs must provide high bandwidth and low latencies. Recent proposals for NOW interconnects, like Autonet [7], Myrinet [1], and ServerNet II [5] are switch-based and use point-to-point links between switching elements instead of the traditional bus used in computer networks. Usually,

---

* This work was supported by the Spanish CICYT under Grant TIC97–0897–C04–01

A.Sivasubramaniam, M.Lauria (Eds.): CANPC'99, LNCS 1602, pp. 47–61, 1999.

they present an irregular topology as a consequence of the needs in a local area network. This irregularity provides wiring flexibility, scalability, and incremental expansion capability required in this environment.

Several deadlock-free routing algorithms have been proposed for NOWs, like the up*/down* routing scheme [7] (used in Autonet networks), the adaptive-trail routing algorithm [6], or the ones proposed for Myrinet [1] and ServerNet II [5]. These algorithms are inherently different from those in regular networks, mainly due to the irregular connections between switches. In these algorithms, routing is considerably restricted in order to avoid deadlocks. Recently, a general methodology for the design of adaptive routing algorithms for irregular networks has been proposed [10, 8]. The resulting algorithms drastically increase the maximum achievable throughput while reducing message latency.

The up*/down* routing algorithm is devised to be implemented in networks with irregular topology. However, because this scheme is based on building a tree with the switches of the network, the up*/down* algorithm can also be used as the routing scheme in any regular network, since any regular network contains an embedded tree. Several routing algorithms have been designed for regular networks, like the well-known XY routing scheme, proposed for 2D meshes. Unlike the up*/down* routing scheme, which provides non-minimal partially adaptive communication, the XY routing strategy is a minimal deterministic routing algorithm.

Regular topologies usually present better performance than irregular ones. For this reason, the designers of large NOWs tend to use the flexibility of their interconnects to choose the regular topology that best fit their purposes - fat trees for the Berkeley NOW and Illinois FM NT clusters, 2-D meshes for the RWCP PM and Vrije University DAS clusters, for example. Thus, we could wonder how much network performance we are losing due to the use of irregular topologies in NOWs. We can, therefore, compare the performance of the up*/down* routing algorithm in a regular topology with the performance achieved by a typical routing algorithm for this kind of topologies. In this paper we perform such a comparison. We analyze the performance of the up*/down* routing algorithm in a 2D mesh topology and compare it with the performance achieved by the XY routing scheme in the same network. Our aim is to answer the following two questions: 1) in a 2D mesh, which of the two routing algorithms achieves better performance?, and 2) where does the up*/down* routing algorithm work better, in a 2D mesh or in an irregular network?. By answering these two questions we will known how much network performance we waste due to the use of irregular topologies in NOWs. We will also know if the wiring flexibility and the incremental expansion capability provided by irregular networks compensate for their lower performance.

The rest of the paper is organized as follows. In Section 2, networks of workstations are briefly introduced. In Section 3, the performance of the up*/down* routing algorithm in several 2D meshes is evaluated and compared with the performance achieved by the XY scheme. Finally, in Section 4 some conclusions are drawn.

2   Networks of Workstations

NOWs are usually arranged as a switch-based network with irregular topology. In these networks each switch is shared by several workstations, which are connected to the switch through some of its ports. The remaining ports are either left open or connected to ports of other switches to provide connectivity between the workstations. This connectivity is usually irregular, but guarantees that the network is connected. Links in a NOW are typically bidirectional full-duplex, and multiple links between two switches are allowed.

Different switching techniques, like wormhole, virtual cut-through, or ATM, are suitable for being implemented in NOWs. Recently proposed networks like Myrinet or ServerNet II use wormhole switching [2].

Routing decisions in irregular networks can be based on source routing or on distributed routing. In the former, the message header contains the sequence of ports to be crossed along the path to the destination [1]. In the latter, each switch has a routing table that stores the output ports that can be taken by the incoming message. Some network mapping algorithm must be executed in order to fill the routing tables before routing can be performed. Regardless of where decisions are taken, a routing algorithm must determine the path to be followed. Several deadlock-free routing schemes have been proposed for irregular networks [7, 1, 5, 6, 10, 8].

2.1   Adaptive Routing

Although up*/down* routing provides some adaptivity, it is not always able to provide a minimal path between every pair of workstations. On the other hand, the adaptivity provided by up*/down* routing is very reduced.

Recently, a design methodology for adaptive routing algorithms on irregular networks has been proposed [10, 8]. This methodology starts from a deadlock-free routing algorithm for a given interconnection network. In a first step, all the physical channels in the network are split into two virtual channels, called the *original* and the *new* channels. In a second step, the routing function is extended so that it can use all the virtual channels. New channels are used with the only restriction that they must bring messages closer to their destination. Original channels are used in the same way as in the original routing function. When a message is injected into the network, it can only leave the source switch by using new channels, since they provide a higher degree of adaptivity and, usually, a shorter path. When a message arrives at an intermediate switch, it first tries to reserve a new channel. If all the suitable outgoing new channels are busy, then an original channel belonging to a minimal path is selected. To ensure that the new routing function is deadlock-free, if none of the original channels provides a minimal path, then the original channel that provides the shortest path will be used as escape path [3]. In case several outgoing original channels belong to shortest paths, only one of them will be selected. Once a message reserves an original channel, it can no longer reserve a new one. This message will be routed through original channels until it arrives at the destination switch.

This design methodology can be applied to any deadlock-free routing algorithm. When applying it to the up*/down* algorithm, the resulting routing scheme can be stated as follows. Newly injected messages can only leave the source switch using new channels belonging to minimal paths. When a message arrives at a switch through a new channel, the routing function gives a higher priority to the new channels belonging to minimal paths. If all of them are busy, then the up*/down* routing algorithm is used, selecting an original channel belonging to a minimal path (if any). To ensure deadlock-freedom, if none of the original channels supplied provides minimal routing, then the one that provides the shortest path will be used. Once a message reserves an original channel, it will be routed using only original channels according to the up*/down* routing function until it is delivered. We would like to remark that this routing algorithm provides fully adaptive minimal routing between all pairs of nodes until messages are forced to move to original channels. When a message starts using original channels, it provides the same adaptivity as the up*/down* routing algorithm.

Note that this routing algorithm can also be implemented using two parallel physical channels instead of splitting link into two virtual channels [10]. This could be easily implemented in networks like Autonet or ServerNet II, which also use distributed routing.

3   Regular versus Irregular Routing Algorithms

The goal of this paper is to answer the following two questions: 1) in a 2D mesh, which of the two routing algorithms, up*/down* and XY, achieves better performance?, and 2) where does the up*/down* routing algorithm work better, in a 2D mesh or in an irregular network?.

To answer these questions we have simulated a NOW with a 2D mesh topology. Thus, it is a network of workstations with regular topology. On this NOW, we have measured the performance of several routing algorithms. First, we have considered the up*/down* and the XY routing algorithms. The up*/down* routing algorithm will we referred to as UD. We have also evaluated the performance of the routing algorithm proposed in Section 2.1, referred to as MA-2vc. As this routing algorithm uses two virtual channels per physical channel, we have also included in this performance evaluation the UD-2vc routing algorithm as well as the XY-2vc routing scheme. These two algorithms behave as the UD and XY schemes respectively, but they use two virtual channels. In both cases, the network is not divided into two virtual networks, but a message arriving at a switch through one of the two incoming virtual channels can be routed through any of the two output virtual channels belonging to the feasible physical channel. Finally, we have evaluated another routing algorithm: the XYadapt algorithm. This routing scheme uses one of the virtual channels for minimal fully adaptive routing and the other one for XY routing [4]. As seen, it is similar to the MA-2vc routing algorithm, except that the latter is based on up*/down* routing and the former on XY routing.

We assume that each switch has 8 ports. When defining the topology of the network, we have connected four workstations to each switch. The remaining switch ports are used to interconnect switches. Note that not all the switches use all of their ports, since switches on the edges of the mesh are only connected to three other switches. Also, corner switches have only two neighbors. We have considered three network sizes in the study: 16 switches (64 workstations), 36 switches (144 workstations), and 64 switches (256 workstations). In the case of the UD, UD-2vc, and MA-2vc routing algorithms, the root of the tree built to compute routing tables has been chosen as the switch whose average distance to the rest of switches is the smallest one. Therefore, the root switch will be the one placed at the center of the mesh.

The virtual channel flow control protocol used in the networks we have analyzed is the one proposed in [9] (see that paper for a complete description of the protocol as well as for an analysis of virtual channels in NOWs). Fly time has been assumed to be one cycle. Input buffer size has been set to 11 flits, while output buffer size has been set to 2 flits.

Instead of analytic modeling, flit-level simulation has been used to evaluate the performance of the different algorithms. The evaluation methodology used is based on the one proposed in [3]. Performance measures are latency and throughput. Message latency, measured in clock cycles, lasts since the message is introduced in the network until the last flit is received at the destination workstation. Traffic is the flit reception rate, measured in flits per switch per cycle. Throughput is the maximum amount of information delivered per time unit (maximum traffic accepted by the network).

3.1 Switch Model

Each switch has a routing control unit that selects the output channel for a message as a function of its destination workstation, the input channel, and the output channel status. Table look-up routing is used. The routing control unit can only process one message header at a time. It is assigned to waiting messages in a demand-slotted round-robin fashion. When a message gets the routing control unit but it cannot be routed because all the alternative output channels are busy, it must wait in the input buffer until its next turn. A crossbar inside the switch allows simultaneous multiple message traversal. It is configured by the routing control unit each time a successful route is established. In the switch model, we have assumed that it takes one clock cycle to compute the routing algorithm. Also, it takes one clock cycle to transmit one flit across the internal crossbar.

3.2 Message Generation

Message traffic and message length depend on the applications. For each simulation run, we considered that message generation rate is constant and the same for all the workstations. Once the network has reached a steady state, the flit generation rate is equal to the flit reception rate (traffic). We have evaluated the full range of traffic, from low load to saturation. On the other hand, we have considered that message destination is randomly chosen among all the workstations in the network. We have also considered the bit reversal, perfect shuffle, and transpose distributions, and also local traffic. For message length, 16-flit and 256-flit messages were considered, and also a mixture of short and long messages (80% 16-flit messages, 20% 256-flit messages). Simulations were run, after a transient period high enough to deliver 60,000 messages, for a number of cycles sufficient for obtaining steady values of network throughput, or, when the network is close to saturation, a number of cycles high enough to deliver 200,000 messages.

3.3   Simulation Results

Figure 1(a) shows the average message latency versus traffic for a network composed of 16 switches. Message length is 16 flits. Message destinations are uniformly distributed among all the workstations in the network. As expected, the up*/down* routing algorithm achieves the highest latency and the lowest throughput. When this routing scheme is implemented using two virtual channels, latency decreases, and achieved throughput increases. However, network performance is lower than the one obtained when using the XY scheme, despite the fact that this latter algorithm does not use virtual channels. This result reflects the concentration of traffic near the root of the tree and the great amount of messages that are routed following non-minimal paths when the UD routing scheme is used. On the other hand, the performance achieved by the MA-2vc routing algorithm is quite the same as the one achieved by the XY-2vc scheme. Latency for the MA-2vc routing scheme is even lower for low and medium network loads. This result means that the MA-2vc scheme routes messages along minimal paths for low and medium network loads, and also that adaptivity contributes to make latency lower, due to the higher number of routing choices with respect to the minimal deterministic routing scheme XY-2vc. Note that when the XYadapt routing scheme is used, latency is decreased, while the maximum achieved throughput is maintained with respect to the XY-2vc algorithm. This means that adding adaptivity to a minimal routing algorithm leads to lower message latencies, even for high network loads. In the case for long messages, shown in Figure 1(b), similar results are obtained. Note that in this case a slightly higher network throughput is achieved because of two reasons: first, large input buffers are more efficiently used by long messages; second, the cost for routing a message and propagate its data along the wires is better amortized by long messages than by short ones.

When network size increases, differences between minimal and non-minimal routing are more noticeable. Figures 1(c) and (d) show the case for a network with 36 switches, while Figures 1(e) and (f) plot results for a 64-switch network. It can be seen that the up*/down* routing algorithm performs even worse as network size increases, due to the use of non-minimal paths in most cases. It can also be seen that as network size increases, the MA-2vc algorithm saturates at lower loads than the XY-2vc, due to the fact that when the network is close to saturation, the minimal adaptive virtual channel of the MA-2vc scheme saturates and messages are routed through the original channel, which does not provide minimal routing in many cases. This leads to a waste of network resources, and therefore, the network saturates prematurely. The XY-2vc scheme achieves a slightly higher latency than MA-2vc for low and medium network loads because of the adaptivity of the latter. However, since XY-2vc is a minimal routing scheme, it achieves a higher throughput. In addition to provide minimal routing, the XYadapt algorithm also provides adaptivity. This makes message latency even lower. However, when the network is practically saturated the XY-2vc obtains a slightly higher throughput than XYadapt because traffic with the latter algorithm concentrates in the center of the network [4]. Finally, note that for large networks, when messages are long, throughput achieved by XY is higher than the one achieved by MA-2vc. This is due to the waste of resources caused by the use of the original virtual channel, as mentioned above. Note that with large networks, differences between the lengths of the paths provided by minimal and non-minimal routing algorithms are larger.

When locality exists in message destination, we expect a higher network throughput, because messages block less often. In the case for message destination randomly chosen within small squares, network throughput is expected to be higher than for larger squares. Figure 2 shows the case for local traffic when the square side is 2 and 4 channels. In Figure 2(a) the average message latency versus traffic for a 16-switch network is shown. Message length is 16 flits. It can be seen that network throughput is more than twice the throughput achieved with a uniform distribution of destinations. In this case, because of the short message paths, routing algorithms that use two virtual channels present lower latency and higher throughput, because channel utilization is higher. Note that the MA-2vc routing scheme achieves lower throughput than the UD-2vc algorithm. The reason for this is the higher adaptivity of the UD-2vc scheme at the source switch. In effect, the MA-2vc routing algorithm considerably reduces adaptivity at the source switch. This reduction in adaptivity is intended to use minimal routing. However, for local traffic with square side equal to 2 channels, paths are very short, and therefore, the benefits of using minimal routing are less noticeable. This is the reason why the UD-2vc routing algorithm achieves a throughput similar to that obtained when the XY-2vc scheme is used. In the case for larger networks (Figure 2(c)), the UD-2vc scheme outperforms the XY-2vc, due to the higher adaptivity provided by the former. With respect to the XYadapt scheme, it presents the best behavior because it provides in all the cases minimal routing at the same time that it is an adaptive routing scheme.

When local traffic spans over a higher distance in the 2D mesh, we obtain different results. Figures 2(e) and (f) show the average message latency versus traffic when local traffic is enclosed in 4-link side squares. In this case, as in the case above, routing algorithms that use two virtual channels achieve higher throughput because of a higher channel utilization. However, distances traveled by messages are longer than in the previous case, and therefore, routing algorithms that provide minimal routing obtain better performance. Moreover, when adaptivity is provided besides minimal routing, a higher throughput is achieved. This is the case for the XYadapt scheme, which obtains the best network performance. The MA-2vc algorithm presents lower message latency and higher throughput than the XY-2vc scheme because of adaptivity. The XY-2vc algorithm always provides minimal routing, unlike the MA-2vc scheme. However, this feature of XY-2vc has little benefits with local traffic, while adaptivity is more important.

We have also compared the performance of XY and UD routing algorithms when the message destination distribution is other than uniform or local traffic. In Figure 3 we can see some simulation results for transpose, perfect shuffle, and bit reversal destination distributions.

The results presented above answer the first question. In a 2D mesh, the XY routing algorithm behaves much better than the UD scheme. In the case for the adaptive routing algorithms, the XYadapt scheme achieves a higher performance than the MA-2vc scheme. Moreover, in several cases, the XY-2vc scheme exhibits better performance than MA-2vc. Nevertheless, XY routing improves with respect to UD by a larger amount than XYadapt does with respect to MA-2vc.

In order to answer the second question (where does the up*/down* routing algorithm work better), we have compared the performance of the UD, UD-2vc, and MA-2vc routing algorithms in both regular and irregular networks. For the latter networks, topology is completely irregular and has been generated randomly. However, for the sake of simplicity, we have imposed three restrictions to the topologies that can be generated. First, we assumed that there are exactly 4 workstations connected to each switch. Also, two neighboring switches are connected by a single link. Finally, all the switches in the network have the same size. We assumed 8-port switches, thus leaving 4 ports available to connect to other switches. In order to make a fair comparison, since switches in a 2D mesh present less connectivity than in the irregular networks due to the edges of the mesh, we have removed in the irregular networks the same number of links that are not present in a 2D mesh of similar size. Thus, for a 16-switch irregular network, we have removed 16 links, while in the case for a 64-switch irregular network we have taken away 32 links. Note that the performance of the network can vary depending on the particular links that are removed. Moreover, removing some specific links may disconnect the network. Thus, in order to make a fair comparison at the same time that the network is not split into two networks, we have removed links starting from the switch with lower ID, and taken away the same links than are removed in a 2D mesh. If the network is disconnected when removing one of the links, that link is not removed and the equivalent link in the switch with the following ID is removed.

Figure 4 shows some of the simulation results. In Figure 4(a) one can see the average message latency versus traffic for a 16-switch network with both regular and irregular topology, when the UD scheme is used with 16-flit messages. This routing algorithm achieves a noticeable higher performance in a regular network: latency is lower for the whole range of traffic and the achieved throughput is higher. The reason for this improvement is that paths followed by messages are shorter in a 2D mesh due to the regularity of the network. Also, removing some links in the irregular network makes distances longer. When the UD-2vc and MA-2vc routing algorithms are used (Figures 4(c) and (e)), similar results are obtained. In the case for the MA-2vc scheme, differences in latency are smaller, especially for low network loads, because this routing algorithm provides minimal routing in most cases. In general, for small networks, with a regular topology we obtain a 20% of improvement in throughput.

We have also considered the case for large networks. Figures 4(b), (d), and (f) show the average message latency obtained for 64-switch networks. UD, UD-2vc, and MA-2vc routing algorithms are used, respectively. When the UD and UD-2vc schemes are implemented, achieved throughput in regular networks is higher. However, with respect to message latency, it is lower for irregular networks for low network loads. This is due to the fact that in an irregular network, some of the paths are very short because the tangle of links provides some short cuts from one part of the network to another. This effect is more noticeable as network size increases. However, in a 2D mesh the length of the paths followed by messages is more uniformly distributed. This causes that in the absence of contention, messages traveling in an irregular network through these short cuts are not disturbed by messages traveling along longer paths, and therefore, their latency is small, reducing the average message latency. This effect is much more noticeable with the MA-2vc routing scheme, which provides minimal routing in most cases. Figure 4(f) shows that when using this routing scheme, performance in a large irregular network is better than in a regular one, especially with respect to message latency. The reason is that the MA-2vc algorithm takes advantage of the short cuts present in the irregular network, routing messages efficiently. However, this routing scheme cannot use any short cut in a regular network because in such a topology there is no short cut. The minimum average distance from one switch to the rest of switches is 4.06 hops in a 64-switch regular network. In an irregular network with same number of switches, this distance is about 3. Therefore, a routing scheme that provides minimal routing in most cases, like the MA-2vc, can take advantage of this shorter distance by using short cuts.

Results when message length is 256 flits instead of 16 flits are similar to those presented above.

4   Conclusions

Networks of workstations are becoming increasingly popular as a cost-effective alternative to parallel computers. Typically, these networks connect workstations using irregular topologies. Irregularity provides the wiring flexibility, scalability, and incremental expansion capability required in this environment. Routing algorithms used in NOWs are inherently different from those used in regular networks, mainly due to the irregular connections between switches. In these algorithms, routing is considerably restricted in order to avoid deadlocks. Recently, we proposed a design methodology as well as fully adaptive routing algorithms for irregular topologies. These algorithms increase throughput considerably with respect to previously existing ones.

Due to the routing algorithms used in NOWs, especially designed to be used in irregular topologies, network performance could be lower than if a traditional routing algorithm were used in a NOW based on a regular topology.

In this paper we have analyzed whether the additional flexibility provided by using irregular topologies is worth the performance degradation due to the use of more general routing algorithms. In particular, we studied the performance of the up*/down* routing algorithm in a 2D mesh topology and compared it with the performance achieved by the XY routing scheme in the same network. We have also compared the performance of the up*/down* routing algorithm in both regular and irregular networks.

Results show that the XY routing algorithm considerably outperforms the up*/down* scheme. However, when a fully adaptive routing algorithm like MA-2vc is used, differences are much smaller. In other words, performance degrades by a significantly lower amount when adaptive routing is used. On the other hand, the up*/down* algorithm performs better in a regular network than in an irregular one. However, in the case for the MA-2vc algorithm, when the network is large, it achieves better performance for irregular networks.

In summary, the wiring flexibility provided by using irregular topologies leads to a significant performance degradation when up*/down* routing is used. However, performance degradation is significantly smaller when the adaptive algorithm previously proposed by us for irregular networks is used. In some cases, an irregular network with our adaptive routing algorithm may outperform a regular one with fully adaptive routing. In general, when our adaptive routing algorithm for irregular networks is used, the higher performance of a regular topology could not compensate for the loss in wiring flexibility with respect to irregular networks, or their capability of adding a single switch at any moment.

References

1. N. J. Boden, D. Cohen, R. E. Felderman, A. E. Kulawik, C. L. Seitz, J. Seizovic and W. Su, "Myrinet - A gigabit per second local area network," *IEEE Micro*, pp. 29–36, February 1995.
2. W. J. Dally and C. L. Seitz, "Deadlock-free message routing in multiprocessor interconnection networks," *IEEE Trans. on Computers*, vol. C-36, no. 5, pp. 547–553, May 1987.
3. J. Duato, "A new theory of deadlock-free adaptive routing in wormhole networks," *IEEE Transactions on Parallel and Distributed Systems*, vol. 4, no. 12, pp. 1320–1331, Dec. 1993.
4. J. Duato, S. Yalamanchili and L. M. Ni, *Interconnection Networks: An Engineering Approach*. IEEE Computer Society Press, 1997.
5. D. Garcia, "Servernet II," in *1997 Parallel Computer Routing and Communication Workshop*, June 1997.
6. W. Qiao and L. M. Ni, "Adaptive routing in irregular networks using cut-through switches," in *Proceedings of the 1996 International Conference on Parallel Processing*, August 1996.

7. M. D. Schroeder et al., "Autonet: A high-speed, self-configuring local area network using point-to-point links," Technical Report SRC research report 59, DEC, April 1990.

8. F. Silla and J. Duato, "Improving the Efficiency of Adaptive Routing in Networks with Irregular Topology," in *1997 Int. Conference on High Performance Computing*, Dec. 1997.

9. F. Silla and J. Duato, "On the Use of Virtual Channels in Networks of Workstations with Irregular Topology," in *1997 Parallel Computer Routing and Comm. Workshop*, June 1997.

10. F. Silla et al., "Efficient Adaptive Routing in Networks of Workstations with Irregular Topology," in *Workshop on Communications and Architectural Support for Network-based Parallel Computing* , February 1997.

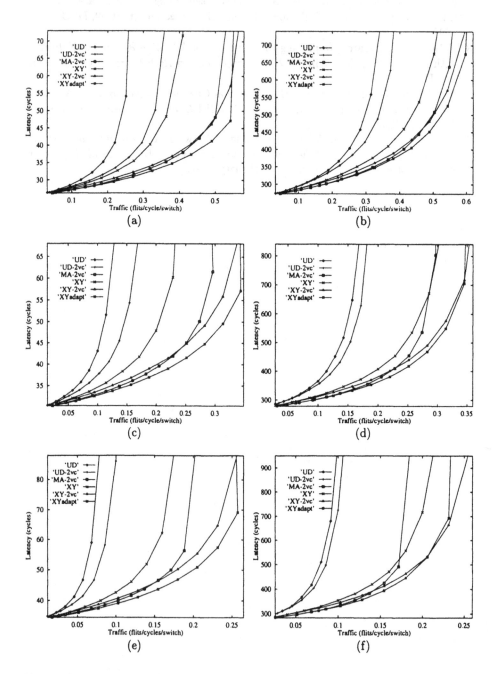

Fig. 1. Average message latency versus traffic. Network size is 16 switches in (a) and (b), 36 switches in (c) and (d), and 64 switches in (e) and (f). Message length is 16 flits in (a), (c), and (e), and 256 flits in (b), (d), and (f).

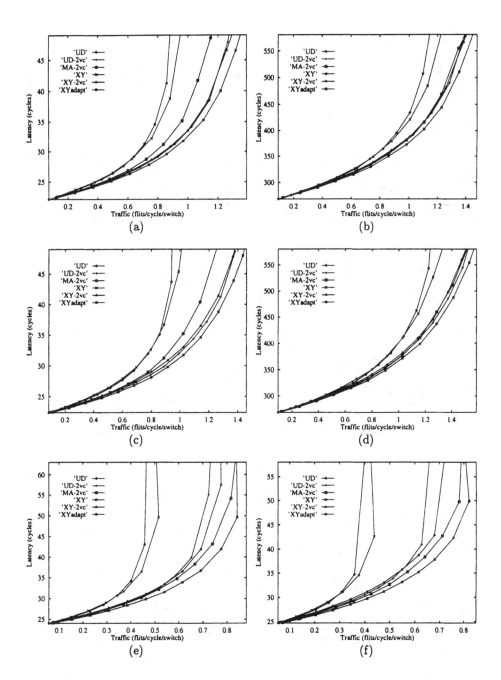

Fig. 2. Message latency versus local traffic. Destinations are chosen within a square centered at the source switch with side equal to 2 links in (a), (b), (c), and (d), and inside a square with side equal to 4 links in (e) and (f). Network size is 16 switches in (a), (b), and (e), and 64 switches in (c), (d), and (f). Message length is 16 flits in (a), (c), (e), and (f), and 256 flits in (b) and (d).

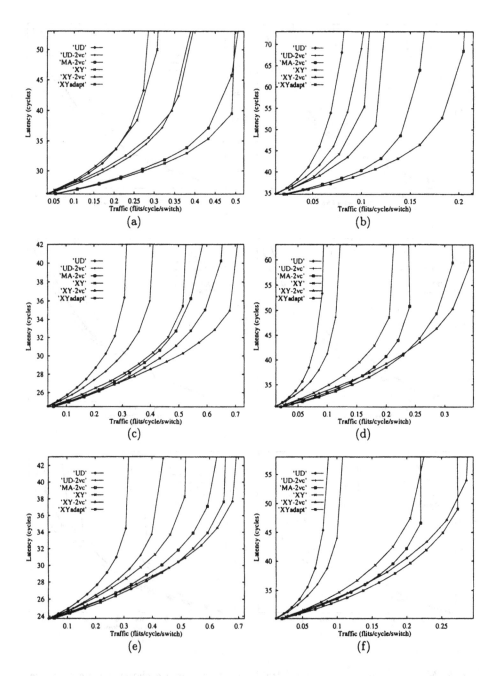

Fig. 3. Average message latency versus traffic for several destination distributions. (a) and (b) transpose. (c) and (d) perfect shuffle. (e) and (f) bit reversal. Network size is 16 switches in (a), (c), and (e), and 64 switches in (b), (d), and (f). Message length is 16 flits.

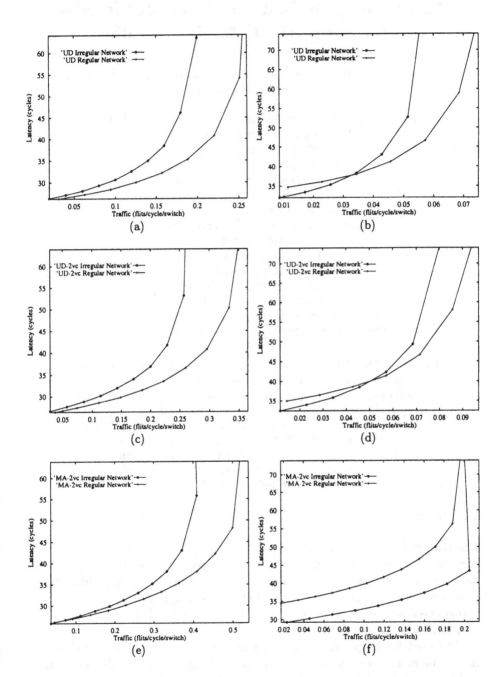

Fig. 4. Average message latency versus traffic for both regular and irregular networks. Network size is 16 switches in (a), (c), and (e), and 64 switches in (b), (d), and (f). Message length is 16 flits. Fly time is 1 cycle. UD, UD-2vc, and MA-2vc routing algorithms are used.

Performance Evaluation of the Multimedia Router with MPEG-2 Video Traffic *

Blanca Caminero[1], Francisco J. Quiles[1], José Duato[2], Damon S. Love[3], and Sudhakar Yalamanchili[3]

[1] Dept. of Computer Science. Escuela Politécnica Superior de Albacete
Universidad de Castilla - La Mancha
02071 - Albacete, SPAIN
{blanca,paco}@info-ab.uclm.es
http://raap.info-ab.uclm.es
[2] Dept. of Information Systems and Computer Architecture
Universidad Politécnica de Valencia
P.O.B. 22012, 46071 - Valencia, SPAIN
jduato@gap.upv.es
http://www.gap.upv.es
[3] School of Electrical and Computer Engineering
Georgia Institute of Technology
Atlanta, Georgia 30332-0250
{dlove,sudha}@ece.gatech.edu
http://www.ece.gatech.edu/research/labs/casl/

Abstract. The Multimedia Router (MMR) architecture is aimed at providing QoS to multimedia traffic in a local area environment, while retaining a compact and simple design. In this paper, we show some preliminary performance evaluation results. The workload was composed of a mix of synthetic CBR traffic and semi-synthetic VBR traffic. The latter was obtained from real MPEG-2 video sequences. We show that, with a simple scheduling algorithm, amenable for single-chip implementation, the link bandwidth utilization is quite satisfactory, while still providing acceptable delays to both CBR and VBR traffic.

1 Introduction

The market for multimedia applications continues to expand. Moreover, the number of systems dedicated to multimedia applications is growing at a fast rate. This is the case for Web servers, video-on-demand servers, video game computers, immersive environments, collaborative design environments, etc. All of them need to transfer great amounts of information, and the number of users is increasing continuously.

The need for higher communication bandwidth is especially crucial in local environments. Virtual meetings, access to medical imaging databases and multi-player 3-D games are applications usually executed in local area environments. These applications individually require substantial bandwidth to meet

---

* This work was supported by the Spanish CICYT under Grant TIC97–0897–C04

A.Sivasubramaniam, M.Lauria (Eds.): CANPC'99, LNCS 1602, pp. 62–76, 1999.
© Springer-Verlag Berlin Heidelberg 1999

interactive and other real-time constraints. Moreover, there are certain kinds of applications, like 3-D image rendering or video encoding, that need the storage capacity or the computing power of a set of workstations in order to achieve good performance, thus increasing the need for higher communication bandwidth [2].

This bandwidth must be provided over a network shared by multiple applications. Traditional router technology developed for high-speed multiprocessor interconnection networks or high-performance local area networks (LANs) are optimized for low latency for best-effort traffic ([3,1]). These networks are not designed to permit concurrent guarantees of communication performance for multiple applications.

On the other hand, ATM provides support for quality of service (QoS), but it has been optimized for wide area networks (WANs). The only known single-chip implementation of ATM in a local environment is ATLAS I [9].

The main goal pursued by the Multimedia Router (MMR) project [5] is to design single-chip routers able to support a large number of multimedia connections while allocating the remaining bandwidth to best-effort traffic. The MMR should handle this hybrid traffic efficiently, satisfying the QoS requirements of multimedia traffic, minimizing the average latency of best-effort traffic, and maximizing link utilization when the network reaches saturation.

The rest of the paper is organized as follows. We will first introduce the Multimedia Router architecture. A more detailed description as well as the MMR design trade-offs can be found in [4,5]. Then, we will present some simulation results, obtained with MPEG-2 video traces. We will next show how some parameters affect performance. Finally, we will draw some conclusions and point out the guidelines of our future research effort.

2   Multimedia Router Architecture

2.1   Application Requirements

The requirements of multimedia traffic are quite different from those arising in other applications like parallel computing, real-time applications, computer communication, remote file servers, etc. The main distinguishing features are:

- Very long data streams
- Wide range of bandwidth requirements
- Large number of concurrent connections
- Jitter sensitive
- Latency tolerant, especially during connection setup
- Short control messages

In some applications, data streams are not compressed because the compression/decompression process reduces quality, thus leading to constant bit rate (CBR) traffic. In other cases, either the applications produce a variable amount of data, or data are compressed to reduce bandwidth requirements, thus leading to variable bit rate (VBR) traffic. Also, multimedia traffic may coexist with best-effort traffic generated by other applications.

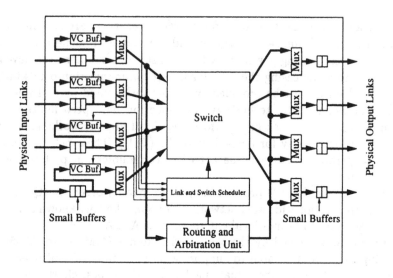

Fig. 1. Multimedia router (MMR) architecture

2.2 Switching Technique and Router Organization

In the Multimedia Router architecture we use the most suitable switching technique for each class of traffic. Multimedia traffic is handled by a simple connection oriented scheme, like pipelined circuit switching (PCS)[7], while best-effort traffic and control messages are transmitted by using virtual cut-through (VCT).

Each physical channel is split into a large number of virtual channels, each one supporting one connection concurrently with each other. The organization of the virtual channel buffers consists of a set of interleaved RAM modules using a simple interleaving scheme. Small buffers with capacity for a few words allow the storage of incoming data while control information is being processed. Figure 1 shows the MMR architecture for 4 physical links, including such a buffer organization. More details can be found in [4, 5].

The MMR uses a credit-based flow control scheme, as in [9], allowing the use of small virtual channel buffers at the price of a higher control overhead. Thus, it uses large flow control units or flits (>64 bits), in order to amortize this control overhead.

The internal switch is a multiplexed crossbar, because of the high number of virtual channels that have to be supported. This switch has as many ports as communication links. The main drawback of a multiplexed crossbar is that arbitration is needed every time an input link switches from a virtual channel to another. Arbitration in the MMR is hidden during the transmission of another flit because flits are large enough.

In order to fully exploit switch and link bandwidth while simplifying router design, the MMR synchronously assigns switch ports and output links to the requesting virtual channels. Flit transmission is organized as a sequence of flit cycles. Although transmission is synchronous inside each router, different routers work asynchronously.

The *routing and arbitration unit* executes the routing algorithm. The routing algorithm determines the path followed by the probes when establishing a connection and by the control and best-effort packets. A deadlock-free fully adaptive routing algorithm proposed for networks with irregular topology [11, 12] will be used to route packets using VCT switching. Exhaustive profitable backtracking (EPB) [6] will be used when establishing connections. A connection is established in PCS by routing a probe from source to destination. This probe contains some control information, the destination address, and information about bandwidth requirements. The destination node returns an acknowledgement to the source node.

2.3   Bandwidth Allocation and Link/Switch Scheduling

The network must provide some mechanisms to guarantee the QoS requirements of different applications. Admission control coupled with policing mechanisms during data transmission within the switch and/or network interface enable provision of certain types of QoS guarantees. Support for QoS guarantees within the MMR takes the form of solutions to three basic problems: bandwidth allocation, link scheduling, and switch scheduling.

Link bandwidth and switch port bandwidth are split into flit cycles. Flit cycles are grouped into *rounds* also referred to as *frames*. The number of flit cycles in a round is an integer multiple K ($K > 1$) of the number of virtual channels per link. Bandwidth for a connection is allocated as an integer number of flit cycles. The allocated flit cycles will be assigned to the requesting connection every round. Thus, a greater value of K provides a higher flexibility for bandwidth allocation. However, it may increase jitter because rounds take longer to complete. Therefore, the selected value for K is a trade-off between flexibility and jitter.

The data structure used for supporting fast scheduling decisions is a set of *status bit vectors*, where each bit in a vector is associated with a single virtual channel. Bit vectors provide information about different conditions for all the virtual channels in the router. We consider the following status bit vectors: flits available, CBR service requested, CBR bandwidth serviced, VBR service requested, VBR bandwidth serviced. A bit in one of these bit vectors is updated every time the status of a virtual channel changes.

When a connection is being established in the MMR, the source node generates a routing probe that carries information about bandwidth requirements. For CBR connections, each probe must carry information about the requested bandwidth, measured in flit cycles/round. Each output link requires an associated register that keeps track of the total number of flit cycles/round that have been allocated. This register is incremented by the requested number of flit cycles when link bandwidth is allocated and decremented when bandwidth is deallocated. A CBR connection can only be allocated if the total number of flit cycles that have been allocated (including the current request) does not exceed the number of flit cycles in a round. Note that a certain number of flit cycles can be reserved for use by all the best-effort packets crossing a particular link in order to prevent starvation of best-effort traffic.

In order to deal with the varying requirements of different VBR connections, a probe establishing a VBR connection will carry the permanent (or average) and peak bandwidth for that connection. In order to support bandwidth allocation for VBR connections, each output link requires two associated registers. The first one keeps track of the total number of flit cycles/round that have been allocated. This is the same register mentioned above for CBR connections. The second one stores the total peak bandwidth requested by the connections using that link, and it is updated only when allocating/deallocating VBR connections. These registers are incremented by the permanent and peak bandwidth, respectively, when a connection is established and decremented by those values when a connection is removed. A VBR connection will only be accepted if the value of the first register (total number of flit cycles/round that have been allocated) plus the permanent bandwidth of the current connection do not exceed the number of flit cycles in a round, and the value of the second register (total peak bandwidth of the connections through that link, including the current request) does not exceed the number of flit cycles in a round times a concurrency factor. This *concurrency factor* is stored in a separate register and is set during power on. A higher concurrency factor means that link bandwidth will be shared by more VBR connections, thus decreasing QoS guarantees.

The *link scheduling algorithm* operates on a round basis. It keeps track of the number of flit cycles assigned to each virtual channel during each round. This algorithm ensures that no virtual channel consumes more bandwidth than allocated. At each router, the link scheduler will assign flit cycles to the flits that arrive during each round, giving priority to CBR connections, and then to VBR connections. Link scheduling is performed for each flit cycle. On each input port the link scheduler provides one or more virtual channels among those ready to transmit a flit during the next flit cycle. *Switch scheduling* refers to the process of determining which input ports are connected to which output ports in a flit cycle. Switch scheduling must be performed in conjunction with link scheduling.

In order to maximize the probability of successfully assigning an output port in a flit cycle, instead of computing a single candidate for each group of virtual channels at an input port, the link scheduler computes a set of candidates. By doing so, if a given virtual channel cannot be serviced due to conflicts, it may happen that another virtual channel in the set of candidates can be serviced.

The router uses an input-driven scheme. The set of candidates for each input link is simply obtained as the result of some operations with bit vectors (for instance, the set of input virtual channels at that link with flits available and CBR service requested and not completely serviced). In this paper, we have used a round-robin selection among the candidates for arbitration. First, an input physical link is selected. A virtual channel is then selected from the set of candidates in this physical link using the link scheduling algorithm and the requested output link is assigned to it. Then, the next input physical link is selected. From the set of candidates for this physical link the router eliminates the virtual channels connected to the already assigned output link. A virtual channel is then selected from the set of candidates in this physical link, and so on. A more effective link/switch scheduling strategy has been recently proposed by us for CBR traffic [5]. This strategy is not available yet in our simulator for VBR traffic, but we plan to support it in the near future.

The scheduling algorithm is completely executed every round, servicing all the active connections. For each round, the scheduling algorithm is invoked every flit cycle. During each flit cycle, physical output links and switch input ports are synchronously assigned to a non-conflicting set of virtual channels for the transmission of a single flit from each virtual channel. Concurrently with this transmission, the scheduling algorithm computes the set of virtual channels that will transmit a flit during the next flit cycle. Then, the router waits until the current flit transmission finishes. The switch is then reconfigured according to the computed output link assignment, the next flit cycle starts, and the switch scheduling algorithm is invoked again, and so on until the round is completed.

3 Simulation Results

3.1 Simulation Conditions and Workload

We have run several simulations in order to assess the performance achieved by our router design. Simulation is event-driven, and the tool is written in C++. Link and switch scheduling are carried out as described in section 2.3. We have simulated a 4×4 router with 256 virtual channels per physical link. Physical links are 16 bits wide. Link bandwidth is 1.24 Gbps, thus the router cycle is 12.9 nanoseconds. Buffer size is not limited. This is similar to the use of flow control. When using flow control, flits are stored in the buffers of the routers the flow traverses, thus there is no practical limit to the size of the buffers. This is conceptually the same as having unlimited buffer space in a single router. All the tests have been simulated for 200 scheduler rounds.

For the first set of simulations, the K parameter is set to 16, thus the round has 4096 flit cycles. Flit size is 1024 bits, leading us to a flit cycle of $12.9 \times 65 = 838.5$ nanoseconds. This is the time available to the router to compute the scheduling for the next flit cycle.

The workload is composed of a mix of CBR and VBR traffic. Simulations do not include best-effort traffic nor control messages yet. CBR traffic is synthetic, and is composed of connections randomly chosen from the following set of average bandwidth requirements: {64 Kbps, 1.54 Mbps, 55 Mbps}. VBR traffic is semi-synthetic. We model it with a pattern similar to the train packets in [8], but with timing parameters obtained from MPEG-2 video traffic.

MPEG-2 video coding standard [13] encodes the video streams as a sequence of different frame types, I, P, and B, ordered with a prefixed and repetitive pattern, called GOP (Group Of Pictures). The GOP we use is IBBPBBPBBPBBPBB. I frames encode an independent frame, that is, I frames do not need any other information but themselves to be decoded. P frames need the last I frame in the sequence to be decoded, because the data they hold is related to that on the I frame. Finally, B frames need information from both previous and following P or I frames to be decoded. The bandwidth needed for each type of frame is different. I frames are the most bandwidth consuming, because they carry more information, and B frames are the least bandwidth consuming. In Figure 2 we show the traffic pattern for a typical MPEG-2 video sequence.

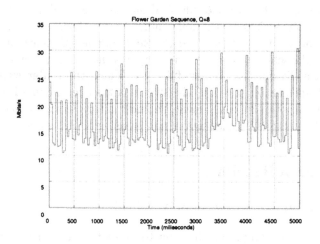

Fig. 2. Example of VBR MPEG-2 video sequence

We model the MPEG-2 video flows by sending a frame every 33 milliseconds, which corresponds to a transmission rate of 30 frames/sec. The frame sizes are obtained from trace files, corresponding to real MPEG-2 video sequences. The flits in a frame are sent uniformly within those 33 msecs. We chose the VBR connections randomly among the ones whose characteristics are shown in Table 1. We considered a concurrency factor of 16, so that it does not posses any restriction other than the availability of enough output link bandwidth for the average bandwidth on the admission of VBR connections. The effect of this factor will be studied in future works.

We generated connection requests randomly, for several workload levels. When simulation starts, the connection admission control may reject some of them, if there is not enough output link bandwidth to serve them. The remaining connections are kept active during all the simulation. It should be noted that the percentage of bandwidth filled with connections may be bigger than the one we request, because we perform surplus round-off, that is, we keep on requesting connections until the filled bandwidth is greater than the requested one. Besides, we take into account the average bandwidth for VBR connections, thus, the effective bandwidth they consume may be bigger than that. Finally, when a connection is requested, the simulator adds the bandwidth consumed by

Table 1. MPEG-2 video sequence statistics

Video Sequences	Image Size (bits)		
	Max.	Min.	Average
Ayersroc	535030	148755	232976
Hook	454560	159622	272738
Martin	444588	116094	199880
Flower Garden	900139	308411	497126
Mobile Calendar	970205	412845	600742
Table Tennis	933043	260002	440547
Football	590532	340246	441459

the overhead caused by control information (selection of virtual channel, flow control...) when deciding whether the connection can be admitted. For example, a CBR connection with a requested average bandwidth of 1.54 Mbps will consume in fact 1.56 Mbps, if flits are 1024 bits long, and 1.73 Mbps if flits are 128 bits long.

3.2 Performance Evaluation

Figure 3 shows the average crossbar utilization for different percentages of VBR connections. Each curve presents the utilization for 20%, 50% and 80% of the requested bandwidth consumed by VBR traffic, respectively. That is, in each curve, the specified percentage of the workload is filled with VBR traffic. The figure shows that the router reaches saturation for utilizations of (approximately) 77%, 80% and 88% , respectively. The reason for that is that VBR connections have bandwidth peaks and, as we use infinite buffers, the flits belonging to a burst will be stored until they can be served. We never discard those flits. So, even in the periods between I frames, where bandwidth requirements are lower, there will be flits in the buffers waiting for being transmitted. As a consequence of this, the performance in terms of jitter and delay may be damaged. This issue will be analyzed later. It should also be noted that the buffers that grow in size always corresponds to virtual channels carrying VBR traffic. This means that CBR traffic always gets its reserved bandwidth serviced, in spite of the presence of VBR traffic.

For the following simulations, we have used a workload where 50% of the requested bandwidth is consumed by VBR connections. We can see in Figure 4 the effect of the size of the round (parameter K) on the average crossbar utilization. Recall that bandwidth allocation is always expressed as a number of flit cycles/round, and that a round has a number of flit cycles equal to an integer parameter K times the number of virtual channels per link. The whole round is equivalent to the total link bandwidth, and by allocating pieces of it (the flit cycles) to the different connections, we reserve part of the link bandwidth for those connections.

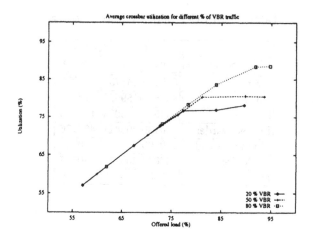

Fig. 3. Average crossbar utilization for different percentages of VBR traffic

The saturation point for $K = 16$ and $K = 4$ is reached around 81% of offered load. For $K = 64$, the utilization still grows a bit more before the switch saturates. We should note here that the offered load for $K = 64$ is a bit lower than the other ones when entering saturation because of our workload generation scheme and the smaller granularity achieved with such a big round. Our workload generator keeps on issuing connection requests until the total permanent bandwidth requested by them is greater than a certain percentage of the link bandwidth. That is, we make a surplus round-off when generating connections. The excess bandwidth will be smaller with this big round, because granularity is also smaller.

Figure 5 shows the percentage of accepted connections for the three values of K that have been considered. For $K = 4$ (i.e., coarse granularity) there are more rejected connections when increasing workload. This is because, as the bandwidth is coarsely allocated, it is more difficult to fit bandwidth requirements with bandwidth reservation. Thus, more connections are rejected. When we increase the value of K, there are less rejections because the bandwidth is more accurately allocated.

Figure 6 shows the effect of the flit size in the average crossbar utilization. We have factored out the overhead caused by control information. We can see that for low workloads, we are able to achieve comparable data utilization for both small and big flits. For higher workload levels, utilization for small flits hardly grows: the router reaches saturation with a data utilization of approximately 70%. But with larger flits we are still able to exploit almost a 10% more of the link bandwidth, reaching almost 80% of utilization. Thus, we can conclude that large flits are the best choice if we only consider efficient link utilization, because as they inject control overhead less frequently, there is more link bandwidth available for data transmission.

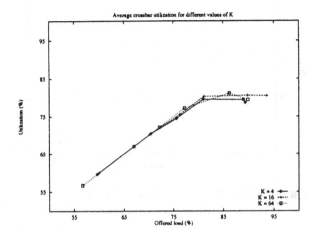

Fig. 4. Effect of the K parameter on crossbar utilization

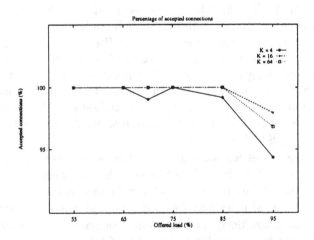

Fig. 5. Effect of the K parameter on the percentage of accepted connections

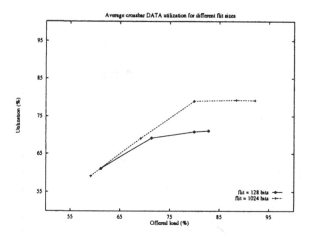

Fig. 6. Effect of flit size on crossbar utilization by data

We have shown that our simple scheduling algorithm is able to reach high crossbar utilizations. But, in order to be able to provide QoS guarantees, we need to know how that workload is delivered.

We have measured the contribution of each router to the global delay experienced by the flits. For every flit, the time elapsed since it is stored at the corresponding input buffer until it leaves the router through the corresponding output link has been recorded. We have obtained the maximum and average delay, and its standard deviation. The results for three levels of workload are presented in Table 2. They have been obtained for $K = 16$, flits of 1024 bits and with the 50% of the workload composed of VBR traffic.

We can see that the delay experienced by CBR flits does not grow significantly when increasing workload. This is because CBR traffic is given the highest priority when competing for resources. On the other hand, VBR traffic suffers extremely high delays for workloads around 80%. Thus, we can conclude that, although our router is able to reach such high utilizations, the delays obtained by VBR flits are unbearable. Those utilization levels should not be achieved if we want to offer QoS to VBR traffic.

Regarding the values for standard deviation, we can see that they remain stable, except for VBR traffic and high workloads. This means that the delays experienced by the flits are rather predictable. Moreover, this suggests that the performance in terms of jitter may be good. This will be studied later.

In order to check how delays are distributed, we have set six delay thresholds (TH1 to TH6), and have recorded the number of flits whose delays are greater than each of those thresholds. TH1 is 10 times the time the crossbar needs to forward a flit, which is 65 router cycles (838.5 nanosecs) in our simulations. TH2 is 2 times TH1, TH3 is 4 times TH1, and so on. Thus, TH6 is 32 times that value ($32 \times$ TH1 = 268.32 microsecs). The results are presented in Table 3 for CBR flits, and in Table 4 for VBR flits. They are given as percentages of the total number

Table 2. Flit delay statistics

	Load (%)	Max. Delay	Ave. Delay	Std. Dev.
Total	59.98	29358	196.38	288.00
	70.20	200073	341.28	288.00
	81.13	26915769	283939.69	1074500784.00
CBR	59.98	3299	127.50	288.00
	70.20	1913	135.26	288.00
	81.13	2969	148.99	289.00
VBR	59.98	29358	253.76	288.00
	70.20	200073	516.50	288.00
	81.13	26915769	521313.74	1074500784.00

of transmitted flits. We can see that almost all the CBR flits experienced delays lower than the first threshold (8.385 microsecs), for both workloads considered. For VBR traffic and 70% load, we can see that almost all the flits suffer delays lower than the sixth threshold (268.32 microsecs). For lower loads most of the flits meet stricter deadlines, as the one imposed by TH5 (134.16 microsecs). The maximum delay for VBR flits is 200073 router cycles, that is, around 2.6 milliseconds (see Table 2). These results are rather encouraging, because a typical deadline for MPEG-2 video transmission is 1 second between endpoints. This is the value for the CTD (Cell Transfer Delay) recommended by the ATM Forum for video distribution services, using MPEG-2 [10].

Table 3. Flit delay distribution for CBR traffic

Load (%)	TH1	TH2	TH3	TH4	TH5	TH6
59.98	0.034	0.00056	0.00011	0	0	0
70.20	0.063	0.00075	0	0	0	0

Table 4. Flit delay distribution for VBR traffic

Load (%)	TH1	TH2	TH3	TH4	TH5	TH6
59.98	6.35	1.17	0.29	0.11	0.045	0.004
70.20	19.50	6.81	2.09	0.64	0.20	0.075

For MPEG-2 video, the unit of information for the applications, from the point of view of the receiver, is the frame. Thus, we have obtained several measures related to the performance of the router with frames. The *delay of a frame* is the time elapsed since the first flit of the frame is stored at the corresponding input buffer of the router, until the last flit of the frame is delivered through an output link. Note that we send all the flits that compose a frame uniformly within the 33 milliseconds of separation between adjacent frames, so every frame will take at least 33 milliseconds in traversing the router. This fixed time is represented in Figure 7 with the straight line. We can see in that figure that the delay introduced by the router is quite small, because for the highest load we tested (75 %) this additional delay is under 200 microseconds.

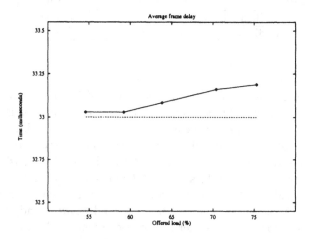

Fig. 7. Average MPEG-2 frame delay

We have also measured the jitter that the frames suffer when traversing the router. In MPEG-2 video transmission, every frame should arrive to its destination 33 milliseconds after the previous frame in the sequence, in order to be displayed properly. Thus, we define the *frame jitter* as the deviation from this 33 milliseconds of required separation. Results are shown in Figure 8. We can see that for loads lower than 70 % the jitter remains low, under 1 microsecond. For higher loads, the jitter increases quite a lot, but it remains under 3.5 microseconds. These are quite encouraging results, because the jitter allowed in MPEG-2 video transmission is around several milliseconds, that is, jitter must be low enough so that a person can see the video sequence smoothly, at a regular rate. Further studies are needed in order to check the distribution of frame delays and jitter.

4   Conclusions and Future Research

Multimedia applications are continuously expanding nowadays. We have introduced a new router architecture designed in order to cope with the requirements of these applications, as well as traditional data communications.

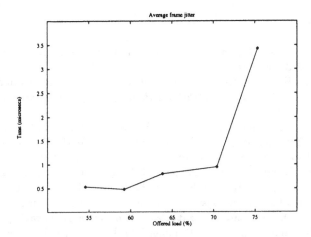

Fig. 8. Average MPEG-2 frame jitter

In this paper, we present some performance evaluation results, related to bandwidth utilization. We also show some preliminary results regarding the delays experienced by flits traversing our router, as well as the jitter introduced. We fed the switch simulator with a set of CBR and VBR connection requests. In order to make realistic tests, we used traces obtained form real MPEG-2 video sequences as VBR traffic.

These results show that our simple design can provide satisfactory bandwidth guarantees to CBR and VBR traffic. Crossbar utilization is good even for high loads. CBR traffic performance is not influenced by the presence of VBR traffic, since its flits are always serviced before the flits corresponding to VBR traffic. VBR traffic can meet strict deadlines at workloads of around 70% the capacity of the link. Frame delay and jitter are also acceptable for the same levels of workload.

Our future research will first test with more detail the performance of our design in terms of jitter guarantees. Also, some more design parameters have to be tested and tuned, such as the effect of the concurrency factor and other scheduling algorithms. Then, we plan to add support for best-effort traffic and control messages. Later on, an analysis of flow control mechanisms has to be carried out. Finally, we would like to analyze the coupling between the admission control algorithm and the link/switch scheduling algorithm in order to improve QoS guarantees and reduce the percentage of missed deadlines.

Acknowledgment

We would like to thank Pedro Cuenca for providing us with the MPEG-2 video traces used as VBR workload, and for his helpful comments about MPEG-2 video characterization.

References

1. N. J. Boden, et al., "Myrinet - A gigabit per second local area network," *IEEE Micro*, pp. 29–36, February 1995.
2. A.A. Chien, J.H. Kim, "Approaches to quality of service in high-performance networks," *Proceedings of the Workshop on Parallel Computer Routing and Communication*, July 1997.
3. W. J. Dally, et al., "The Reliable Router: A reliable and high-performance communication substrate for parallel computers," *Proceedings of the Workshop on Parallel Computer Routing and Communication*, pp. 241–255, May 1994.
4. J. Duato, S. Yalamanchili, B. Caminero, D. Love, F. J. Quiles, "MMR: Architecture and Trade-offs in a High Performance Multimedia Router," Technical Report, Computer Architecture and Systems Laboratory, Georgia Institute of Technology. Available from `http://www.ece.gatech.edu/research/labs/casl/papers/`.
5. J. Duato, S. Yalamanchili, M.B. Caminero, D. Love, and F.J. Quiles, "MMR: A high-performance multimedia router. Architecture and design trade-offs," *Proceedings of the 5th Symposium on High Performance Computer Architecture (HPCA-5)*, January 1999.
6. P. T. Gaughan and S. Yalamanchili, "Adaptive routing protocols for hypercube interconnection networks," *IEEE Computer*, vol. 26, no. 5, pp. 12–23, May 1993.
7. P. T. Gaughan and S. Yalamanchili, "A family of fault-tolerant routing protocols for direct multiprocessor networks," *IEEE Transactions on Parallel and Distributed Systems*, vol. 6, no. 5, pp. 482–497, May 1995.
8. R. Jain and S. Routhier. "Packet trains – Measurement and a new model for computer network traffic," *IEEE Journal on Selected Areas in Communications*, pp. 986–995, September 1986.
9. M. G. H. Katevenis, et al., "ATLAS I: A single-chip ATM switch for NOWs," *Proceedings of the Workshop on Communications and Architectural Support for Network-based Parallel Computing*, February 1997.
10. M Schwartz and D. Beaumont, "Quality of service requirements for audio-visual multimedia services," ATM Forum, ATM94-0640, July, 1994.
11. F. Silla, et al., "Efficient adaptive routing in networks of workstations with irregular topology," *Proceedings of the Workshop on Communications and Architectural Support for Network-based Parallel Computing*, pp. 46–60, February 1997.
12. F. Silla and J. Duato, "Improving the efficiency of adaptive routing in networks with irregular topology," *Proceedings of the 1997 Conference on High Performance Computing*, December 1997.
13. "Generic coding of moving pictures and associated audio," Recommendation H.262, Draft International Standard ISO/IEC 13818-2, March, 1994.

A Scalable Flow Control Algorithm for the Fast Messages Communication Library

Roberto Canonico, Rosario Cristaldi, and Giulio Iannello

Dipartimento di Informatica e Sistemistica
Università di Napoli Federico II
v. Claudio, 21 – 80125 Napoli
{canonico,rcristal}@grid.unina.it, {iannello}@unina.it

Abstract. The evolution of the Fast Messages (FM) communication library has shown the importance of flow control to deliver the raw hardware performance of currently available interconnection networks to the applications. However, the credit-based solution used in FM to provide flow control, though simple and efficient for systems of limited dimension, does not scale well when the dimension of the parallel system increases. In this paper, we propose an extension to the FM flow control algorithm where credits can be assigned on-demand to communicating nodes. The experimental results reported in the paper demonstrate that the performance of this new scheme is virtually insensitive to system dimension providing that messages are long enough and there are not communication hot spots in the system. In presence of more general communication patterns, the proposed dynamic credit assignment mechanism can be used to implement adaptive credit allocation policies.

1 Introduction

The availability of new technologies for high speed Local Area Networks (LANs) offers comparable latency and bandwidth to the proprietary interconnect traditionally found in massively parallel processors. This has made increasingly attractive building large parallel systems from commodity components like workstations and PCs. However new hardware technologies are not sufficient to solve the communication problem for these systems. The development of high performance communication libraries capable to deliver the raw network performance to the applications has been recognized as a key factor for the success of cluster architectures.

A number of research projects have been started to study the design of high performance communication software for high speed, low latency networks: Active Messages (AM) [2], Fast Messages (FM) [10,11], U-Net [3], VMMC-2 [1], BIP [12]. A distinguishing aspect of the FM project is an accurate choice of the services to be provided at the library interface. Relying on the favorable characteristics of the interconnection network used in the project, the Myrinet LAN [4], FM designers decided to provide services like reliable and in-order delivery. Since Myrinet is characterized by very low error rate, absence of buffering

A.Sivasubramaniam, M.Lauria (Eds.): CANPC'99, LNCS 1602, pp. 77–90, 1999.
© Springer-Verlag Berlin Heidelberg 1999

in the network fabric, and link-level flow control, providing these services essentially requires the introduction of a flow control scheme to prevent the overflow of internal buffers. These design choices proved to be successful in transferring the very high performance available at the FM interface to the applications through a higher-level communication library such as MPI [9].

These results indicate that, for reliable networks, a fundamental component of a high performance communication library is the flow control algorithm. To attain its performance levels FM uses a very simple credit-based protocol where credits correspond to free buffer space. Senders are allowed to transmit packets as long as they have enough credits for the target node. Credits are refilled by receivers when they drop under a given threshold. The protocol, called in the following *Static Credit Protocol* (SCP), is equivalent to the *Credit Update Protocol* (CUP) proposed in [8] for ATM networks. In both protocols the buffer space available at the receiver is statically partitioned at initialization time among all potential senders. This means that senders have less credits and must process refill packets more often, as long as the number of nodes in the system grows up. The corresponding bandwidth decrease limits the scalability.

In this paper, we propose an extension to the credit-based flow control algorithm used by FM allowing the number of credits of a given sender to be temporarily increased on-demand. The performance of this new protocol, called Credit On-Demand (COD), is virtually insensitive to system dimension, providing that two constraints are satisfied. Messages are required to be long enough to observe remarkable improvements in bandwidth and there must not be communication hot spots in the system. The first condition is really not a constraint since short messages cannot reach peak bandwidth anyway. As to the second condition, message-passing algorithms are usually designed to minimize conflicts at network interfaces, which means that a wide class of algorithms can benefit of the on-demand flow control scheme. For more general communication patterns, the proposed protocol represents a very flexible basic mechanism on top of which adaptive credit allocation policies [8] can be implemented.

The Credit On-Demand protocol guarantees reliable and in-order delivery of messages and introduces a negligible overhead, achieving the same peak bandwidth of SCP.

We will present here in detail a simplified version of COD that requires the knowledge of the message length when message transmission is started. A more general version of the protocol that releases this constraint has been developed, but it will be only sketched here for space reasons. A detailed discussion of this version can be found in [5].

The rest of the paper is organized as follows. In section 2 we informally describe the flow control algorithm used in the FM library, and discuss its scalability with respect to experimental data. In section 3 we present our on-demand algorithm and prove its correctness. In section 4 we present experimental data confirming the effectiveness of the proposed approach and pointing out its practical limitations. In section 5 we report about related work, and in section 6 we conclude the paper.

2   Credit-Based Flow Control in FM

According to the Fast Messages programming model [10], the parallel system consists of n nodes each running at most P independent processes (*contexts* in FM terminology). Messages can be sent to any process and they have an associated *handler* function, which is invoked on message reception as in the Active Messages model [2]. Message reception is performed through the extract primitive which implements a flexible polling mechanism. Messages are sent and received as *streams* of bytes and primitives are provided for the piecewise manipulation of data, both on the send and on the receive side. Hence, messages can be gathered and scattered on-the-fly so that their size and content can be decided dynamically during message transmission. More details on the library interface can be found in [10].

Internally the library segments messages into packets of fixed size L_p. The sender host injects the packets into the network copying them through the I/O bus. Since programmed I/O is used, the packets are copied directly from user memory to an adapter's memory region managed as a circular queue. At the receiver side, incoming packets are extracted from the network into another circular queue allocated into the adapter's memory and then DMAed to a properly allocated region into the host kernel memory. The latter region is also managed as a circular queue.

Since FM guarantees message delivery, a flow control scheme must be implemented in order to avoid queues' overflow.

Both queues in the adapter's memory at the sender and receiver sides are protected by overrun simply blocking the queueing of new packets when the queues are full. Conversely, a credit-based algorithm is used between communicating nodes to manage the queue allocated into the receiver's kernel memory.

Let D be the size of this region and $N = \lfloor D/L_p \rfloor$ the number of packets it can contain. The N available packet slots correspond to as many *credits* that are equally divided among all potential senders (which are $n \cdot P$ since a process can send to itself). A sender is allowed to send packets to a given node only if it has enough credits corresponding to that node. When packets are extracted by the kernel area, the receiver check how many credits still has the sender. When a given *low water mark* is reached, it sends back to the sender a special *refill* packet with the freed credits. The low water mark lwm is set for all senders to a fraction of the initial credits, so that on one hand refill packets are not sent too often, and on the other hand the communication pipeline is not interrupted for lack of credits at the sender side. Senders use piggybacking instead of special refill packets to refill freed credits to their targets.

Since the queue allocated into the kernel region is the target of DMA operations, it has to be pinned down at the initialization time by the operating system. Hence, the dimension of this area cannot grow indefinitely and in some cases the operating system limits its size to a few hundreds kilobytes. The total amount of credits available for all senders is then upper bound and it decreases as L_p increases. Correspondingly, as the number of nodes and the number of contexts per node increase, the credits initially assigned to each sender decrease,

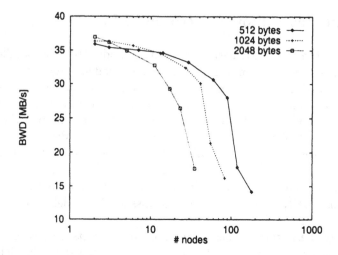

Fig. 1. Bandwidth vs. number of nodes for different packet sizes (messages are 64 Kbytes long).

which means that credits must be refilled more often. This implies that actual bandwidth decreases as L_p, n, and P increase.

We carried on a set of measurements that confirms this expected behavior. For the experiments reported here and in section 4, we used a setup consisting of Sun Ultra 1 workstations connected by Myrinet and running FM 2.0 under Solaris 2.5. The DMA region allocated by the operating system to buffer incoming packets has a size of 384 Kbytes. The measured peak bandwidth B_0 ranges between 36 to 37 MB/s for packet sizes between 512 and 2048 bytes. We simulate the scaling of the system dimension by using a modified version of FM allowing the assignment of an arbitrary number of credits to every node.

In figure 1 the measured bandwidth for packets of 512, 1024 and 2048 bytes is shown when the number of nodes n increase. For all packet sizes, the bandwidth decreases linearly until a given value of n is reached. For larger values of n the slope of the curve increases and measured bandwidth gets worse rapidly.

For instance, when packets are 1024 bytes long, the decrease is moderate and linear up to 40 nodes (assuming one context per node). At this point $lwm = 4$. Since the time needed to send 4 packets is comparable with the round trip time, a sender transmitting many packets in a row can receive the refill packet after running out of credits. This means that the sender blocks waiting for fresh credits and this explains the steep decrease in bandwidth.

These results confirm that the credit-based flow control algorithm of FM does not scale well with the number of nodes in the system. Up to a given system size this is due to the higher rate at which refill packets must be sent, for larger systems this is due to the longer waiting times before receiving refill packets.

3   On-Demand Credit Management

In this section we present an on-demand flow control algorithm, called Credit On-Demand (COD), that improves the performance of SCP, the algorithm originally used by FM. All algorithms discussed will be presented giving a list of the variables used by the generic process i and the pseudo-code executed when i transmits or receives a packet. Each code segment is assumed to be executed atomically. We assume also that after initialization all processes synchronize so that all variables are guaranteed to assume consistent values. Correctness will be proved giving an invariant that captures the basic properties of the algorithm, and showing that such an invariant holds at any time, before and after execution of code segments.

Since COD is based on SCP, we present first the latter algorithm and briefly discuss its correctness.

The SCP algorithm used by the FM implementation on Myrinet is presented in figure 2. Note that the initial value of all variables is independent of the array index. Note also that when a packet is transmitted only variables concerning the receiver process r are accessed. Similarly, when a packet is received only the variables of the sending process s are accessed. This is a general property of all algorithms presented in this section and from now onward we will omit the array index in pseudo-code.

Since the algorithm of figure 2 is quite standard, we only point out a few aspects that can help the presentation of the on-demand algorithm.

First we note that flow control for refill packets is managed in a special way. One special credit is reserved for these kind of packets at initialization time (see initialization of N_0) and then refill packets are sent when needed without further checking. It can be easily proved that there is always space for a refill packet in the kernel memory, providing that the inequality $N_0 > 2\,lwm$ holds at any time. Since this condition is assumed to be satisfied in all the algorithms presented in this paper, we will not discuss the matter any further.

Second, the precondition to packet transmission means that if there are no more credits ($n_{send}[r] = 0$), the sender process s loops extracting packets until a credit refill is received from r and the precondition is restored. Note that the process cannot loop indefinitely, since r send a refill packet every $N_0 - lwm$ received packets at least.

Third, the correctness of the algorithm requires that all the variables assume always non-negative values and, for each possible pair of processes (s, r), holds the invariant:

$$n_{send}^{(s)}[r] + n_{refill}^{(r,s)} + n_{network}^{(s,r)} = n_{recv}^{(r)}[s] \tag{1}$$

where the parenthesized upperscripts denote to which process the referred variable belongs, the symbol $n_{refill}^{(r,s)}$ denotes the number of credits that r has possibly refilled to s, but s has not yet received, and the symbol $n_{network}^{(s,r)}$ denotes the number of packets sent by process s, but not received yet by process r. Relation (1) means that the overall number of packets that s is allowed to send to r plus those in transit between s and r (including packets already DMAed in

variable (at process i)	initial value	description
N_0	$\lfloor \lfloor D/L_p \rfloor /(n\,P) \rfloor - 1$	#credits initially assigned to any sender
$n_{send}[r]$	N_0	#credits available to i to send packets to r
$n_{recv}[s]$	N_0	#credits available to s to send packets to i
$n_{freed}[s]$	0	#credits consumed by s and already freed by i
lwm	$\lfloor N_0/2 \rfloor - 1$	low water mark

packet transmission to process r: % PRE: $n_{send}[r] \geq 1$
    $n_{send}[r] := n_{send}[r] - 1$
    if $n_{freed}[r] > 0$ **then**   % there is freed buffer space
        piggyback to the packet $n_{freed}[r]$ credits
        $n_{recv}[r] := n_{recv}[r] + n_{freed}[r]$ % update available credits
        $n_{freed}[r] := 0$
    endif

packet reception from process s:
    if packet contains a credit refill **then**
        $n_{send}[s] := n_{send}[s] +$ credits refilled
    endif
    if not a refill packet **then**
        $n_{recv}[s] := n_{recv}[s] - 1$
        $n_{freed}[s] := n_{freed}[s] + 1$
        if $n_{recv}[s] = lwm$ **then**   % credits must be refilled
            send a refill packet with $n_{freed}[s]$ credits
            $n_{recv}[s] := n_{recv}[s] + n_{freed}[s]$ % restore the window size
            $n_{freed}[s] := 0$
        endif
    endif

Fig. 2. Variables, events and pseudo-code of the FM flow control algorithm executed by a generic process i in the system.

the kernel memory of r, but not extracted yet) must be equal to the number of available slots in the kernel memory of r.

The code reported in figure 2 guarantees that the invariant holds at any time. The formal proof is trivial and we omit it for the sake of brevity.

We are now ready to present the on-demand flow control algorithm. The general idea is to have a buffer space in the kernel region which is not statically assigned to a process, but it can be used on-demand to temporarily increment the credits assigned to a particular sender. Increasing the credits solves both problems described in section 2, making peak bandwidth essentially independent of the number of processes in the system. More specifically, credits should be increased so that, on one hand the low water mark can be placed at a value that does not cause a break in the data flow outgoing from the source node, and on the other, the value of p, i.e. the number of packets transmitted between two consecutive refills, is high enough not to cause a bandwidth decrease.

Since just one or at most a few processes at a time can have their credits increased, we need a mechanism to both acquire and release credits dynamically.

The start and the end of a message transmission are the natural boundaries at which credits can be effectively acquired and released. Besides simplicity, the main advantage of this choice is that virtually all senders can use a larger number of credits, providing that communication schedules minimizing conflicts at the network interfaces are adopted. Since parallel algorithms are usually designed assuming for the parallel system a fully connected model [6], this requirement turns out to be satisfied in many cases. In particular this is true in typical collective communication patterns where processes exchange large data sets [7], and more generally in scientific applications. However, this approach presents two main drawbacks. The first one is that messages have to be long enough to take advantage of the credit increment. In section 4, we will show that this issue is not critical by giving a quantitative evaluation of the impact of message length over performance. The second drawback is that this simple, per message policy cannot guarantee a fair credit assignment among senders in presence of general communication patterns. In section 5, we will discuss the matter further.

In designing a per message on-demand credit-based algorithm for the Fast Messages library, however, a problem arises. Since messages can be gathered on-the-fly, their length may not be known in advance and only when the transmission ends both sender and receiver know that the additional credits acquired when transmission started must be released. This makes difficult for the sender to discard all the additional credits acquired without introducing additional control messages. We therefore designed a simplified version of the on-demand algorithm assuming that the first packet of any message contains the exact length in packets of the message itself. We also designed a more general version of the algorithm that releases this assumption. For space reasons we give here only some hints on the latter version. Interested readers may find a complete discussion in [5].

In figures 3 and 4 is presented the first variant of the algorithm. The variables that remain unchanged with respect to the original FM flow control algorithm are not shown in the table. Note that the array indexes s and r have been omitted in the pseudo-code and in the related discussion.

Constant values N_{opt} and lwm_{opt} have to be determined experimentally and are not shown in the table. The values used in our experiments will be given in the next section. The proper initial value to be given to N_0 and N_{avail} are not independent and depend on many factors. They must be determined so that $n P (N_0 + 1) + N_{avail} = \lfloor D/L_p \rfloor$.

The basic idea of the algorithm is that the receiver gives additional credits to the sender when the first packet of a long enough message is received. The criteria to decide which is the threshold length, how many additional credits have to be assigned, and if the low water mark has to be risen depend on many parameters and they will not be discussed here. Possible choices that lead to good results in practical cases are suggested in the pseudo-code.

variable (at process i)	initial value	description
N_0	see text	#credits initially assigned to any sender
N_{opt}	see text	minimum additional #credits that guarantees peak bandwidth (constant)
$N_{add}[s]$	0	additional #credits temporarily assigned to s
N_{avail}	see text	#credits not assigned to any process
lwm_{opt}	see text	minimum value of low water mark that does not introduce holes into the communication flow (constant)
$lwm[s]$	$\lfloor N_0/2 \rfloor - 1$	low water mark currently assigned to s
$len[s]$	0	length (#packets, included header and tail) of FM message that is being received

packet transmission to process r: % PRE: $n_{send}[r] \geq 1$
  $n_{send} := n_{send} - 1$
  if $n_{freed} > 0$ **then**   % there is freed buffer space
    if $len = 0 \vee len \geq N_{add}$ **then**   % on-demand credit scheme
      piggyback to the packet $n_{freed}[s]$ credits   % not used or all available
      $n_{recv} := n_{recv} + n_{freed}$ % credits must be refilled
      $n_{freed} := 0$
    else   % partial refill
      piggyback to the packet $\min(n_{freed}, len - \max(0, n_{recv} - N_0))$ credits
      $n_{recv} := n_{recv} + \min(n_{freed}, len - \max(0, n_{recv} - N_0))$
      $n_{freed} := n_{freed} - \min(n_{freed}, len - \max(0, n_{recv} - N_0))$
      $lwm := \lfloor N_0/2 \rfloor - 1$ % ensures $lwm < n_{recv}$
    endif
  endif

Fig. 3. Additional variables and pseudo-code for packet transmission in the first variant of the on-demand flow control algorithm.

The number of credits is restored to its original value N_0 when the last packet of the message is received. However this can be safely done only if the current number of credits available to the sender does not exceed N_0. This is ensured by the refill policy used when the on-demand scheme is in use. If there are still enough packets to be sent ($len \geq N_{add}$) the number of credits is restored to its maximum value ($N_0 + N_{add}$). Otherwise, only the fraction of credits that guarantees correctness is restored. See reference [5] for the details of the formal proof.

Before ending the section, we briefly discuss how the on-demand scheme can be implemented when the assumption that message length is known in advance cannot be made.

This time, the correctness of the algorithm cannot be based on condition (1) for two reasons. On one hand, variables $n_{send}^{(s)}[r]$ and $n_{recv}^{(r)}[s]$ cannot be updated

packet reception from process s:
  if packet contains a credit refill **then**
    $n_{send} := n_{send} +$ credits refilled
  endif
  if not a refill packet **then**
    $n_{recv} := n_{recv} - 1$
    $n_{freed} := n_{freed} + 1$
    if $len \neq 0$ **then**   % not first packet
      $len := len - 1$ % on-demand scheme used
    else if first packet **then**
      if message length in packets $> 2\,(N_0 - lwm)$ **then**
        $len :=$ message length in packets $- 1$ % long enough message
        $N_{add} := \min(N_{avail}, N_{opt}, len + 1)$ % on-demand scheme used
        $N_{avail} := N_{avail} - N_{add}$
        $lwm := \min(lwm_{opt}, \lfloor (N_0 + N_{add})/2 \rfloor - 1)$
        $n_{freed} := n_{freed} + N_{add}$
      endif
    endif
    if last packet **then**   % $len = 0$
      $N_{avail} := N_{avail} + N_{add}$
      $N_{add} := 0$
      $lwm := \lfloor N_0/2 \rfloor - 1$
      $n_{freed} := N_0 - n_{recv}$
    endif
    if $n_{recv} \leq lwm$ **then**   % credits must be refilled
      if $len = 0 \lor len \geq N_{add}$ **then**   % on-demand scheme not
        send a refill packet with $n_{freed}[s]$ credits   % used or all credits
        $n_{recv} := n_{recv} + n_{freed}$ % must be refilled
        $n_{freed} := 0$
      else   % partial refill
        send a refill packet with $\min(n_{freed}, len - \max(0, n_{recv} - N_0))$ credits
        $n_{recv} := n_{recv} + \min(n_{freed}, len - \max(0, n_{recv} - N_0))$
        $n_{freed} := n_{freed} - \min(n_{freed}, len - \max(0, n_{recv} - N_0))$
        $lwm := \lfloor N_0/2 \rfloor - 1$ % ensures $lwm < n_{recv}$
      endif
    endif
  endif

Fig. 4. Pseudo-code executed at packet reception in the first variant of the on-demand flow control algorithm.

simultaneously to discard the credits in excess because this time processes s and r are informed that message transmission is terminated at different times. On the other hand, it may happen that, after s has sent the last packet, it may receive old refills containing credits in excess that must be discarded too. In place of condition (1), we may require that the following weaker condition is satisfied at any time:

$$n_{send}^{(s)}[r] + n_{refill}^{(s,r)} - \Delta + n_{network}^{(s,r)} = n_{recv}^{(r)}[s], \qquad (2)$$

where Δ is a non negative term such that $n_{refill}^{(s,r)} - \Delta \geq 0$. Note that Δ basically represents credits in excess refilled by r, but not received yet by s. This new invariant coincides with condition (1) if $\Delta = 0$, whereas it implies $n_{network}^{(s,r)} \leq n_{recv}^{(r)}[s]$, when $\Delta > 0$. This guarantees that r has always enough space to receive all packets sent by s.

The details of the protocol can be found in [5]. There we show that it can be efficiently implemented and that its costs are constant, unless s sistematically overstimates message length when message transmission starts.

4   Experimental Results

From experiments reported in section 2, we observed that peak bandwidth can be attained if at least 50 credits are assigned to each sender, and the lower water mark is set to 20. We then assigned these values to N_{opt} and lwm_{opt}, respectively.

We measured the bandwidth attainable by the COD protocol between one sender and one receiver versus the number of nodes in the system and repeated the experiments for different message lengths and packet sizes. The results corresponding to a packet size of 1024 bytes are reported in figure 5, compared with the bandwidth achieved by SCP in the same conditions. For the sake of brevity, we do not report the graphs corresponding to other packet sizes, since they show very similar behaviors.

The data corresponding to 64 KBytes messages are reported in figure 5(a). Although the bandwidth decreases even when COD is used, the improvement with respect to SCP is more than 40% in the worst case. Moreover, the threshold at which the sender remains idle waiting the refill packet increases. The situation is much better for longer messages. When message length is 256 KBytes (figure 5(b)), the bandwidth is independent of the system size if COD is used, while it can decrease more than 50% with the SCP algorithm. These results indicate that the COD algorithm has beneficial effects even for middle size messages (64 KBytes).

5   Related Work and Discussion

In highly reliable, high performance networks like Myrinet, host-to-host flow control is introduced at the software level essentially to guarantee reliability at the communication library interface through buffer overflow avoidance. Even

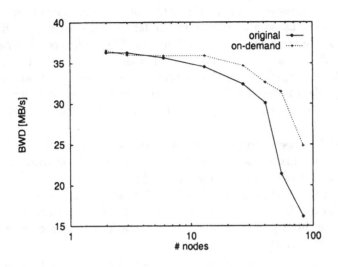

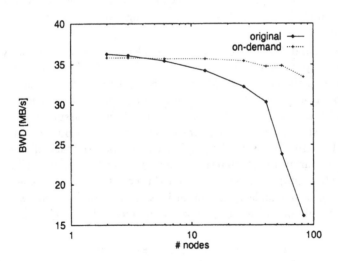

Fig. 5. Bandwidth vs. number of nodes with and without the on-demand protocol: (a) 64 Kbytes messages; (b) 256 Kbytes messages.

though simplified versions of the schemes available for non-reliable networks [13] can be reused in this context, credit-based protocols have been preferred in most cases.

The Active Messages library [2] provides buffer management and reliability and uses a credit-based algorithm very similar to that used in FM. *Reply* messages are exploited to refill consumed credits. The designers of U-Net [3] did not include flow control and reliable buffer management in the library since it was initially developed for ATM networks that are themselves non-reliable. In VMMC-2 [1] data is deposited directly in receiver's memory and flow control is up to higher level software. BIP [12] is a minimal library and does not guarantee reliability.

In the FM project, after an initial attempt to use a rate-based sliding window protocol requiring acknowledgements [11], the SCP protocol described in sections 2 and 3 has been used. The protocol proved to be successful because it is well suited to the characteristics of the Myrinet network. However, the high bandwidth available at the network level makes the management of buffer space internal to the library very critical, and the static policy used by SCP limits performance scalability.

Recently Kung et al. have proposed an adaptive credit allocation policy in the framework of a per Virtual Channel (VC), link-by-link, credit-based protocol for ATM networks, called Credit Update Protocol (CUP) [8]. The adaptive policy dynamically adjusts the buffer space allocated to an individual VC according to the actual bandwidth usage of the VC, achieving a more efficient use of available buffer space.

This proposal differs from our Credit On-Demand protocol in many respects. First, relevant parameters like Round Trip Time (RTT) and packet size are very different in the two cases. Moreover, RTT between hosts cannot be upper bounded like that between switches because of contention in the network and non-coordinated scheduling at the hosts. Hence, many assumptions which the policy proposed in [8] relies upon are no longer valid in our scenario. Second, while in CUP credits assigned to a VC cannot be got back if the VC stops transmitting, our protocol guarantees that the sender always either uses the assigned credits (simplified version) or returns credits in excess (general version). This property is particularly desirable in scientific applications where it may happen that pair of processes do not communicate for a relatively long time interval.

Another deep difference is that COD is essentially intended to be a mechanism that senders can use to dynamically acquire and release additional credits from their targets. In section 3 we have used the mechanism to implement a per message credit allocation policy and suggested simple criteria to decide how buffer space could be shared between all potential senders at initialization time. While these choices can suffice when regular communication patterns are used, more dynamic, adaptive policies could be needed to deal with general situations.

COD, especially in its general version, can be used as a basis to implement these policies. It allows credits to be acquired and (partially) released by senders at any time. For instance, in both versions of the algorithm the receiver can recover at any time at most $\min(n_{freed}, N_{add})$ credits simply decreasing variables n_{freed} and N_{add}. Moreover, in the general version, the sender can release credits at any time without substantial changes in the protocol [5]. This ability to dynamically change the credit assignment can be used to improve the fairness of the assignment policy when multiple senders compete for additional credits.

6   Conclusions

In this paper we have proposed the Credit On-Demand protocol, a variant of the static flow control protocol used by FM, that makes better use of available buffer space at the receivers. COD allows senders to require additional credits when they begin transmitting a message, and release them when message transmission terminates. We have reported experimental data that demonstrate that COD improves scalability and uses the resources available in the system more efficiently.

The limitations of our proposal are that it is effective only for long enough messages, and that there must not be communication hot spots in the system. These limitations however can be overcome because COD is a flexible mechanism that can be combined with more sophisticated, adaptive assignment policies.

Acknowledgements

This work has been carried out partially under the financial support of the Ministero dell'Università e della Ricerca Scientifica e Tecnologica (MURST) in the framework of the Project MOSAICO (Design Methodologies and Tools of High Performance Systems for Distributed Applications), of the Consiglio Nazionale delle Ricerce (CNR) in the framework of the project ADESSO. and of the University of Napoli Federico II in the framework of the Short-Term Mobility Programme.

We especially thank Andrew Chien for making available the FM and MPI-FM sources to a few selected groups outside the University of Illinois.

References

1. C. Dubnicki, L. Iftode, E. Felten, and K. Li, "Software support for virtual memory-mapped communication", *Procs. of the 1996 International Parallel Processing Symposium*, Aug. 1996.
2. T. von Eicken, D. Culler, S. Goldstein, and K. Schauser, "Active Messages: a mechanism for integrated communication and computation", *Procs. of the International Symposium on Computer Architecture*, May 1992.
3. T. von Eicken, A. Basu, V. Buch, and W. Vogels, "U-Net: a user-level network interface for parallel and distributed computing", *Procs. of the 15th ACM Symposium on Operating System Principles*, Dec. 1995.

4. N.J. Boden, D. Cohen, R.E. Felderman, A.E. Kalawik, C.L. Seitz, J.N. Seizovic, and W.-K. Su, "Myrinet–a gigabit-per-second local-area network", *IEEE Micro*, 15(1), February 1995.

5. R. Canonico, R. Cristaldi, and G. Iannello, "Credit On-Demand: a scalable flow control protocol for the Fast Messages communication library", Tech. Report, DIS, Sept. 1998.

6. D.E. Culler, R.M. Karp, D.A. Patterson, A. Sahay, K.E. Schauser, E. Santos, R. Subramonian, and T. von Eicken, "LogP: towards a realistic model of parallel computation", *Procs. of the 4th SIGPLAN Symp. on Principles and Practices of Parallel Programming*. ACM, May 1993.

7. R.M. Karp, A. Sahay, E.E. Santos, and K.E. Schauser, "Optimal Broadcast and Summation in the LogP Model", *Procs. of the 5th Annual ACM Symp. on Parallel Algorithms and Architectures*, pages 142–153, June 1993.

8. H.T. Kung and R. Morris, "Credit-Based Flow Control for ATM Networks", *IEEE Networks*, March/April 1995.

9. M. Lauria and A. Chien, "MPI-FM: High performance MPI on workstation clusters", *Journal of Parallel and Distributed Computing*, vol. 40(1), January 1997, pp. 4–18.

10. M. Lauria, S. Pakin, and A.A. Chien. "Efficient Layering for High Speed Communication: Fast Messages 2.x", *Procs. of the 7th High Performance Distributed Computing Conference (HPDC7)*, Chicago, Illinois, July 28-31, 1998.

11. S. Pakin, M. Lauria, and A.A. Chien. "High performance messaging on workstation: Illinois Fast Messages (FM) for Myrinet", *Procs. Supercomputing 95*, Dec. 1995.

12. L. Prylli, "Draft: BIP messages user manual for bip 0.94", `lhpca.univ-lyon1.fr/bip.html`, 1997.

13. A. Tanenbaum, *Computer Networks*, Prentice Hall International, 3rd Edition, 1996.

High Performance Sockets and RPC over Virtual Interface (VI) Architecture

Hemal V. Shah[1], Calton Pu[2], and Rajesh S. Madukkarumukumana[1,2]

[1] M/S CO3-202, Server Architecture Lab,
Intel Corporation,
5200 N.E. Elam Young Pkwy, Hillsboro, OR 97124.
{hemal.shah,rajesh.sankaran}@intel.com
[2] Department of Computer Science & Engineering,
Oregon Graduate Institute of Science and Technology,
P.O. Box 91000, Portland, OR 97291.
{calton,rajeshs}@cse.ogi.edu

Abstract. Standard user-level networking architecture such as Virtual Interface (VI) Architecture enables distributed applications to perform low overhead communication over System Area Networks (SANs). This paper describes how high-level communication paradigms like stream sockets and remote procedure call (RPC) can be efficiently built over user-level networking architectures. To evaluate performance benefits for standard client-server and multi-threaded environments, our focus is on off-the-shelf sockets and RPC interfaces and commercially available VI Architecture based SANs. The key design techniques developed in this research include credit-based flow control, decentralized user-level protocol processing, caching of pinned communication buffers, and deferred processing of completed send operations. The one-way bandwidth achieved by stream sockets over VI Architecture was 3 to 4 times better than the same achieved by running legacy protocols over the same interconnect. On the same SAN, high-performance stream sockets and RPC over VI Architecture achieve significantly better (between 2-3x) latency than conventional stream sockets and RPC over standard network protocols in Windows NT^{TM} 4.0 environment. Furthermore, our high-performance RPC transparently improved the network performance of Distributed Component Object Model (DCOM) by a factor of 2 to 3.

1 Introduction

With the advent of System Area Networks (SANs), low latency and high bandwidth communication has become a reality. These networks have opened new horizons for cluster computing. But, the centralized in-kernel protocol processing in legacy transport protocols such as TCP/IP prohibits applications from realizing the raw hardware performance offered by underlying SANs. In order to address this problem, Virtual Interface (VI) Architecture standard was developed. However, building high-level applications using primitives provided by

A.Sivasubramaniam, M.Lauria (Eds.): CANPC'99, LNCS 1602, pp. 91–107, 1999.

VI Architecture is complex due to lack of transport functionality such as flow control, communication buffer management, fragmentation/re-assembly.

On the other hand, stream sockets and remote procedure calls (RPCs) provide simple and easy to use communication abstractions for distributed applications and distributed object computing frameworks such as DCOM [5], Java RMI [9], CORBA [12]. Stream sockets provide a connection-oriented, bi-directional byte-stream model for inter-process communication. RPC mechanism enables a program to call procedures that execute in other address space and it hides networking details from applications.

This paper provides prototype designs and implementations of 1) stream sockets over VI Architecture and 2) RPC over VI Architecture. The design goals considered were:

- Performance: deliver close to raw end-to-end performance to multi-threaded client/server applications.
- Legacy support: support RPC/sockets application programming interfaces as much as possible.
- CPU overhead: minimize CPU cycles spent per byte transferred.

Optimizations for special cases such as single-threaded applications and modifying kernel components such as virtual memory management system can be used to further improve performance. Most of these techniques trade off application transparency and ease of use, and thus, were not considered as design goals.

This paper contributes VI Architecture specific design techniques, developed for optimizing stream sockets and RPC performance, such as credit based flow control, decentralized user-level protocol processing, caching of pinned communication buffers, and deferred processing of completed send operations. On Windows NT^{TM} 4.0, user-level stream sockets and RPC over VI Architecture achieve significantly better performance (2-3x improvement in latency and 3-4x improvement in one-way and bi-directional bandwidths) than stream sockets and RPC with legacy network protocols (TCP/IP) on the same SAN. For small messages, RPC over VI Architecture achieves an end-to-end latency comparable to the latency achieved by the local RPC implementation on the same system. Further, this translated into 2-3x improvement in DCOM network performance transparently.

The rest of the paper provides the details of the design and evaluation of stream sockets and RPC over VI Architecture. The outline of the remaining paper is as follows. Section 2 provides an overview of VI Architecture. The design and performance evaluation of stream sockets over VI Architecture is described in Section 3. Section 4 describes the design of RPC over VI Architecture and evaluates its performance. Section 5 provides a summary of the related work. Finally, conclusions and future work are presented in Section 6.

2   Virtual Interface (VI) Architecture

VI Architecture is a user-level networking architecture designed to achieve low latency, high bandwidth communication within a computing cluster. To a user process, VI Architecture provides direct access to the network interface in a fully protected fashion. The VI Architecture avoids intermediate data copies and bypasses operating system to achieve low latency, high bandwidth data transfer. The VI Architecture Specification 1.0 [15] was jointly authored by Intel Corporation, Microsoft Corporation, and Compaq Computer Corporation.

Virtual Interface Architecture uses a VI construct to present an illusion to each process that it owns the interface to the network. A VI is owned and maintained by a single process. Each VI consists of two work queues: one send queue and one receive queue. On each work queue, descriptors are used to describe work to be done by the network interface. A linked-list of variable length descriptors forms each queue. Ordering and data consistency rules are only maintained within one VI but not between different VIs. VI Architecture also provides a completion queue construct used to link completion notifications from multiple work queues to a single queue.

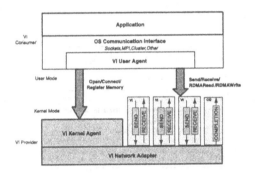

Fig. 1. VI Architecture

Memory protection for all VI operations is provided by protection tag (a unique identifier) mechanism. Protection tags are associated with VIs and memory regions. The memory regions used by descriptors and data buffers are registered prior to data transfer operations. Memory registration gives VI NIC a method to translate a virtual address to a physical address. The user receives an opaque memory handle as a result of memory registration. This allows a user to refer to a memory region using a memory handle/virtual address pair without worrying about crossing page boundaries and keeping track of the virtual address to tag mapping.

The VI Architecture defines two types of data transfer operations: 1) traditional send/receive operations, and 2) Remote-DMA (RDMA) read/write operations. A user process posts descriptors on work queues and uses either polling or blocking mechanism to synchronize with the completed operations. The two descriptor processing models supported by VI Architecture are *the work queue model* and *the completion queue model*. In the work queue model, the VI consumer polls or waits for completions on a particular work queue. The VI consumer polls or waits for completions on a set of work queues in the completion queue model. The processing of descriptors posted on a VI is performed in FIFO order but there is no implicit relationship between the processing of descriptors posted on different VIs. For more details on VI Architecture, the interested reader is referred to [6, 15]. The next two sections describe design and implementation of stream sockets and RPC over VI Architecture.

3   Stream Sockets over VI Architecture

Stream sockets provide connection-oriented, bi-directional byte-stream oriented communication model. Windows Sockets 2 Architecture utilizes sockets paradigm and provides protocol-independent transport interface. Figure 2 shows an overview of Windows Sockets 2 architecture [16]. It consists of an application programming interface (API) used by applications and service provider interfaces (SPIs) implemented by service providers.

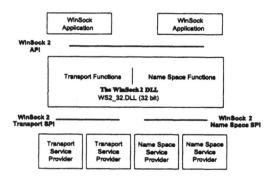

Fig. 2. Windows Sockets 2 Architecture

This extensible architecture allows multiple service providers to coexist. The transport service providers implement the actual transport protocol and the name space providers map WinSock's name space SPI to some existing name space. In this research, Windows Sockets 2 Architecture is used to provide high performance VI-based stream sockets. The new transport service provider was completely implemented at user-level.

3.1   Design and Implementation

User-level decentralized protocol processing, credit-based flow control, caching of pinned communication buffers, and minimization of CPU overhead are the main techniques used in our stream sockets over VI Architecture implementation. These techniques along with the design are described next.

Endpoint Mappings and Connection Management The connection-oriented design provided by VI Architecture maps well to stream sockets. Each stream socket (endpoint) is mapped to a VI. Each endpoint consists of send/receive descriptors, registered send/receive buffers, and information for credit based flow control. Each endpoint has a queue of received buffers containing data yet to be read by the application. In order to reduce number of memory registrations, global pools of send/receive descriptors are created and registered within a process during service provider initialization. During creation of an endpoint, descriptors are assigned from these global pools. Upon destruction of an endpoint, descriptors are returned back to the global pools. A queue of pending connection requests is maintained at each endpoint. A dedicated thread manages connection requests on the endpoint. IP port numbers are used as discriminators in underlying connection establishment between VIs.

Data Transfer and Flow Control The reliability mode used in data transfers is *Reliable Delivery*. Reliable delivery VI guarantees that the data submitted for transfer is delivered exactly once, intact, and in the order submitted, in the absence of errors. Transport errors are extremely rare and considered catastrophic. In network interfaces that emulate VI functionality, reliable delivery is commonly implemented in NIC firmware or software. In native VI NICs (such as GNN1000 [8]), the hardware provides reliable delivery. Due to the use of reliable delivery VIs, fragmentation of the messages can be handled without using sequence numbers. Furthermore, the transport service provider need not worry about managing acknowledgements and detecting duplicates. The timeout and retransmission mechanisms are not incorporated in the transport service provider as transport errors are rare and connection is broken when transport errors occur.

Three types of messages used in data transfer are *CreditRequest*, *CreditResponse*, and *Data*. The transport service provider is responsible for managing end-to-end flow control between two endpoints. For providing end-to-end flow control, a credit-based scheme is used. If the number of send credits is sufficient, then the sender prepares and sends the packet. Otherwise, the sender sends a credit request (*CreditRequest*) and waits for the credit response (*CreditResponse*). Upon receiving credit response, it continues sending packets. In response to sender's request for credit update, the receiver sends the credit response only when it has enough receive credits (above the low water mark). In the case of not having enough credits when the credit request arrives, the receiver defers the sending of credit response until sufficient receive credits are available. As application consumes the received data, receive credits are regained. Credit-based flow control scheme and use of reliable delivery VIs provide low overhead user-level protocol processing.

Descriptor Processing In VI Architecture, a data transfer operation is split into two phases: initiation of the operation (posting a descriptor) and completion of the operation (polling or waitiing for a descriptor to complete on a work queue). Due to push model of processing and high-speed reliable SANs, each send descriptor completes quickly once it reaches the head of the send queue. So in order to reduce interrupts, polling is used for checking completion of send descriptors. Checking completion of a send descriptor is deferred until either there are not enough send credits available or the entire message is posted. This type of deferred de-queuing of send descriptors reduces CPU overhead compared to when polling immediately after posting each send descriptor.

The transport service provider maintains a small-sized LRU cache of registered application buffers. This allows zero-copy sends for frequently used send buffers. The application data is copied into pre-registered send buffers only when the application buffer is not found in the cache and is not added to the cache. To allow application specific tuning, the maximum number of LRU cache entries and the minimum size of registered application buffer are kept configurable.

Receive descriptors need to be pre-posted prior to posting of the matching send descriptors on the sender side. The data is always copied from the registered received buffers to the buffers supplied by the application for receiving data. The copying of data on the receiver side can be overlapped with VI NIC processing and physical communication. The receiver waits when there is no data available on the socket. When the receiver wakes up due to completion of a receive descriptor, the receiver de-queues as many completed receive descriptors as possible. This scheme for processing receive descriptors reduces the number of interrupts on the host system.

The transport service provider for stream sockets over VI Architecture was implemented at user-level. This allows decentralized protocol processing on per process basis. The user-level buffer management and flow control scheme do not experience kernel like restrictive environment. The communication subsystem becomes an integrated part of the application and this allows for an application specific tuning. The next subsection provides experimental evaluation of stream sockets over VI Architecture.

3.2   Experimental Evaluation

In the experiments involving micro-benchmarks, a pair of server systems, with four 400 MHZ Pentium^R II Xeon^{TM} processors (512K L2 cache), Intel AD450NX 64-bit PCI chipset, and 256 MB main memory, was used as a pair of host nodes. GigaNet's cLAN^{TM} GNN1000 interconnect (full duplex, 1.25 Gbps one-way) [8] with VI functionality implemented on NIC hardware is used as VI NIC. The software environment used for all the experiments included Windows NT^{TM} 4.0 with service pack 3 and Microsoft Visual C++ 6.0. As a default, the Maximum Transfer Unit (MTU) per packet used by the stream sockets over VI Architecture was 8 K bytes and credit-based flow control scheme reserved an initial receive credits of 32 for each connection. Unless stated, all the experimental results were obtained using these default values.

Round-Trip Latency In distributed applications, round-trip latencies of small messages play an important role in the performance and scalability of the system. In order to measure round-trip latency, a ping-pong test was used in the experiments. Figure 3 compares the application-to-application round-trip latency achieved (averaged over 10000 runs) by raw VI Architecture primitives, stream sockets over VI Architecture (GNN1000), TCP/IP over Gigabit Ethernet, and TCP/IP over GNN1000. The round-trip latency achieved by stream sockets over VI Architecture is 2-3 times better than the round-trip latency achieved by both TCP/IP over Gigabit Ethernet and TCP/IP over GNN1000. Moreover, the average round-trip latency achieved for a given message size is within 50% of the round-trip latency achieved using raw VI architecture primitives.

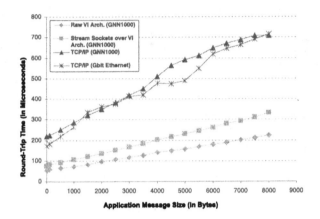

Fig. 3. Round-Trip Latency

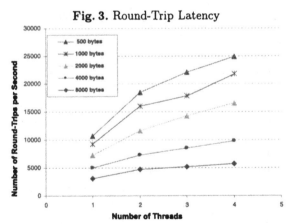

Fig. 4. SMP Scalability

In order to measure SMP scalability of stream sockets over VI Architecture, a multi-threaded ping-pong test (where each thread independently ping-pongs messages on a dedicated socket) was used. Figure 4 provides the SMP scalability for various message sizes. The metric used to measure scalability was the number of aggregate round-trips per second. Due to availability of multiple CPUs, most of the protocol processing was performed in parallel. The primary reasons for limited scalability for large messages were the use of single VI NIC for processing the messages sent and received by multiple threads and availability of single I/O channel on host system (PCI bus). VI NIC performs the tasks of multiplexing, de-multiplexing, putting user-level data on the wire, copying received data into user-level buffer, and data transfer scheduling. Hence, for large messages, the VI NIC processing overhead can become significant. This suggests that having multiple VI NICs and multiple I/O channels can further improve SMP scalability.

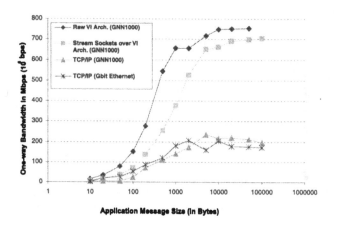

Fig. 5. One-way Receiver Bandwidth

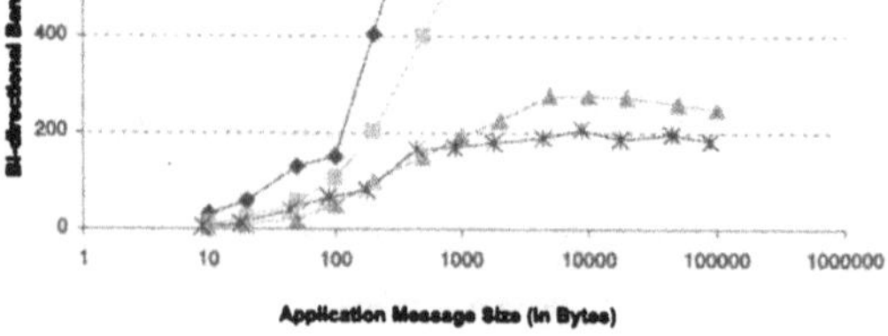

Fig. 6. Bi-Directional Bandwidth

Bandwidth Figure 5 provides comparison of application-to-application one-way bandwidths (measured using a stream of 10000 messages) achieved by raw VI Architecture, stream sockets over VI Architecture (GNN1000), TCP/IP over Gigabit Ethernet, and TCP/IP over GNN1000. For large messages, the one-way bandwidth achieved by stream sockets over VI Architecture is 3 to 4 times better

than the same achieved by running legacy protocols (TCP/IP) over both the
same SAN and Gigabit Ethernet. The one-way bandwidth achieved by stream
sockets over VI Architecture is within 10% of the one-way bandwidth achieved
by the raw VI Architecture primitives using same descriptor processing models
and synchronization mechanisms.

Similarly, Figure 6 compares the bi-directional bandwidths achieved by various messaging layers. The bi-directional bandwidth test has two threads (one
sender and one receiver) using two separate communication endpoints. The
sender thread sends a stream of messages on one endpoint and the receiver
thread receives a stream of messages on another endpoint. The receiver bandwidths achieved on both nodes were added to obtain bi-directional bandwidth.
Similar to one-way bandwidth, for large messages, the bi-directional bandwidth
achieved by stream sockets over VI Architecture is 3-4 (4-5) times better than
the same achieved by running legacy TCP/IP protocol over GNN1000 (Gigabit
Ethernet). For large messages, the bi-directional bandwidth achieved by stream
sockets over VI Architecture stays within 10% of the bi-directional bandwidth
achieved by using raw VI Architecture primitives. Figure 7 shows the number
of CPU cycles spent per byte transferred at different messaging layers. These
experiments demonstrate that stream sockets over VI architecture not only
achieve substantially better performance than legacy transport protocols, but
also spend significantly less host CPU cycles per byte transferred than TCP/IP.
Table 1 summarizes 4-byte round-trip latency and 50000-byte one-way bandwidth achieved by various messaging layers.

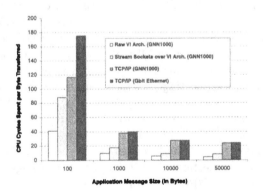

Fig. 7. CPU Overhead

4   RPC over VI Architecture

In order to examine the advantage in efficiently supporting an off-the-shelf RPC
system over user-level networking architectures, we instrumented the Microsoft
Remote Procedure Call (MSRPC) and DCOM facilities available in Windows

Table 1. Performance of Various Messaging Layers

Messaging Layer	4-byte Round-trip Latency (in μs)	50000-byte One-way Bandwidth (in 10^6 bps)
Raw VI Architecture Primitives	52.4	753.2
Stream Sockets over VI Architecture	74.9	697.3
TCP/IP over GNN1000	219.1	211
TCP/IP over Gigabit Ethernet	170.5	175

NT^{TM} 4.0. Experimental results in our earlier research [10] have shown that the latency incurred in MSRPC over conventional high-speed networks such as Gigabit Ethernet is dominated by the overhead in the legacy transport protocol (TCP/IP) stack. The primary focus of this prototype effort was to transparently improve the performance of RPC and DCOM applications over SANs by reducing the transport protocol overheads.

4.1 Operational Overview

MSRPC system is primarily composed of the IDL compiler generated proxy and stubs, the RPC runtime and the various dynamically loadable transport modules. The remoting architecture in DCOM [5] is abstracted as an Object RPC (ORPC) layer built over MSRPC. As a natural consequence, DCOM wire protocol performance directly follows the performance of MSRPC. MSRPC provides a high performance local RPC transport implementation for procedure calls across address spaces on the same machine. For procedure calls across the network, the transport interface in MSRPC supports both connectionless and connection-oriented transport interfaces. Figure 8 shows the operational view of the MSRPC system supporting multiple transport providers. Building high performance RPC over our stream sockets prototype was definitely a viable option. Rather, we added a connection-oriented MSRPC loadable transport directly over VI architecture to avoid additional layering overheads. Our prototype RPC transport[1] makes use of the low-latency and high reliability properties of SANs. The following sub-sections describe in detail the design and implementation trade-off made in the RPC transport for SANs.

4.2 RPC Transport Design for SANs

The main objective for the transport design was to improve the network performance of multi-threaded RPC and DCOM client/server applications. Any performance improvement possible by modifying the MSRPC runtime and/or the

---

[1] Rajesh S. Madukkarumukumana implemented the RPC transport at Oregon Graduate Institute of Science & Technology (OGI). Access to MSRPC source was provided under Microsoft Windows NT^{TM} source code agreement between Microsoft and Oregon Graduate Institute for educational research purposes.

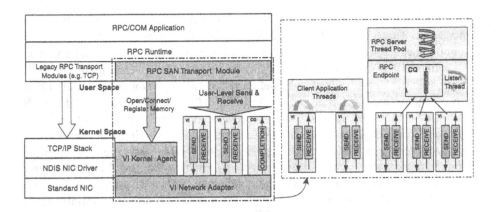

Fig. 8. MSRPC Operational Overview

marshaling engines was traded-off for application transparency and simplicity. These design choices were further motivated by the fact that the legacy network protocol stack contributed to the most part of the standard RPC latency. To co-exist with other transports, the SAN transport supports a new RPC protocol sequence (ncacn_san_vi) and is registered with the system using the standard WinNT^{TM} registry. Our transport uses a connection-oriented design for performance and utilizes the higher reliability modes offered by SANs. The transport module performs various operations like static/dynamic endpoint mapping, listening for connections, data transfers, connection tear-downs, etc. The transport module also provides the RPC runtime system information like the MTU of the transport and the buffer size needed to manage each endpoint and connection.

Endpoint Mapping In response to the RPC binding calls from the application, the MSRPC runtime calls the transport module to setup static and dynamic endpoints. The RPC transport takes machine name as the network address and accepts any string as an endpoint. The endpoint strings are used as discriminators in connection establishment between VIs. Dynamic endpoints use universally unique identifiers (UUIDs) as discriminators. On the server side, the receive queues of all VI connections created under an RPC endpoint are attached to a Completion Queue (CQ). The send queue for each VI connection is managed independently. The completion queue provides a mechanism to poll or wait for receive completions from multiple VIs associated with a given endpoint. This is equivalent to a traditional select functionality, but has the distinct advantage that the receive operation (after the select) does not need a kernel transition to de-queue the completed receive buffer. Since each send queue is managed separately, send operations can be performed independently on any connection. Connection requests from the RPC runtime on behalf of any client application thread is mapped directly to a unique VI. The client side does not use completion queues (CQs), but manages the receive and send queues for each connection independently. The connection management and flow control design are discussed next.

Connection Management and Flow Control Today, most SANs provide a message-oriented reliable transport service, but do not provide flow control or support for out-of-band data. In addition to this, user-level networking architectures like VI Architecture require explicit registration of communication buffers. Compared to the centralized in-kernel implementation of flow control and buffering in legacy transport protocol stacks (TCP/IP), the RPC transport for SAN uses a de-centralized approach for user-level connection management and flow control. Upon endpoint creation request from the server side RPC runtime, the transport creates a CQ and registers the needed receive buffers and descriptors. The endpoint accepts connection requests by creating/binding VI handles with pre-posted receive buffers. After connection setup, a three-trip protocol between the client and the server-transports negotiates the MTU and the available credits on either side. The server-side RPC runtime is notified of newly accepted connections by using callbacks.

Similar to stream sockets over VI Architecture, the credit based flow control scheme uses three types of messages: *Data* (contains requests/replies from MSRPC runtime), *RTS* (sent to get more credits from receivers), and *CTS* (sent in response to an *RTS* message). The flow control information consists of packet sequence number, number of available credits and the sequence number of the last received packet. The transport encodes the flow control information into the *ImmediateData* field of VI descriptors. The sender is allowed to send a data packet only if there are enough credits available. If enough credits are not available, more credits can be requested by sending an RTS request message and waiting for a CTS reply message. An automatic RTS/CTS credit synchronization happens whenever the number of send credits goes below low watermark. Due to lightweight nature of this RTS/CTS scheme and the efficient re-use of receive buffers, automatic credit update schemes were not considered. The service-oriented abstraction and synchronous nature of RPC keep the buffer management much simpler than stream sockets where receive buffers are asynchronously consumed by the application.

Buffer Management and Data Transfer The RPC transport achieves zero-copy sends of marshaled buffers passed from the RPC runtime by pinning them first if needed, then fragmenting and queuing it on the send queue of the appropriate VI. Polling is used to complete send operations without kernel transitions. To avoid the costly registration and de-registration of buffers on each send operation, a cache of previously marshaled buffers is maintained in LRU fashion. Since RPC runtime itself uses cached buffers to marshal data on a per connection basis, a large percentage of cache hits was observed in the experiments. Any small-sized send buffer (typical in RPC) that misses this cache is copied to a pre-registered send buffer before posting the send descriptor.

The RPC transport interface supports two types of receive semantics for network I/O: *ReceiveAny* and *ReceiveDirect*. The *ReceiveAny* interface uses a single thread at a time to service a set of clients connected to an endpoint. In legacy transport protocols such as TCP/IP, the *ReceiveDirect* path dedicates a thread per connection and saves an extra kernel call compared to the *ReceiveAny* path. The use of CQs and user-level receive operations in our transport allows efficient implementation of *ReceiveAny*. This reduces the performance advantages of additionally implementing *ReceiveDirect*. Both the client and server perform a single copy of data from the receive buffers to RPC runtime buffers. The RPC runtime is called back to do any re-allocation of the marshaled buffer for re-assembly of multiple fragments. After copying the message, the de-queued receive descriptors are re-posted immediately on the receive queue to keep the flow-control credits fairly constant.

The use of reliable delivery VIs (as discussed in Section 3.1), efficient caching of marshaled send buffers, zero-copy user-level sends and single copy receive completions in the RPC transport contributes to the high performance achieved. In addition, to enable DCOM applications to transparently run over SANs, the DCOM Service Control Manager (SCM) in WinNT^{TM} was modified to listen on the new RPC protocol (in addition to other legacy protocols) for COM object invocation requests. The performance analysis of RPC and DCOM applications over the SAN transport is discussed next.

4.3   Experimental Results

In order to evaluate the RPC and DCOM performance improvements over the user-level RPC transport, a set of experiments was carried out using the same experimental setup described in Section 3.2. All DCOM and RPC latency measurements used bi-directional conformant arrays as method parameters. Figures 9 and 10 compare the round-trip RPC and DCOM method call latencies (averaged over 10000 runs) across various RPC transports respectively. On the same SAN, RPC and DCOM over VI Architecture achieve significantly (2-3x) better latency than RPC and DCOM over legacy network protocols (TCP/IP). Furthermore, application-to-application latency achieved by RPC and DCOM is comparable to the latency achieved by local RPC (LRPC) and COM.

RPC and distributed object abstractions are becoming norm to build multithreaded client/server applications. While several previous research efforts [1, 3, 11, 17] have shown the performance improvement possible through efficient thread and function dispatching in specialized environments, our research focuses more on transparently improving the performance of commercial multi-threaded implementation like MSRPC.

The RPC transport implementation creates a new VI connection to the server endpoint for each client application thread using the same RPC binding handle. The de-centralized user-level protocol processing done independently on a per connection basis eliminates major synchronization and multiplexing overheads otherwise required for buffer management in the transport. Figure 11 shows the scalability achieved on a 4-way SMP system with multiple application threads using a single RPC binding handle over the RPC transport. This demonstrates the efficiency of credit based flow control and buffer management. Figure 12 shows that the host CPU cycles spent per byte transferred using the high performance RPC transport is substantially lower than using legacy transport protocol

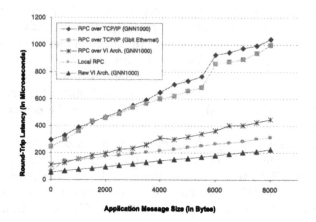

Fig. 9. Round-Trip Latency

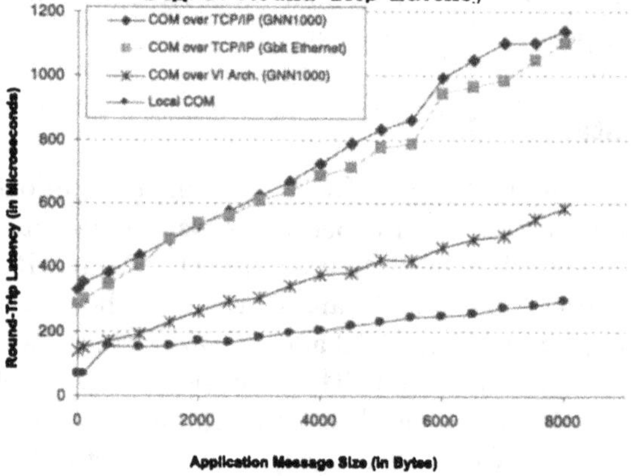

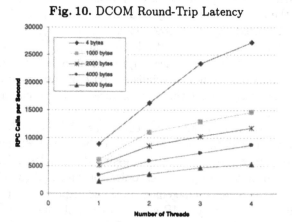

Fig. 10. DCOM Round-Trip Latency

Fig. 11. SMP Scalability

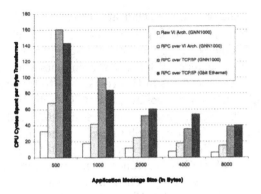

Fig. 12. CPU Overhead

(TCP/IP) over the same SAN and Gigabit Ethernet. Table 2 summarizes 4-byte round-trip latencies and 8000-byte round-trip latencies achieved by various RPC transports.

Table 2. MSRPC Performance Across Various Transports

Messaging Layer	4-byte Round-trip Latency (in μs)	8000-byte Round-trip Latency (in μs)
Local RPC (LRPC)	62.7	314.8
RPC over VI Architecture (GNN1000)	111.21	448.1
RPC over TCP/IP (GNN1000)	297.1	1039.7
RPC over TCP/IP (Gigabit Ethernet)	243.5	995.8

5   Related Work

Damianikis et al. [4] described the implementation of high performance stream sockets compatible abstraction over virtual memory mapped communication (VMMC) in the SHRIMP multi-computer using a custom designed network interface. Thorsten von Eicken et al. [7] showed how traditional protocols (TCP/IP, UDP/IP) can be efficiently supported over U-Net (a user-level networking architecture). Fast sockets [14] were implemented to provide low overhead protocol layer on top of high performance transport mechanism (active messages). Pakin et al. [13] implemented user-level sockets library over low-level FM messaging layer. In all of these previous efforts, the focus was on to build efficient socket abstractions using custom low overhead messaging layer. In this paper, we add-on to their findings by developing techniques for efficient stream sockets implementation over standard user-level networking architecture (VI Architecture).

Muller et al. [11] showed how specialization techniques like partial evaluation can be applied to improve RPC performance. Cheriton et al. [17] proposed a specialization methodology for applications to modify and tune the RPC system to meet specific requirements. While these techniques are possible in custom application environments, our focus in this research is to transparently improve performance of applications using commercial RPC systems. Bilas and Felten [1] described a SunRPC implementation over the SHRIMP multi-computer, but concentrated on achieving the best absolute performance in single threaded environments. Zimmer and Chien [18] described in detail the impact of inexpensive communication to MSRPC performance by implementing a RPC datagram transport over Fast Messages (FM). Their implementation exposed the pessimistic assumptions made by the MSRPC runtime about datagram transports. Chang et al. [3] proposed a software architecture for zero-copy RPC in Java across user-level network interfaces. Their work showed interesting RPC latency improvements, but required manual generation of proxy/stub code. Our user-level RPC transport's connection-oriented design and credit based flow control utilizes reliable delivery mode offered by SANs to achieve significant performance improvements transparently.

6   Conclusions and Future Work

User-level networking architecture like VI Architecture provides low level primitives for high performance communication over SANs. Building high-level scalable distributed applications require this type of communication performance without sacrificing ease of programming. This paper demonstrates how high level communication abstractions like stream sockets and RPC can be efficiently implemented over VI Architecture. Our prototype implementations achieve significantly better performance (3-4x bandwidth improvement for stream sockets, 2-3x latency improvement for stream sockets, MSRPC, and DCOM) over legacy network protocols (TCP/IP) on the same SAN. We are currently investigating variants of credit based flow control and optimized large data transfers with RDMA operations provided by VI Architecture. A possible direction for future work is to extend support for overlapped and asynchronous operations in stream sockets and RPC over VI Architecture. Another interesting direction is to experiment with high level RPC and distributed objects based applications such as transaction processing monitors, web servers, and N-tier applications over VI Architecture.

Acknowledgements

We would like to thank many people at Intel corporation especially Natalie Bates, Ellen Deleganes, Chris Dodd, David Fair, Ed Gronke, Roy Larsen, Dave Minturn, George Moakley, Wire Moore, Justin Rattner, Greg Regnier, and Brad Rullman for their helpful suggestions and support.

References

1. Angelo Bilas and Edward W. Felten: Fast RPC on the SHRIMP Virtual Memory Mapped Network Interface. J. of Parallel and Distributed Computing. **40(1)** (1997) 138–146
2. M. Blumrich et al.: A Virtual Memory Mapped Network Interface for the Shrimp Multicomputer. In Proceedings of the 21st Annual Symposium on Computer Architecture. (1994) 142–153
3. Chi-Chao Chang and Thorsten von Eicken: A Software Architecture for Zero-Copy RPC in Java. CS Technical Report 98-1708, Cornell University. (1998)
4. Stefanos N. Damianakis, Cezary Dubnicki, and Edward W. Felten. Stream Sockets on SHRIMP. In Proceedings of 1st International Workshop on Communication and Architectural Support for Network-Based Parallel Computing. (1997)
5. DCOM Architecture. Microsoft Corporation. (1997)
6. Dave Dunning et al.: The Virtual Interface Architecture: A Protected, Zero Copy, User-level Interface to Networks. IEEE MICRO. **18(2)** (1998) 66–76
7. Thorsten von Eicken et al.: U-Net: A User-Level Network Interface for Parallel and Distributed Computing. Proceedings of the 15th ACM Symposium on Operating System Principles. (1995) 40–53
8. GigaNet Incorporated. GigaNet cLAN Product Family. http://www.giganet.com/products.
9. Java^{TM} Remote Method Invocation Specification. ftp://ftp.javasoft.com/docs/jdk1.2/rmi-spec-JDK1.2.pdf.
10. Rajesh S. Madukkarumukumana, Calton Pu, and Hemal V. Shah: Harnessing User-level Networking Architectures for Distributed Object Computing over High-Speed Networks. In Proc. of 2nd USENIX Windows NT Symposium. (1998) 127–135
11. Gilles Muller et al.: Fast, Optimized Sun RPC Using Automatic Program Specialization. In Proceedings of the International Conference on Distributed Computing Systems (ICDCS-18). (1998) 240–249
12. Object Management Group: The Common Object Request Broker: Architecture and Specification. 2.0 Edition. (1995)
13. Scott Pakin, Vijay Karamcheti, and Andrew A. Chien: Fast Messages: Efficient, Portable Communication for Workstation Clusters and MPPs. IEEE Concurrency. **5(2)** (1997) 60–73
14. Steven H. Rodrigues, Thomas E. Anderson, and David E. Culler: High-Performance Local Area Communication with Fast Sockets. USENIX 1997 Conference. (1997)
15. Virtual Interface Architecture Specification. Version 1.0. http://www.viarch.org/. (1997)
16. Windows Sockets 2 Service Provider Interface. ftp://ftp.microsoft.com/bussys/winsock/winsock2/.
17. Matthew J. Zelesko and David R. Cheriton: Specializing Object-Oriented RPC for Functionality and Performance. In Proceedings of the International Conference on Distributed Computing Systems (ICDCS-16). (1996)
18. Oolan M. Zimmer and Andrew A. Chien: The Impact of Inexpensive Communication on a Commercial RPC System. Concurrent System Architecture Group Memo, University of Illinois at Urbana-Champaign and University of California at San Diego. (1998)

The Scheduled Transfer (ST) Protocol

Ian R. Philp and Yin-Ling Liong

Network Engineering Group, MS B255
Los Alamos National Laboratory
Los Alamos, NM 87545
philp@lanl.gov, yliong@cae.wisc.edu

Abstract. This paper describes the Scheduled Transfer (ST) protocol that can be used by applications to bypass the operating system (OS) for network communications. The design of ST has been influenced by two overriding goals. First, we want ST to be used to move data between multiple vendors' machines and over different media; therefore, we have proposed ST as an ANSI standard and defined a network protocol that is independent of the underlying physical layer. Second, ST has been designed to operate in a large, heavily-loaded scientific computing environment, and this goal is manifested in several ways. ST has been designed to minimize receive processing, relieving network congestion that could occur if the receiver exerts backpressure into the network. ST provides a mechanism by which upper layer protocol (ULP) headers can be separated from application data, a capability that is generally necessary to avoid a subsequent memory-to-memory copy in the host. ST includes support for reassembly of application messages that are striped across multiple physical interfaces. ST also includes a flow control mechanism that relieves the ULP from this responsibility and provides the opportunity for the implementor to offload this function to the network interface (NI).

1 Introduction

Recent advances in commercially available network technologies, e.g., HIPPI-800 and 6400 [11], ATM/SONET [2], Myrinet [3], and Gigabit Ethernet [10], have presented the possibility of connecting PC-class machines and high-end workstations to interconnects that have bandwidths approaching and sometimes exceeding the main memory bandwidth of the host. This contrasts with the situation just a few years ago when memory bandwidths were frequently many times the network bandwidth. Because the time spent in physical transmission of a message has dropped so significantly, software overheads in the host system have been exposed as the major bottleneck in achieving low-latency, high-bandwidth communications.

Typical operating system- (OS) implemented network protocol stacks result in unnecessary memory-to-memory copies and excessive interrupts that can limit application-achievable throughput to a fraction of what is theoretically achievable and increase end-to-end latency by an order of magnitude. A solution to this

A.Sivasubramaniam, M.Lauria (Eds.): CANPC'99, LNCS 1602, pp. 108–121, 1999.
© Springer-Verlag Berlin Heidelberg 1999

problem is to bypass the host OS for common send and receive operations while still maintaining all the features found (and expected) in an OS-implemented protocol stack: the ability to share the network and protection and fairness among applications.

OS bypass techniques have been studied extensively in recent years. Some of the protocols that have been proposed are: SHRIMP [4], Hamlyn [5], APIC [6], Osiris [7], AM [8], U-net [9], FM [13], PM [12, 14], and VIA [15].

This paper describes the Scheduled Transfer (ST) OS bypass protocol [11]. The design of ST has been influenced by two overriding goals. First, we want ST to be used to move data between multiple vendors' machines and over different media; therefore, we have proposed ST as an ANSI standard and defined a network protocol that is independent of the underlying physical layer.

Second, ST has been designed to operate in a large, heavily loaded scientific computing environment. OS bypass protocols all attempt to provide low-latency, high-bandwidth communications to the application, but ST has paid specific attention to integrating these functions with the upper and lower layer protocols without tying itself to any particular technology.

In a heavily loaded environment, there is a possibility that the receiving network interface (NI) is the bottleneck in the communications path. If the receiving NI cannot keep up with the incoming traffic, it may either drop packets or exert backpressure into the network. Dropping packets requires that higher layer protocols detect and retransmit the dropped packets, while exerting backpressure into the physical interconnect causes congestion and will likely degrade other communication paths. To avoid this situation, ST has been designed to simplify the receiving NI's job by pushing parts of the protocol processing back to the sender.

Attention has also been paid in integrating ST with upper layer protocols (ULPs) by providing the capability to separate ST and ULP protocol headers from application data, a capability that is generally necessary to avoid subsequent memory-to-memory copies of the data in the host [12]. ST includes support for reassembly of application messages that are striped across multiple physical interfaces. ST also includes a flow control mechanism that relieves the ULP from this responsibility and provides the opportunity for the implementor to offload this function to the NI [13, 14].

We are currently implementing ST on a Myrinet-connected cluster of Intel PCs running Linux that we plan to use for visualization rendering. ST will be used as the OS bypass protocol on the ASCI [1] (Accelerated Strategic Computing Initiative) Blue Mountain machine at Los Alamos National Laboratory (LANL), a cluster of 48 128-processor SGI Origin 2000 symmetric multiprocessors (SMPs). We are also working with IBM, Compaq/DEC, Sun, and PMR to develop a HIPPI-6400/ST network interface card that will connect directly into each vendors' memory system. A major goal of this effort is to be able to move data between the ASCI machine and the IBM-based archival storage system.

Table 1. An ST API.

st_connect()	Initiate an ST Virtual Connection
st_accept()	Accept an ST Virtual Connection
st_disconnect()	Tear down an ST Virtual Connection
st_map_addr()	Pin memory on the local host
st_unmap_addr()	Unpin memory on the local host
st_send()	Send a user message via a Write sequence
st_recv()	Receive a user message via a Write sequence
st_request_pmr()	Request a remote Persistent Memory Region (PMR)
st_get_pmr_request()	Get the request PMR parameters
st_grant_pmr()	Grant a local Persistent Memory Region (PMR)
st_put()	Put a user message into a remote PMR
st_get()	Get a user message from a remote PMR
st_fetchop()	Get an 8-byte datum from a remote PMR and perform an operation on it
st_done()	Test whether a send,recv,put,get,fetchop has completed
st_end()	End a Transfer (a send/recv or PMR)

2   ST Overview

Table 1 shows the ST API calls we have used in our implementation. We note that an ST API is planned by the ANSI committee and may look different from our API.

ST is a connection-oriented protocol, that is, a Virtual Connection (VC) is set up between two endpoints before any data are transmitted. The first three API calls in Table 1 set up and tear down ST VCs, and the parameters for the VC setup are shown in Table 2. The *client_addr* and *serv_addr* structures contain IP addresses and 16-bit ports, just like TCP. The ports are used to select upper layer services. The calls return an integer identifier for the VC (*vc*). VC setup is handled by the two hosts' OSs; therefore VC resources (e.g., ports) may be viewed as protected entities.

The st_map_addr() call results in a system call which pins down an area of memory in the application and informs the NI of the physical addresses of the pages.

ST supports five types of data movement sequence: Write, Read, Put, Get, and FetchOp. A Write sequence corresponds to the well-known send/receive message passing model used in, for example, sockets and MPI. The Write sequence is intended to be used as a zero-copy protocol for large messages where the receiver specifies the location where the message is to be received. A Read sequence is similar to a Write sequence except the receiver of the data initiates the Transfer. The st_send() and st_recv() API calls map to an ST Write sequence, and their parameters are shown in Table 2. The *vc* parameter is the VC identifier. *vaddr* and *len* specify the region of memory to be sent/received into and must have been previously pinned with st_map_addr(). The *tag* allows multiple sends and receives on the same VC to be matched. The send and receive calls may be blocking or non-blocking, and the *send_id* and *recv_id* are identifiers that are used in the st_done() call to test for the non-blocking Transfers' completion.

Put, Get, and FetchOp sequences are used in conjunction with ST Persistent Memory Regions (PMRs) and correspond to the one-sided-communication model where the initiator of the sequence is aware of the location of the data in the other end. A Put sequence writes data into a specified location in a remote PMR, a Get sequence reads data from a remote PMR, and a FetchOp reads 8 bytes of data from a remote PMR and performs some operation (e.g., clear or increment) on it. Before these three sequences can be initiated, a chunk of remote memory is set up in the other end and pinned down in memory, hence the term persistent memory. Put, Get, and FetchOp operations are designed for low-latency communications because once the PMR is set up, the sequences proceed without any additional control messages. In particular, the Put sequence is intended to be used for low-latency message passing where a small message is placed into a message passing buffer in the receiver and then copied into the application data structure. PMR sequences are also useful for implementing shared memory software packages over non-shared-memory clusters.

Table 3 shows the API calls for a Put sequence. As in the Write sequence, a VC is set up and an area of memory is mapped with st_map_addr(). The sender requests a PMR on the receiving side with the st_request_pmr() call. The VC, the requested length of the PMR, and a tag are specified by the sender. The receiver gets the request parameter *len* with the st_get_pmr_request() call, and grants the PMR request with st_grant_pmr(). The receiver specifies its virtual address and length of the PMR (which may be less than the requested length) and receives an identifier *pmr_id* for the PMR. The remote virtual address *r_vaddr* and length *r_len* and *pmr_id* are returned to the sender in the st_request_pmr() call. The sender then is able to put data to the receiver's memory with the st_put() call. The sender specifies the VC and PMR where the data is to be put. It also specifies the local *vaddr* and *len* as well as the receiver's virtual address *r_vaddr*. A *put_id* is returned for the non-blocking put call, and its completion is tested with st_done(). The Get and FetchOp sequences are similar to the Put sequence.

Table 2. An example ST Write sequence.

Sender
rc = st_connect(&client_addr, &serv_addr, &vc);
rc = st_map_addr(vaddr, len);
rc = st_send(vc, vaddr, len, tag, &send_id, ST_NON_BLOCKING);
rc = st_done(vc, send_id, ST_BLOCKING);
Receiver
rc = st_accept(&client_addr, &serv_addr, &vc);
rc = st_map_addr(vaddr, len);
rc = st_receive(vc, vaddr, len, tag, &recv_id, ST_NON_BLOCKING);
rc = st_done(vc, recv_id, ST_BLOCKING);

Table 3. An example ST Put sequence.

Sender
rc = st_connect(&client_addr, &serv_addr, &vc);
rc = st_map_addr(vaddr, len);
rc = st_request_pmr(vc, len, &r_vaddr, &r_len, tag, &pmr_id);
rc = st_put(vc, vaddr, len, r_vaddr, pmr_id, &put_id, ST_NON_BLOCKING);
rc = st_done(vc, put_id, ST_BLOCKING);
Receiver
rc = st_accept(&client_addr, &serv_addr, &vc);
rc = st_map_addr(vaddr, len);
rc = st_get_pmr_request(vc, &len, tag);
rc = st_grant_pmr(vc, vaddr, len, tag, &pmr_id);

2.1   The ST Header and Operations

The ST standard defines a network protocol that is independent of the underlying physical media. ST uses a 40-byte protocol header (Figure 1) that is used for all ST *control* and *data* operations (Table 4). Control operations (all operations except the *Data* operation) are used to set up and tear down Virtual Connections, Transfers, and Persistent Memory Regions (see below) as well as to query the other end's state. Control operations may include a 32-byte optional payload that can be used by the ULP in any way it chooses. Data operations include an ST header followed by up to 4 gigabytes of data. Figure 2 shows how the st_send() and st_receive() API primitives are translated into an ST Write sequence which is explained further below.

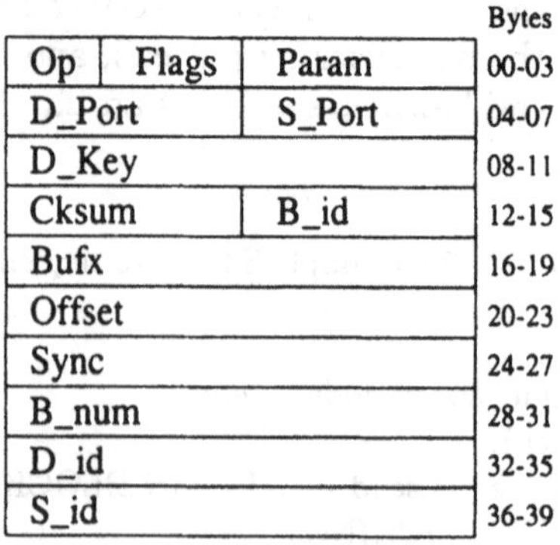

			Bytes
Op	Flags	Param	00-03
D_Port		S_Port	04-07
D_Key			08-11
Cksum		B_id	12-15
Bufx			16-19
Offset			20-23
Sync			24-27
B_num			28-31
D_id			32-35
S_id			36-39

Fig. 1. The 40-byte ST header.

2.2   The ST Data Hierarchy

Each ST operation is identified by the 5-bit *Op* field in the ST header and fills in a subset of the rest of the ST header fields. The first five operations in Table 4 are the connection setup and teardown sequences. An ST Virtual Connection (VC) between two hosts is identified by the two 16-bit ports (D_Port and S_Port) and two 32-bit keys (D_Key). All subsequent operations must carry both ports (source and destination) and the destination's key.

Multiple user messages, called *Transfers*, may be transmitted on a VC with no OS intervention. A Transfer can be a Write, Read, or Persistent Memory Sequence. The next seven ST operations are used to set up and tear down Transfers. These operations exchange the size of the Transfer (up to 2^{64} bytes) and choose the Transfer identifiers (S_id and D_id) of the two endpoints. In particular, a Write sequence is initiated by exchanging a Request_to_Send (RTS), Request_Answer (RA) pair (Figure 2). A Read sequence begins with a Request_to_Receive (RTR) operation followed by the RTS/RA Write Sequence pair. A PMR is set up with a Request_Memory_Region (RMR), Memory_Region_Available (MRA) exchange.

Transfers are segmented into *Blocks*, which are the unit of flow control and retransmission. A Block is enabled for transmission in a Write/Read sequence with the Clear_to_Send operation (CTS), which fills in the Block number (B_num) field in the ST header. The CTS operation also fills in the Bufx and Offset parameters, which are the ST virtual address of the beginning of the Block in the receiver.

Blocks may be further segmented into Scheduled Transfer Units (STUs). STUs are the basic unit of transmission, and each STU contains a Bufx and Offset that tell the receiver where the STU should be placed. An STU is the same as a Data operation in Figure 2. Note that the first STU in a Block contains the same (Bufx, Offset) as specified in the CTS, but that subsequent STUs contain different (Bufx, Offset) values. STUs also contain sequence numbers that allow detection of missing and duplicate fragments.

A Bufx identifies an *ST Buffer* which corresponds to a physically contiguous region of memory (a page) in the end host; the Offset is the offset within the Buffer. ST defines the Bufx, Offset virtual address to achieve independence from the architecture-specific virtual address size (i.e., 32-bit vs. 64-bit) and pagesize parameters that are implicit in each host's virtual addresses.

The st_map_addr() call results in a system call that pins down the region of user memory specified by a virtual address and length. The OS informs the NI of the mapping in terms of (Bufx, physical address) pairs and returns the list of Bufx values to the ST API. There is a one-to-one mapping of Bufx values to physical pages. Note that the Bufx values are not returned to the application in the st_map_addr() call. The ST API handles all translations between virtual addresses and (Bufx, Offset) values, a necessary conversion since the NI only knows about Bufx's. The strategy of ST is to place the responsibility for mapping Buffers on the application/middleware. There is no attempt in the ST API to dynamically determine which Buffers should be mapped and which should not.

The model used is that the application/middleware maps the Buffers it wants to use and then sends/receives multiple messages to/from those Buffers.

Applications are able to control interrupts because ST supports silent delivery of data (the NI does not forward any ST headers to the host), polling (ST headers are forwarded to the host, but no interrupt is generated), and interrupt-driven (ST header delivery plus an interrupt) interfaces. These options are specified in the Flags field in the ST header. Because interrupts may be generated on a per-STU basis, an application can arrange to receive interrupts on each STU, at the end of each Block, at the end of the Transfer, or not at all. ST also includes a checksum that enables its use in an internetworking environment.

Table 4. ST operations.

Request_Connection
Connection_Answer
Request_Disconnect
Disconnect_Answer
Disconnect_Complete
Request_To_Send
Request_Answer
Request_To_Receive
Request_Memory_Region
Memory_Region_Available
End
End_Ack
Get
FetchOP
FetchOP_Complete
Clear_To_Send
Request_State
Request_State_Response
Data

2.3 Tiling

One of the major concerns in the design of ST is preventing network congestion caused by bottlenecked receive processing. If the receiving host or NI is unable to keep up with the incoming network load, it must either drop packets or exert backpressure into the network, causing congestion on other independent VCs. The general approach ST has taken to alleviate this potential problem is to push parts of the protocol processing back to the data source. In ST, a message is only injected into the network when the receiver is as ready as possible to forward the packet into the receiving host's memory.

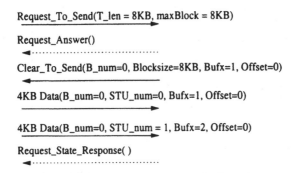

Request_To_Send(T_len = 8KB, maxBlock = 8KB)

Request_Answer()

Clear_To_Send(B_num=0, Blocksize=8KB, Bufx=1, Offset=0)

4KB Data(B_num=0, STU_num=0, Bufx=1, Offset=0)

4KB Data(B_num=0, STU_num = 1, Bufx=2, Offset=0)

Request_State_Response( )

Fig. 2. An ST Write Sequence.

This goal is achieved in ST in two ways. First, the sender includes in each STU the starting ST virtual address in the receiving host's memory where the STU is to be placed. Including this address relieves the receiver from reassembly processing. Second, each STU is required not to cross a receiver's Buffer (page) boundary. This ensures that the receiver can move each STU into host memory in one direct memory access (DMA) operation.

During Write and Read sequences the receiver includes in the CTS operation the beginning address for the Block. In PMR sequences, the beginning address for the PMR is sent in the MRA control operation that enables the PMR. Given the starting address of the Block or PMR it is then the sender's responsibility to calculate the correct ST virtual address subject to the above two rules. We call this process *tiling* the STUs into the receiver's Buffers.

ST tiling is very useful when applications stripe messages across multiple physical interfaces. Striping introduces yet another level of fragmentation of a user message and presents significant reassembly problems for most protocols since the fragments arrive at different interfaces. ST easily handles reassembly because the source, by including the (Bufx, Offset) pair in each STU, effectively handles all reassembly processing.

In Figure 2, the RTS is sent in response to the st_send() API call. The RTS contains the length of the Transfer (8KB) and the preferred Block size (also 8KB). The RA operation is optional and is used in case the CTS cannot be returned soon enough to avoid an RTS timeout. When the receiver has posted the st_recv() API call and the API has matched the st_recv() with the RTS, it sends out a CTS with the Block size (8KB) the Block number (B_num) and the starting address of the Block (Bufx=1, Offset=0). The sender then sends the data with two Data operations each of size 4KB. In this example, we have assumed the Buffer (page) size is 4KB. The sender has segmented the Block into two STUs according to the above tiling rules. The Request_State_Response (RSR) is also optional and can be requested in the Flags field of each Data operation. The RSR indicates the highest number Block which has been received and provides a mechanism for the sender to retransmit lost or damaged Blocks.

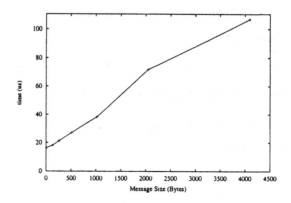

Fig. 3. One-way Put latency vs. message size.

2.4   Integration with the Upper Layer Protocol

ULPs typically place data correctly by passing ULP protocol headers along with the application data. This presents another problem in achieving zero-copy on the receive side because the ULP protocol headers may be mixed in with application data. If the application requires the data to be presented contiguously in its address space, a data copy will be required to remove the protocol headers. To prevent this situation, there must be some way of removing the ST and ULP protocol headers from the application data stream [12].

The ST headers are removed and placed in the *Scheduled Header Queue*, a region in application (or middleware) memory specifically registered with the NI for notification of ST operation completion. ULP headers may be removed in two ways. First the ULP header can be included in the 32-byte optional payload of the RTS control message that initiates a Write Transfer. Second, if the ULP header is too large to fit in the optional payload, it can be sent via a Put operation to the receiving message passing library's buffers, and then the Transfer can be initiated by the receiver as a Read Transfer.

3   Implementation Results

We have implemented ST on a Myrinet-connected cluster of 300MHz Pentium II processors. Figure 3 shows the one-way latency for a Put operation vs. message size. The latency for a zero-sized Put is just over 16 us. Figure 4 shows the achieved bandwidth for a Write sequence for various message sizes. The peak bandwidth of the Myrinet link is 1.2 Gbps and the theoretical bandwidth of the PCI bus is just over 1 Gbps. The main limitation for Write bandwidth is we do not yet pipeline the messages through the Myrinet card [14]. We expect to achieve significant performance improvements once we implement these techniques.

As mentioned previously, the key performance goal of ST is to minimize the receiving NI's processing. Here, we only discuss the processing of a Write

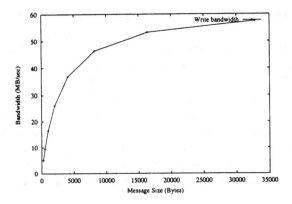

Fig. 4. Put bandwidth vs. message size.

sequence and show how this is done. The processing for Data operations that are part of PMR sequences is slightly different, but has almost the same overhead.

In our current implementation, the processing of Request_to_Send (RTS) and Clear_to_Send (CTS) operations is done in host software. When an application calls st_send(), the ST API generates an RTS operation that includes the length of the message and a 32-bit tag that is included in the 32-byte optional payload. The RTS operation is passed through the sender's NI to the receiver's NI which then forwards it to the receiving application's *Scheduled Header Queue* (SHQ), a region of memory in the receiving ST API. The receiving application makes the st_receive() call, and the receiving ST API matches it with the RTS in the SHQ (of course the RTS and st_receive() may occur in any order). The receiving ST API generates one or more CTS operations that each include the appropriate (Bufx, Offset) and size of the Block.

When each CTS operation is sent through the receiving NI, it creates an entry in its *Mx Validation Table* which it will later use to validate each Data operation as it comes in from the sender. Figure 5 shows the entries in the Mx table and the relevant entries in an incoming Data operation. The receiving NI actually keeps three tables. The Mx table, the VC table, and the Bufx table. The VC table keeps track of all active VCs and which application they are associated with. Each entry in the VC table is of the form: (Local-Port, Local-Key, Remote-Port, Remote-Key, pid) where pid is the process ID of the application. Our VC table is a hash table indexed by the low order bits of the 32-bit Local-Key; since the local OS chooses the key, good hashing performance is guaranteed. The Bufx table keeps track of all Bufx mappings and which application they are associated with. Each entry in the Bufx table is of the form: (Bufx, physical address, length, pid). Our Bufx table is also a hash table indexed by the low-order bits of the 32-bit Bufx value. Again, the local OS chooses the Bufx values to guarantee good lookup performance.

When the CTS operation passes through the receiving NI, it does as much work as it can to simplify the incoming Data operation processing. First, it chooses a free Mx value which is used to index into the Mx table and inserts the VC parameters (Local-Port, Remote-Port, Local-Key) into the table entry. It looks up the VC parameters in the VC table and validates that the application that sent the CTS owns that VC. The NI then inserts in the Mx entry the Seq-id (Transfer ID) and B_num from the CTS and initializes the STU_num field to 0. Based on the size of the Block, the NI creates a valid Bufx range for the Data operations and validates, via a Bufx table lookup, that the application has mapped these Bufx values. The Mx value is included in the CTS operation and is returned to the receiver in every Data operation (in the B_id field) for that Block.

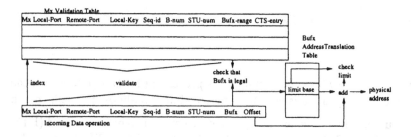

Fig. 5. NI validation of Data operations.

When a Data operation arrives at the receiving NI, the NI looks up the Mx entry and compares the Data operation's parameters with those in the Mx table. All the validation fields shown in Figure 5 should match. The STU_num field is treated differently because it changes with each Data operation. We assume in-order delivery of STUs within a Block and check that all Data operations have been received by incrementing STU_num after each Data operation is checked. Finally, the Bufx in the Data operation is checked against the Bufx-range in the Mx entry and the physical address of the Bufx is found from a lookup in the Bufx table. The Offset and size of the STU operation are used to check whether the STU fits within the Bufx, and the STU is DMAed into host memory. The last STU of a Block contains a Last bit in the Flags field. When this STU is received and validated, the NI deletes the Mx entry and sends a message to the host SHQ that notifies the receiving ST API that the Block has been received correctly.

To summarize, the receiving NI fully validates each Data operation before sending it to its host's memory, but does as much validation as it can before the Data operation is received. When the Data message does arrive, the NI indexes into the Mx table, validates seven fields, increments the STU_num, indexes into the Bufx table, and then validates the Offset. At this point the NI has the correct physical address in the host and can DMA the STU to the correct location in application memory.

4   Related Work

The SHRIMP [4] interface, developed at Princeton, allows an application to map a local page into one remote page, with changes being automatically propagated. It is therefore intended to be used in a shared memory environment, with synchronization implemented at the application level.

The Osiris [7] project at the University of Arizona and the ATM Port Interconnect Controller (APIC) [6] project at Washington University at St. Louis are OS bypass mechanisms over ATM and provide no end-to-end flow control. The U-Net [9] project at Cornell was originally developed over ATM, but has now been ported to Myrinet. U-net also provides no end-to-end flow control.

Berkeley Active Messages (AM) [8] is similar to ST in that it uses different protocols for long and short messages, with the ability of the sender to place long messages in a *sender-specified* memory location at the receiver. However, AM does not provide end-to-end flow control and hence message progress is coupled with ULP scheduling on the host processor.

The Hamlyn [5] project at HP Labs is the most similar to ST. Hamlyn never sends a message unless there is a pinned application buffer at the receiver. The sender is responsible for placing the address in the receiver in each sent message. The Hamlyn paper describes the RATS library which sits on top of Hamlyn, but the distinction between the two is not clear. Apparently RATS is responsible for end-to-end flow control and for communicating the receiver address to the sender. Hamlyn does not provide support for placing data into locations specified by ULPs.

Illinois Fast Messages (FM) [13] is a portable message passing interface which has been implemented on a number of platforms, including Myrinet. It is optimized for latency and uses PIO to move data to the NI from the sending application. All messages are buffered on the receiving side, which requires a copy into the application data structure. FM also provides end-to-end flow control and decouples message progress from host processor scheduling by having the NI DMA data into the FM buffers on the host. The FM over Myrinet implementation uses window-based flow control, where the receiving FM buffer is partitioned between all senders; it is not clear to what size of system this approach scales.

The original PM [14] protocol, whose name is apparently a pun on AM and FM, is developed at RWCP in Japan. PM provides buffering which requires copies into application data structures and flow control. The flow control algorithm is more scalable than that of FM and guarantees in-order delivery. However, it does permit lost messages due to buffer overflow (it is based on go-back-N) and therefore requires retransmissions. Unfortunately, lost messages are most likely to occur under heavy load, and these retransmissions only make the load heavier. In a later paper [12], PM added the *rendezvous* protocol which achieves zero-copy in essentially the same way as the ST Write protocol. The sender in PM does not segment its PDUs to prevent crossing of receiver page boundaries. This segmentation is thus left to the receiving NI. PM also does not provide Get, FetchOp, or Read sequences.

The Virtual Interface Architecture (VIA) [15] project is a consortium between Intel, Microsoft, and Compaq. VIA attempts to define an OS bypass mechanism, but does not provide any method for interoperability because it does not define a network protocol. Because the protocol has not be defined it is somewhat difficult to predict what capabilities/features VIA will eventually support. The VIA standard does indicate that end-to-end flow control will not be provided; it states that the NI shall drop any packets for which there are not queued receive buffers. The most complete section of the VIA document is the API, called the Virtual Interface Primitive Library (VIPL). We believe that the VIPL may become an industry standard API and plan to implement it over ST.

5   Summary and Future Work

In addition to providing low-latency, high-bandwidth message passing, ST attempts to minimize the NI processing for Data operations as much as possible. The goal is to avoid dropping data in the receiving NI or applying backpressure into the network by allowing the NI to forward packets to the correct location in the host as quickly as possible. This is achieved by pushing reassembly processing back to the sender of the data and by doing as much validation as possible at the receiver before the data arrives. This sender-based reassembly technique also enables striping messages over multiple interfaces.

In the future, we plan to investigate the performance gains achieved by placing RTS/CTS processing on the NI. This processing is substantial compared with incoming Data processing and presents a problem in that the NI may be busy and unable to immediately service incoming Data operations. We plan to investigate NI hardware capabilities such as priorities for the different types of processing to deal with this problem.

One shortcoming of ST is that it does not support a zero-copy scatter (it does support a zero-copy gather); this is due to the restriction that all intermediate Blocks of a Transfer must be the same size (the first and last may be smaller). We also plan to investigate mechanisms by which zero-copy scatter can be supported without changing the nature of the protocol.

Acknowledgments

The ST protocol was developed in the T11.1 ANSI committee chaired by Don Tolmie of LANL. We also acknowledge the following major contributors who have spent a great deal of time and effort towards the successful definition and implementation of the protocol: Greg Chesson, Jim Pinkerton, Jeff Young (SGI), Bob Willard (DEC), Roger Ronald (PMR), Michael McGowen, John Gibbon (Essential Communications), Craig Warner (HP), Don Woelz (Genroco).

References

1. The Accelerated Strategic Computing Initiative (ASCI). Available at http://www.llnl.gov/asci.
2. ATM Forum Specifications. Available at http://www.atmforum.com.
3. N. Boden, D. Cohen, R. Felderman, A. Kulawik, C. Seitz, J. Seizovic, and W. Su. "Myrinet: A Gigabit-Per-Second Local Area Network", *IEEE Micro* 15(1), Feb. 1995, pp. 29–36.
4. M. Blumrich, C. Dubnicki, E. Felton, and K. Li. "Protected, User-Level DMA for the SHRIMP Network Interface", In *Proceedings 2nd International Symposium on High Performance Architecture*, San Jose, CA, Feb. 3–7, 1996, pp. 154-165.
5. G. Buzzard and D. Jacobson and S. Marovich and J. Wilkes. "Hamlyn: A High-Performance Network Interface with Sender-Based Memory Management", Technical Report, Hewlett-Packard, July 1995.
6. Z. D. Dittia and J. R. Cox, Jr. and G. M. Parulkar. "Design of the APIC: A High Performance ATM Host-Network Interface Chip", In *Proceedings IEEE Infocom '95*, 1995, pp. 179-187.
7. P. Druschel and L. L. Peterson and B. S. Davie. "Experiences with a High-Speed Network Adapter: A Software Perspective", In *Proceedings ACM Sigcomm '94*, Aug. 1994.
8. T. von Eicken, D. Culler, S. Goldstein, and K. Schauser. "Active Messages: A Mechanism for Integrated Communication and Computation", In *Proceedings of the International Symposium on Computer Architecture*, 1992.
9. T. von Eicken, A. Basu, V. Buch, and W. Vogels. "U-net: A User-Level Network Interface for Parallel and Distributed Computing", In *Proceedings of the 15th ACM Symposium on Operating Systems Principles*, December 1995.
10. Gigabit Ethernet Alliance. http://www.gigabit-ethernet.org.
11. HIPPI Standards documents. Available at http://www.lanl.gov/hippi.
12. F. O'Carroll, H. Tezuka, A. Hori, and Y. Ishikawa. "The Design and Implementation of Zero Copy MPI Using Commodity Hardware with a High Performance Network", In *ACM SIGARCH ICS'98*, pp. 243–250, July 1998.
13. S. Pakin, M. Lauria, and A. Chien. "High Performance Messaging on Workstations: Illinois Fast Messages (FM) for Myrinet", In *Proceedings of Supercomputing '95*, San Diego, CA, 1995.
14. H. Tezuka, A. Hori, Y. Ishikawa, and M. Sato. "PM: An Operating System Coordinated High Performance Communication Library", In *High-Performance Computing and Networking '97*, April 1997.
15. The Virtual Interface Architecture (VIA) Specification. Available at http://www.viarch.org/.

The NIP Parallel Object-Oriented Computational Model

Paul Watson and Savas Parastatidis

Department of Computing Science,
University of Newcastle upon Tyne,
NE1 7RU, UK
{Paul.Watson,Savas.Parastatidis}@newcastle.ac.uk

Abstract. Implicitly parallel programming languages place the burden of exploiting and managing parallelism upon the compiler and runtime system, rather than on the programmer. This paper describes the design of NIP, a runtime system for supporting implicit parallelism in languages which combine both functional and object-oriented programming. NIP is designed for scaleable distributed memory systems including networks of workstations and custom parallel machines. The key components of NIP are: a parallel task execution unit which includes an efficient method for lazily creating parallel tasks from loop iterations; a distributed shared memory system optimised for parallel object-oriented programs; and a load balancing system for distributing work over the nodes of the parallel system. The paper describes the requirements placed on the runtime system by an implicitly parallel language and then details the design of the components that comprise NIP, showing how the components meet these requirements. Performance results for NIP running programs on a network of workstations are presented and analysed.

1 Introduction

This paper describes work aimed at reducing the effort required to develop efficient programs for parallel architectures, in particular those with scaleable distributed memory architectures. Many practitioners believe that the widely used message passing methodology, currently embodied by PVM [1] and MPI [2], is too complex and time-consuming [3].

The design of an alternative, an implicit parallel system in which it is the compiler and runtime system rather than the programmer that are responsible for the creation and management of parallelism, has been investigated. The runtime system, called NIP, has been designed and a prototype of it has been implemented. NIP removes from the programmer the burdens of dividing a program into parallel tasks, sharing work evenly across all the nodes, organising communication between tasks, making the data available to tasks that require it, and synchronising tasks. This paper describes the design of the NIP system, its prototype implementation, and gives a preliminary performance evaluation.

This paper makes the following contributions:

A.Sivasubramaniam, M.Lauria (Eds.): CANPC'99, LNCS 1602, pp. 122–136, 1999.
© Springer-Verlag Berlin Heidelberg 1999

- It investigates the issues and options in the design of systems for executing parallel functional plus object programs on distributed memory parallel systems.
- It introduces an efficient method of lazily extracting parallel work from loops.
- It describes the design of an all-in-software, object-based DSM that uses an optimised version of the entry consistency protocol.

The rest of the paper is organised as follows: Section 2 discusses high-level programming languages which support implicit parallelism. The requirements placed on NIP and an overview of its structure are introduced in Section 3. In Section 4, the NIP execution model and the techniques it incorporates are described in more detail, including: a mechanism for cheaply, lazily extracting parallelism from loops, a lazy task execution mechanism, and dynamic load balancing. Next, the Distributed Shared Memory is presented (Section 5), including a method for optimising performance by combining object locking with cache coherency. Preliminary performance results for the NIP prototype implementation are described in section 6. In Section 7, related work is discussed. Finally, conclusions from the work are drawn in Section 8.

2 Parallel Programming Languages

In the opinion of many software developers, functional programming languages have a number of advantages over conventional, imperative languages including their expressiveness, and their amenity to reasoning about semantics. However, they also have further advantages for parallel computation. In particular, functional programs contain far fewer constraints on execution order than do their imperative counterparts. This is because all expressions in a functional program are referentially transparent [4]. Therefore, the order of their execution cannot affect the result of the execution, and this increases the scope for parallel execution. A number of parallel functional programming systems have been developed over the last 20 years [5-7] to exploit these advantages.

Unfortunately, the very property that makes functional programs so well matched to parallel systems-referential transparency-makes the programming of certain important classes of computations unnatural, contorted and complex. In particular, many computations (or parts thereof) are naturally expressed through an object-oriented programming style in which objects encapsulate state which may be updated through method calls. Method calls to objects may not be referentially transparent, as identical calls can return different values, and therefore these types of computations cannot be directly expressed in a functional program.

As it was felt that functional programming was ideal for many types of computations, and well suited to parallelism, it was not rejected entirely as the preferred programming methodology for NIP over object-orientation. The UFO (United Functions and Objects) [8] programming language was adopted as it brings together the functional and object programming styles in an elegant way.

In UFO, a clear distinction is made between objects containing mutable state and objects containing state that does not change after construction. The latter can be used to write purely functional programs but the two types of objects can also be freely combined within a program. In order to gain the benefits of parallel functional programming described above, as much as possible of the computation should be expressed through purely functional objects. However, where it is natural to do so, mutable objects can be constructed and manipulated.

The semantics of UFO state that the execution of *function calls* (methods that cannot alter the state of an object) on the same object may be executed in parallel. However, a *procedure call* (a method that can alter the state of an object) should prevent other procedure or function calls from being executed on the same object at the same time.

As a language that supports implicit parallelism, UFO does not provide the means for a programmer to explicitly create parallel tasks. Instead, the syntax and semantics of the language provide opportunities for the compiler and runtime system to create and exploit parallel tasks: () In UFO, all calls (functions and procedures) are strict on all their arguments—the arguments must be first evaluated before the call can proceed. If there are two or more arguments, the option of evaluating them in parallel is available. () Where there is a loop, tasks can be created to execute independent iterations in parallel.

The NIP runtime system was designed and implemented to support the execution of programming languages like UFO.[1] However, the mechanisms and solutions in NIP could have application across a wide range of parallel languages, especially those based on functional or object-oriented programming.

3   NIP Design Overview

The goal of NIP is to execute compiled UFO programs exploiting parallelism as efficiently as possible. This section gives an architectural overview of NIP. It begins with a description of NIP running on an abstract parallel system and then describes how it maps onto a distributed memory parallel system such as a network of workstations.

3.1   The NIP Abstract Parallel System

The NIP runtime system can be considered as an abstract parallel system consisting of a *load balancer* and an *object memory* (Fig. reffig.abstractmachine). The unit of execution is a *task* and there is a limit to the number of tasks that can be executing in parallel at a particular time. When the limit is reached, the system is considered 'busy' as the parallelism it offers is fully exploited. The load balancer is responsible for keeping the system at the 'busy' state by creating new tasks when necessary, as is now described.

---

[1] A full description of the UFO language is outside the scope of this paper. The interested reader is referred to [8].

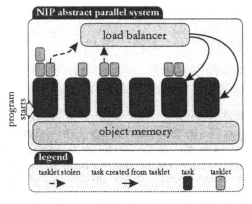

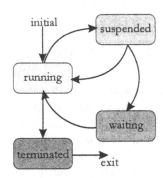

Fig. 1. The NIP abstract machine   **Fig. 2.** Task states

The UFO programmer can develop an application for the NIP abstract parallel system without being concerned about how to exploit parallelism. The UFO compiler will identify those parts of the computation that can be evaluated in parallel. However, it will not create new tasks for them; instead, it will plant code to create *tasklets*. Tasklets are small representations of pieces of computation that could be evaluated in parallel. Computationally, tasklets are cheaper to create than tasks. When more work is required to keep the system busy, the load balancer can use the information encapsulated in a tasklet in order to create a new task.

NIP will automatically create a single task when the execution of the UFO program starts. If the program is parallel, the task will produce tasklets which the load balancer converts into tasks until the system is 'busy.' The newly created tasks may also themselves produce tasklets that are available to the load balancer. If a tasklet has not been converted to a parallel task by the time the result of its computation is required, the task that created the tasklet removes it and executes the computation serially. The technique used by the load balancer to dynamically create tasks only when necessary is called *lazy task creation* [9] and it is discussed in detail in Section 4.

3.2   Task States

A task may be in any of the four states shown in Figure 2. When a task is created, it always starts in the 'running' state. However, there may be situations when the task will have to become 'suspended' (e.g., a task may have to wait for the result of a stolen tasklet). In such a case, if necessary, the load balancer will try to create a new task in order to keep the system as close to the 'busy' state as possible. If a task can exit the 'suspended' state and the parallel system is not 'busy,' the load balancer will return the task to the 'running' state. Otherwise, the task will enter the 'waiting' state. When the load balancer requires a task to run, it first checks whether there are any tasks in the 'waiting' state, before creating a new one from a tasklet, and if so it moves the task to the 'running' state. Finally, a task that completes its execution enters the 'terminated' state and the load balancer destroys it.

3.3   Object Memory

Every task in the NIP abstract parallel system may access any object in the object memory by executing a method on it. There is no need for tasks to synchronise their method calls on objects as the object memory takes care of synchronisation issues while trying to maximise the parallelism in memory operations. The memory model follows the UFO semantics and allows any number of tasks to call methods on an object at the same time if the methods do not change the state of the object. However, the memory model guarantees that only one task at a time is allowed to change the state of an object. The design and implementation of the memory model is discussed in detail in Section 5.

3.4   NIP on Distributed Memory Systems

Every node in the distributed memory parallel system (e.g., all the workstations in a network of workstations) runs an instance of a *NIP Node*. A NIP Node consists of a collection of components, each one assigned specific duties. The components of all the NIP Nodes in the system communicate with each other by exchanging messages. The components are:

- The *Node Manager* component directs the operations of the rest of the components in a NIP Node. It routes the messages received by other NIP Nodes to the appropriate component and it maintains NIP system and node specific information (e.g., list of NIP Nodes, number of processors available on the current node, etc.).
- The *Load Balancer* is responsible for maintaining information about the tasks running on the current NIP Node. It uses the information to make decisions on whether or not more tasks are required on the NIP Node.
- The *DSM Manager* is the component responsible for managing the local memory of the NIP Node.
- The *Communicator* is a wrapper around the underlying communication layer.

All the NIP Nodes in the system collaborate to execute a program. On every NIP Node there is a limit on the number of tasks that may be executed in parallel but the number may not be the same for all NIP Nodes. Usually, the limit is equal to the number of processors available on a node.[2]

---

[2] NIP supports multiprocessor as well as uniprocessor nodes.

4   The NIP Execution Model

On every NIP Node, the Load Balancer component deals with the creation and execution of tasks. The set of Load Balancer components in the parallel system co-operate with each other in order to try to ensure that nodes always have tasks to execute. In this section, a novel variant of the *lazy task creation* [9] technique is introduced, the task execution mechanism is described, and the dynamic load balancing scheme used by NIP is presented.

4.1   Lazy Task Creation

Lazy task creation attempts to reduce the cost of creating tasks for concurrent execution. In [9], a technique is described where every task maintains a queue of *continuations*. A continuation represents a *lazy future call*, a piece of computation that can be executed in parallel. As computational resources become available, a continuation is stolen and a new task is created. When the task requires the result from a continuation, it removes the continuation from the queue and executes it *inline*. The task creating a continuation is called *producer* while a processor stealing a continuation is called *consumer*. The continuation queue is guarded by a lock in order to avoid simultaneous access by the producer and consumer. Mohr et al. show that it is beneficial to use continuations in order to represent potentially parallel pieces of computation that may be converted to tasks at runtime rather than creating tasks for all of them.

An important issue for efficient parallel computation is the cost of the inline execution of the continuation, which should not be much greater than the cost of executing the same computation in a purely serial environment. Therefore, in a parallel system using a lazy task creation scheme, it is very important that the cost of creating continuations and executing them inline is minimised.

Analysis of the existing lazy task creation technique identified three causes of inefficiency:

1. The continuation queue is maintained on a heap and, therefore, the creation and destruction of continuations are expensive operations because memory must be allocated/freed on a heap.
2. For iterative computations where each iteration can be executed in parallel, the number of continuations created equals the number of iterations. As the creation of each continuation has a finite cost, this is a large overhead. For example, if a function is mapped onto an N–element vector, then N continuations will be created.
3. On a shared-memory multiprocessor, a processor must access the continuation queue in order to find a task to execute. When accessing the queue, a lock must be acquired, which introduces significant overhead. The cost of these lock operations has been stated as the main performance disadvantage of lazy task creation in [10].

```
class ParallelMap
{
public:
  ParallelMap(Vector, Function);
  Task stealIteration();
Private:
  int      stealIndex();
  Vector   vector;
  Function function;
  int      index = 0;
}                              (a)
```

```
// create task
Task ParallelMap::stealIteration()
{
  tmpi = stealIndex();
  if (tmpi == -1)
     return nothing
  else
     return newTask(vector,
                    function,
                    tmpi);
}                              (c)
```

```
// execute loop inline
ParallelMap(Vector v, Function f)
{
  vector   = v;
  function = f;
  // Add tasklet to tasklet queue
  activate();
  while (true)
  {
    tmpi = stealIndex();
    if (tmpi == -1)
      break;
    else
      vector[tmpi] =
              f(vector[tmpi]);
  }
  // Wait for the results of any exported tasks
  wait();
}                              (b)
```

```
int ParallelMap::stealIndex()
{
  startCriticalSection();
  if (index == vector.length())
  // No work left. Remove tasklet from queue
     deactivate();
     stolen = -1;
  else
     stolen = index;
     index++;
  endCriticalSection();
  return stolen;
}                              (d)
```

```
map(Function f, Vector v)
{
  for int i = 1 to v.length()
    v[i] = f(v[i]);
}                              (e)
```

Fig. 3. Pseudo-code for an iterative Tasklet

4.2   Lazy Task Creation in NIP

In NIP, a variation of the lazy task creation technique is used. The NIP Lazy Task Creation scheme has a simpler and more portable design than the original technique. In NIP Lazy Task Creation, tasklets are used as the representations of the potentially parallel parts of the computation. The new technique reduces the effects of the sources of inefficiency identified in the previous section:

1. Tasklets are allocated in the stack frame of the task that creates them but, unlike in previous schemes, the tasklet queue is not allocated on a heap. Instead, the tasklets are directly linked and the Load Balancer only maintains pointers to the first and the last tasklet in the queue. This reduces the memory allocation/deallocation costs. When new tasklets are created the links must still be updated but this is a relatively small cost.
2. Only one tasklet is created for a complete iterative computation (e.g., a for-loop) rather than one for each iteration. Once the tasklet is created, the iterations can be executed serially by the task that created the tasklet, while one or more iterations can be *stolen* by the Load Balancer for execution elsewhere. For example, consider a program in which a function f is mapped onto each element of a vector. In pseudo-code, a serial version of the algorithm would be as shown in Figure 3e. In the NIP version (again

in pseudo-code), an instance of the `ParallelMap` class (Figure 3a) is constructed. This has as variables the function, the vector, and an index variable which, as will be seen, is shared between the inline code and the task-stealing code. The class constructor initialises the tasklet, publicises it to the Load Balancer by adding it to the local tasklet queue (`activate()`), and then executes the loop inline (Figure 3b). Once the loop is completed the tasklet is removed from the local queue and waits for the results of any stolen iterations to be returned. The Load Balancer can steal iterations by calling the `stealIteration()` method (Figure 3c); a stolen iteration is turned into a task which can be exported for parallel execution. The inline execution and Load Balancer can never execute the same iteration because the critical section in the `stealIndex()` method (Figure 3d) guarantees unique manipulation of the `_index` variable. As an optimisation, to increase the granularity of tasks, more than one iteration can be stolen at a time by the Load Balancer. These *iterative tasklets* are important for reducing costs in a language like UFO which directly supports iteration. However, in languages which do not directly support iteration and offer solely recursion (e.g., most functional languages), techniques for transforming recursion into iteration [11] can still allow this optimisation to be exploited.

3. The tasklet queue is guarded by a lock but a task only needs to acquire this lock when it adds/removes a tasklet to/from the queue. Each tasklet retains a private lock, which must be acquired by the task when it removes part of the computation in order to execute it inline. The Load Balancer needs to acquire both locks when it creates a new task from a tasklet. First, it needs to locate a tasklet to use, so it must acquire the queue's lock. Then, it needs to acquire the lock—private to the tasklet—in order to steal part of the computation. This 2–level locking scheme allows the Load Balancer to create a new task without blocking the rest of the tasks from executing their tasklets inline. Furthermore, on a multiprocessor node, the tasks do not block each other when accessing their tasklets.

4. The Load Balancer is designed so that when it is active, it cannot be interrupted by a task. Therefore, the lock operations can be optimised by using a boolean variable instead of a mutex as the tasklet's private lock, providing the target platform is composed from uniprocessor workstations where the memory operation of setting the value of a boolean variable is atomic.

5. Finally, tasklets can be designed to be reusable. So, once a tasklet is created it may be used many times in different parts of the computation.

The NIP lazy task creation technique has been implemented in C++ for portability. This differs from earlier schemes (e.g., [9, 12]) which require a customised compiler.

4.3   Task Execution

As mentioned in Section 3, a task is the unit of execution in the NIP abstract parallel system. However, in most operating systems, the unit of execution is either a *process* or a *thread*. In view of the lower overheads associated with the creation, switching, and termination of threads on the distributed systems that NIP targets, threads were preferred over processes as the execution medium for tasks. The Load Balancer component is responsible for the creation, suspension, and termination of threads.

4.4 Dynamic Load Balancing

The set of Load Balancer components in the parallel system co-operate with each other in order to try to ensure that nodes always have tasks to execute. Every Load Balancer implements a simple algorithm to keep its local NIP Node busy with tasks. The algorithm utilises information on tasks and tasklets that the Load Balancer maintains for the NIP Node.

When the number of tasklets on a node changes from zero to one, the Load Balancer broadcasts a notification message to the rest of the NIP Nodes. When the last tasklet is removed from a node a notification message is also broadcast. Every Load Balancer component maintains a *tasklet availability* vector with a boolean entry for each of the other NIP Nodes in the system. The boolean entry indicates whether the corresponding NIP Node has any tasklets or not, and it is updated upon the receipt of a notification messages. When a NIP Node runs out of tasklets and there are no tasks in the 'waiting' state, the Load Balancer checks the tasklet availability vector and sends a request for tasks to a node with a non-empty tasklet queue.

5 The NIP Distributed Shared Memory

The target architecture for NIP is a distributed memory parallel machine that does not directly offer shared memory (e.g., a network of workstations). A systems providing global access to objects was required for NIP as a task can be executed on any node and it may require access to objects created on other nodes (Section 3).

It would have been possible to utilise a conventional, general, all-in-software Distributed Shared Memory (DSM) system to implement the memory model required for NIP.[3] However, a NIP-specific DSM system, the NIPDSM, can support the semantics of the NIP computational model more efficiently than conventional DSM systems. The NIP computational model imposes certain restrictions on the way objects can be accessed (Section 3) and NIPDSM exploits these restrictions—as is described in the rest of this section—in a way that cannot be achieved by a conventional DSM system.

In this section, an architectural overview of the NIPDSM is presented and the motivation behind the design decisions is explained. The memory consistency protocol used in NIPDSM and the way caching is used to improve performance are described. The aspects of the NIPDSM system that exploit the NIP object access semantics are highlighted throughout the section.

---

[3] For a good discussion of DSM and a variety of existing systems, the reader is referred to [13].

5.1 NIPDSM Architecture

Most conventional software-based DSM systems provide a *single address space* view to parallel applications (e.g., [14, 15]). In this approach, a parallel application running on a distributed memory machine consists of a collection of threads or processes that use read and write operations on virtual addresses-in the same manner as a serial program.

This memory model is not ideal for parallelism as interleaving of read and write operations are allowed without any restrictions, although programmers can serialise memory operations using *memory lock* operations. The DSM provides the memory lock operations but it is still the responsibility of the parallel application programmers to use them correctly in order to protect shared memory regions from simultaneous access problems. Failure to do this often results in software errors which are very hard to discover.

NIPDSM investigates an alternative approach, using the semantics of the object memory of the NIP abstract system, where it is the memory that deals with serialisation in memory access rather than the application. The NIPDSM provides an *object view* of the distributed memory; the unit of sharing is the object. The ways in which objects can be accessed by the parallel application are restricted (Section 3). There are a few similarities between the NIPDSM object space, the *tuple space* of Linda [16], and the data-structured DSM systems like Emerald and Clouds [17, 18] but there are significant differences as well, as will be described.

The NIPDSM is organised as a collection of objects which are shared amongst the participating NIP nodes. A parallel application cannot directly access memory locations but instead it calls methods objects. Depending on whether or not a method updates the state of the object, it is characterised as a *read method* (a *function* in UFO) or as a *write method* (a *procedure* in UFO). An object with only read methods is considered to be *immutable* while an object with at least one write method is considered to be *mutable*. NIPDSM implements the UFO semantics as an object can have multiple concurrent readers but only one writer.

Synchronisation of simultaneous accesses to a mutable object is achieved automatically via the use of a lock which is private to that object. Therefore, there is no need for the application to deal with synchronisation. Nevertheless, an interface to the private lock of each object is available in order to support optimisations by the UFO compiler, when it is more efficient to wrap contiguous method calls on the same object within a single pair of lock/unlock operations.

5.2 Object Replication and Consistency Model

Objects in NIPDSM can be cached in multiple nodes; consequently, provision must be made for their state to be kept consistent across the nodes. Many *consistency models* have been proposed in the literature [15, 19, 20] and are used in conventional DSM systems. The choice of the consistency model for the NIPDSM was important not only because of the performance implications but also because the semantics of the NIP computational model have to be met. It was decided that the *entry consistency* model [15] was close to the requirements of the NIPDSM and a novel variation of the original model optimised for NIP was designed and implemented.

Entry consistency is a relaxed model—it defers memory updates to/from replicated regions until they are necessary. Like most relaxed models, entry consistency requires that applications follow certain rules in the way in which they access the shared memory in order to guarantee *strict consistency* semantics in the way the memory operates—a read memory operation always returns the most recent value. An application must associate any shared variables with synchronisation objects, which are used to define critical sections. The shared variables must only be accessed within these critical sections. The burden of defining the critical sections and associating the shared variables with synchronisation objects falls to the application programmer [21].

The semantics of the NIP computational model allow us to simplify the model as there is no need for critical sections at the application level. Every mutable object has a lock which is used whenever a method is applied to the object. This lock provides the synchronisation required when accessing the object's state. Additionally, as will be described, the same lock is used for consistency-related operations ensuring that the object's state is always kept up-to-date. In contrast, in most conventional DSM designs, memory consistency related operations require the manipulation of separate locks; one used by consistency-related operations and one for synchronisation-related operations.

5.3   Managing Consistency

In this section, the NIPDSM approach to maintaining the consistency of the state of the objects is described. An object in the NIPDSM is always assigned to a single *Manager Node*. The Manager Node maintains information about the object and is responsible for satisfying cache requests from other NIP Nodes. When an object is cached on a node, the node becomes either a *Read Proxy Node* or a *Write Proxy Node* for the object. The following rules apply:

- The Manager Node of an object allows the execution of tasks local to that NIP Node which call write and/or read methods on the object when there are no proxies for that object.
- The Manager Node allows the execution of read methods on an object if Read Proxies exist for that object.
- A Write Proxy allows the execution of local tasks that call write and/or read methods on the object.
- A Read Proxy allows the execution of local threads that call only read methods on the object.
- A node can be a Manager Node, a Read or Write Proxy for any number of objects but can never be more than one of these at the same time for a particular object.
- An object in the NIPDSM always has one Manager Node and it may have zero or one Write Proxy, or zero or many Read Proxies at any given time.

5.4 Implementation

The Manager Node remains the same throughout an object's lifetime. This is in contrast with Bershad's implementation of the entry consistency model [21] where the Manager Node—in NIPDSM terms—is the node with write permission to the object and a distributed directory scheme is used to keep track of the Manager Node. In NIPDSM, the overhead associated with maintaining the distributed directory is avoided in order to simplify the implementation, while optimisations are introduced to reduce the number of messages exchanged.

Every object is assigned a unique object ID, the *NIPDSM Pointer*, when it is created. The NIPDSM Pointer provides access to an object's methods, acting like a virtual memory pointer, and it is used by the NIPDSM system in all locking and caching operations.

Unlike most conventional DSM systems, NIPDSM does not depend on the operating system to detect memory accesses and trap cache misses. This is possible because an object can only be accessed via method calls and therefore only via the use of a NIPDSM Pointer. The advantages of this approach are:

- The NIPDSM system is portable, as no operating system specific calls are required.
- Conventional DSM systems use the underlying operating system's page fault mechanism in their implementation. The page fault mechanism usually involves traps to the kernel and the invocation of user-defined handlers. In contrast, NIPDSM uses the lock operations required by the consistency protocol to detect object accesses. These lock operations would have been required even if NIPDSM were to use the underlying operating system's page-fault mechanism.

A compiler can further optimise an object's access time. Once a method is called on an object and the lock is acquired, the local virtual memory address of the object is returned to the calling thread. As the object is locked, it is safe to use the virtual memory address to access the object instead of the NIPDSM Pointer.

6 Performance Results

In this section, preliminary performance results from the execution of the prototype implementation of NIP are presented. Eight PentiumII 233MHz workstations with 64MB of memory, interconnected by a 100Mbps Fast Ethernet network were used as the test-bed. Each of the workstations was running an instance of the Linux operating system (RedHat 5.1, kernel 2.0.35).

The test is the implementation of the UFO example shown in Figure 3e) where a function f is mapped on the elements of a vector both sequentially, and in parallel using NIP. The sequential program was implemented in standard C while the parallel version was implemented in C++ using the implementation

Tasklet creation and destruction	$1.364 usecs$
Overhead per iteration	$0.16 usecs$

Table 1. Tasklet-related costs.

Vector Size	Function granularity($msecs$)											
	Single iteration stolen						Group of iterations stolen					
	0.03	0.3	1.5	3.02	6.04	60.4	0.03	0.3	1.5	3.02	6.04	60.4
100	0.39	0.95	2.01	3.29	5.74	6.73	0.96	1.36	3.11	4.25	5.26	6.23
200	0.74	1.07	1.99	3.57	5.60	6.50	0.59	1.98	4.64	5.09	6.14	6.24
500	0.81	1.11	2.20	3.76	6.65	7.57	1.00	3.10	6.92	7.32	7.50	7.57
1000	0.90	1.17	2.38	3.83	6.64	7.18	1.34	4.45	7.31	7.21	7.52	7.57

Table 2. Speedup on 8 nodes.

of the ParallelMap tasklet class (Figure 3 in Section 4.2). The egcs 1.1b compiler was used for the compilation of the two versions of the program. Finally, the implementation of the TCP/IP protocol provided by Linux was used for inter-node communication rather than an optimised, low-cost communication subsystem like U-Net [22].

The costs of using the tasklet were measured by comparing the timing results from the execution of the sequential and NIP versions of the program. The overhead incurred because of the creation and destruction of the tasklet and the cost per iteration of using the tasklet are presented in Table 1.

The ParallelMap tasklet only allowed one iteration to be stolen at a time. An optimised version of the tasklet was also tested that allowed a group of iterations to be stolen at a time and therefore increased the granularity of the tasks created. The number of iterations stolen was calculated at runtime as $n = vectorsize\ /\ (number\ of\ nodes * 2)$. Table 2 presents the speedups achieved over the sequential version of the program when using different vector sizes and different granularities of the mapped function on 8 workstations. The results show that NIP performs reasonably well even for relatively small granularities.

7   Related Work

Lazy Task Creation and Distributed Shared Memory have been and still are very active areas of research. In this section, the relation of NIP to particularly relevant previous work is discussed.

Mohr et al. [9] describe *Lazy Task Creation* as a technique for increasing the granularity of parallel programs by creating new tasks only when computational resources become available. Lazy Task Creation suffers from overheads caused by the use of the heap and by global lock operations. The NIP Lazy Task Creation scheme only uses the stack, introduces a locking scheme that permits more parallelism (Section 4.2), and creates only one tasklet for iterative computations.

Goldstein et al. [12, 23] produced a compiler-supported technique, which they call *Lazy Threads*, that allows threads to be executed like sequential function calls when computational resources are not available. Unlike NIP, the technique requires a new stack manipulation scheme, a customised compiler, shared memory, and it uses a *polling* scheme to process the queue of available work.

In the area of DSM systems, Bershad et al. in [23] first introduced the *Entry Consistency* model and used it to implement the Midway DSM system. In Midway, an explicit association of data with synchronisation variables has to be made. In NIPDSM, every object has its own private lock allowing full inter-object parallelism to be exploited, and the locking operations are called implicitly when objects are accesed. Unlike NIPDSM, Midway does not allow overlapping of communication and computation.

Other page-based or object-based DSM systems cannot directly support the semantics imposed by the NIP computational model. For example, page-based DSM systems cannot directly support object consistency while existing object-based DSM systems do not provide entry consistency or the overlapping of communication and computation.

8   Conclusions and Further Work

In this paper, the design of the NIP system for executing parallel UFO programs has been described. UFO combines elements of both object-oriented and functional programming, marrying the implicit parallelism of functional languages with the encapsulation of state manipulation offered by object-oriented languages. Whilst this paper focuses on UFO as the high level language, the issues, design and implementation are applicable to other similar parallel languages, and to any others which offer features found within UFO (e.g., iteration, encapsulation of state within objects).

Work on NIP is progressing in a number of directions. First, the behaviour of a wider range of parallel programs is being analysed. Also, a set of advanced caching features are being designed to improve the efficiency of the NIPDSM by copying and caching groups of objects rather than single objects. Finally, we are investigating the mapping of other high level languages onto NIP; the initial focus is on extracting implicit parallelism from Java programs.

References

1. V. S. Sunderam. PVM: A framework for parallel distributed computing. *Concurrency: Practice and Experience*, 2(4):315–339, Dec 1990.
2. M.P.I. Forum. MPI: A message-passing interface standard. *Journal of Supercomputer Applications and High Performance Computing*, 8(3/1), 1994.
3. T. Sterling, P. Mesina, and P.H. Smith. *Enabling Technologies for PetaFLOPS Computing*. MIT Press, 1995.
4. M.C. Henson. *Elements of Functional Languages*. Blackwell Scientific Publications, 1987.

5. K. Hammond. Parallel functional programming: an introduction. In *PASCO'94 - Conference on Parallel Symbolic Computation*. World Scientific, 1994.

6. J. Darlington and M.J. Reece. ALICE: A multiple-processor reduction machine for the parallel evaluation of adaptive languages. In *FPCA'81*, 1981.

7. I. Watson, V. Woods, P. Watson, R. Banach, M. Greenberg, and J. Sargeant. Flagship: a parallel architecture for declarative programming. In *15th Annual Symposium on Computer Architecture*, 1988.

8. J. Sargeant. United functions and objects: An overview. Technical Report UMCS-93-1-4, Dept. of Computer Science, University of Manchester, 1993.

9. E. Mohr, D.A. Kranz, and R.H.J Halstead. Lazy task creation: A technique for increasing the granularity of parallel programs. *IEEE Transactions on Parallel and Distributed Systems*, 2(3):264–280, 1991.

10. O. Kaser, C. R. Ramakrishnan, I. V. Ramakrishnan, and R. C. Sekar. EQUALS - a fast parallel implementation of a lazy language. *Journal of Functional Programming*, 7:183–217, 1997.

11. R.M. Burstall and J. Darlington. Some transformations for developing recursive programs. *Journal of the ACM*, 24(1):44–67, 1977.

12. S. C. Goldstein, K. E. Schauser, and D. E Culler. Lazy threads: Implementing a fast parallel call. *Journal of Parallel and Distributed Computing*, 37(1):5–20, 1996.

13. J. Protic, M. Tomasevic, and V. Milutinovic, editors. *Distributed Shared Memory - Concepts and Systems*. IEEE Computer Society, 1998.

14. P. Keleher, A.L. Cox, S. Dwarkadas, and W. Zwaenepoel. Treadmarks: Distributed shared memory on standard workstations and operating systems. In *1994 Winter USENIX Conference*, 1994.

15. B.N. Bershad and M.J. Zekauskas. Midway: Shared memory parallel programming with entry consistency for distributed memory multiprocessors. Technical Report CMU-CS-91-170, School of Computer Science, Carnegie Mellon University, 1991.

16. S. Ahuja, N. Carriero, and D. Gelernter. Linda and friends. *Computer*, 19(8):26–34, 1986.

17. E. Jul, L. Henry, N. Hutchinson, and A. Black. Fine-grained mobility in the emerald system. *ACM Transactions on Computer Systems*, 6(1):109–133, 1988.

18. U. Ramachandran and M.Y.A. Khalidi. An implementation of distributed shared memory. *Software Practise and Experience*, 21(5):443–464, 1991.

19. P. Keleher, A.L. Cox, and W. Zwaenepoel. Lazy release consistency for software distributed shared memory. In *19th Annual International Symposium on Computer Architecture*, volume 2, pages 13–21, 1992.

20. S.V. Adve and K. Gharachorloo. Shared memory consistency models: A tutorial. *Computer*, 29(12):66–77, 1996.

21. B.N. Bershad, M.J. Zekauskas, and W.A. Sawdon. The midway distributed shared memory system. In *IEEE COMPCON Conference*, 1993.

22. T. von Eicken, A. Basu, V. Buch, and W. Vogels. U-net: A user-level network interface for parallel and distributed computing. In *15th ACM Symposium on Operating Systems Principles*, 1995.

23. S.C Goldstein. *Lazy Threads: Compiler and Runtime Structures for Fine-Grained Parallel Programming*. PhD thesis, Computer Science, Graduate Division, University of California at Berkeley, 1997.

The Aleph Toolkit: Support for Scalable Distributed Shared Objects

Maurice Herlihy *

Computer Science Department, Brown University, Providence, RI 02912

Abstract. The shared object model is an appealing programming abstraction for distributed computing. By hiding the details of the network and data distribution, it allows the programmer to focus on higher-level concerns, and makes the program structure robust in the presence of changes in distribution patterns or environment. Nevertheless, it is not at all clear that the distributed shared object model can be adapted to the needs of modern large-scale distributed applications.

The Aleph Toolkit is a collection of Java packages intended to support the construction of distributed shared objects in a way that addresses networking-related performance issues. This paper describes the design and rationale for the Aleph API, as well as our preliminary experience implementing a distributed shared object system in Java.

1 Introduction

The shared-object model is an attractive approach to structuring distributed applications. Existing shared-object systems, however, often lack the flexibility to meet the demands of large-scale networked applications. We believe that a toolkit approach is the most promising way to achieve an adequate level of flexibility and application-specific customization. Instead of providing a monolithic collection of services, a toolkit encapsulates individual services behind interfaces, allowing applications to select (or develop) customized implementations of each service.

The Aleph Toolkit is a collection of Java packages intended to support the construction of customized distributed shared objects. Aleph supports both "push-based" and "pull-based" communication, and "data-shipping" and "control-shipping" patterns. The major components of the Aleph run-time system are defined by Java interfaces, allowing programmers to substitute customized implementations that adapt to the needs of applications, or exploit specialized hardware.

This paper describes the overall design and rationale for the Aleph API and internals, as well as our early experience implementing a distributed shared object system in Java. The interesting aspects of this system include the modular decomposition, and the provision of services (such as ordered anonymous multicast) that differ from those provided by similar systems.

---

* This work is supported by AFOSR Agreement F30602-96-2-0228, DARPA Order D885.

A.Sivasubramaniam, M.Lauria (Eds.): CANPC'99, LNCS 1602, pp. 137–149, 1999.

2   Programming Models

We are interested in scalable distributed applications that require rapid access to complex objects. Examples of such applications include electronic commerce and trading systems, traffic information systems, and interactive communication systems such as conferencing or whiteboards. Such applications often have a critical need to control the ways in which data objects are moved through the system. In an ideal world, an object's clients would have instant access to the object's current state. Often, however, it is not possible to provide clients with a completely accurate view of the object, thus the application must allow the client's views of the object to diverge from the ideal view in a controlled way.

We call this class of issues the *data fidelity problem*. The conventional way to implement distributed shared objects, in which cached copies are moved among clients on demand, is clearly inadequate to these challenges. Instead, application designers must determine an application-specific notion of fidelity: how closely clients' views must track the object's actual state.

A simple stock trading example illustrates many of these issues. Each stock's price is represented as a distributed *quote* object, where each client accesses the object through a proxy. If there is a single server, the number of clients is small, and each client is interested in a different stock, then quotes could be kept up-to-date by having proxies periodically poll the server (a "pull-based" approach). If the number of clients is large, or the clients have similar interests, then it is more sensible for the server to multicast changes to quotes (a "push-based" approach). If certain clients want to be notified when certain stocks change by specified percentages, then it makes sense for the server to unicast updates to those clients' proxies. Even more elaborate schemes could be imagined: updates may be distributed among a hierarchy of caching servers, clients could be organized into multiple multicast groups depending on their interests, and so on.

Programming models based on explicit message passing (such as PVM [12] or MPI [11]) are widely used for scientific and engineering applications. Although message-passing has proved useful for relatively small-scale and regularly-structured applications, we believe it is poorly suited to structuring large-scale or long-lived applications. The principal limitation of the message-passing model is that it burdens the programmer with responsibility for all interprocessor communication, synchronization and caching. This burden is particularly cumbersome for large-scale applications or those with irregular or dynamically changing communication structures.

The work described here has been influenced by several kinds of distributed shared object systems. *Distributed shared memory* (DSM) systems, whether page-based or object-based, implement a "data-shipping" model, in which the bits representing the object are moved among client caches on demand. A variety of techniques have been proposed for maintaining consistency among the cached copies [1]. Many existing DSM systems provide only limited *flexibility*: although most DSM systems support a fixed number of cache coherence protocols, the stock quote example given above illustrates the need to define and implement application-specific notions of consistency that cannot be anticipated by the designers of the DSM system. A second limitation is that the data-shipping model is simply not appropriate for some kinds of shared objects, including objects that represent caches or encapsulate services, or objects whose contents are subject to security constraints. For example, consider a system that allows users to open chat windows on one another's displays. One might like to treat another user's display as an object providing methods to open and close chat windows, but such a display object could not be treated simply as a data structure to be paged across the network. Similar considerations apply to the system's authentication server, which encompasses sensitive information such as passwords.

By contrast, *remote method invocation* (RMI) systems [19, 21] implement a "control-shipping" model for objects. Calls to an object's methods are transformed, via a stub, to messages forwarded to a remote site that encapsulates the object's state. The RMI approach works well for objects that encapsulate services or resources, but additional techniques are needed to deal with objects for which flexible caching policies are important for performance.

Each of these choices, push vs. pull, or data-shipping vs. control-shipping, is sensible under certain circumstances. The range of choices suggests that a toolkit approach is an attractive way to allow object implementers to "mix-and-match" module implementations to meet application-specific requirements and to track changes in the underlying hardware, reducing or eliminating the need to restructure the application each time.

3   Aleph API

The *Aleph toolkit* is a collection of Java packages (JDK 1.1) that provides platform-independent support for distributed shared objects. Our emphasis is not merely on *portability*, *i.e.*, adapting code written for one platform to another, but on *interoperability*: the ability to run computations that span multiple heterogeneous platforms.

A distributed program runs on a number of logical processors, called *Processing Elements* (PEs). Each PE is a Java Virtual Machine, with its own address space. Each PE is created as part of a *PEgroup* (aleph.PEGroup)[1] When the PE group is started, the Aleph run-time system supervises a handshake protocol ensuring that each PE is initialized knowing the address of every other PE within its group. Any PE in a PE group can shut down the entire group. It is also possible to create *long-lived* PEs that do not belong to any group. Such long-lived PEs are useful for long-lived services and applications.

The next section gives an overview of the Aleph communication primitives. We focus on the meaning of these primitives, and on how their use affects program structure.

---

[1] A PE group is not a process group in the sense used by Isis [7] and related systems.

```
public class RegisteredObject {
  static Hashtable registry;      // register objects here
  static PE[] peers;              // all PEs
  public RegisteredObject(String label) {  // constructor
    RegisterMessage m = new RegisterMessage(label, this); // construct
                                                          message
    for (int i = 0; i < peers.length; i++) // send it out
      m.send(peers[i]);
    ...
  }
  ...
  // Message defined by static inner class
  private static class RegisterMessage extends aleph.Message {
    String label; RegisteredObject object; // new data fields
    public RegisterMessage(String label,    // constructor
                           RegisteredObject object) {
      this.label = label; this.object = object;
    }
    public void run() {          // actually register the object
      registry.put(label, object);
    }
  }
}
```

Fig. 1. Illustrating use of aleph.Message

3.1 Message Passing

Direct message-passing is the simplest form of communication between PEs. It is
the basis for point-to-point (unicast) communication, and is used extensively in
the Aleph internals. Messages in Aleph are modeled loosely on *active messages*
[24]. Each message encompasses a method and its arguments, and that method is
called when the message is received. We define an abstract class aleph.Message
that implements Serializable and Runnable. A new message class is defined by
extending aleph.Message, including a void run() method to be called by the
receiver. When a message is received, its run method is executed to completion.
Messages sent from one PE to another are received in FIFO order, and their run
methods are executed in that order.

We say that a message is *blocking* if its run method could be blocked for an
unpredictable duration. We emphasize that a message is not necessarily blocking just because it calls a synchronized method, because many synchronized
methods impose only a bounded delay. For example, if P sends Q a message
requesting exclusive access to an object, that message is blocking because an
application running at Q may not be ready to release the object. When Q eventually sends a reply message containing that object to P, the reply would not be
considered blocking, even if the reply's run method calls a synchronized method

to place the object in a shared hash table, because that insertion cannot be blocked for an arbitrary duration.

Blocking messages belong to the class `aleph.AsynchMessage`, a subclass of (non-blocking) `aleph.Message`. When a PE receives a blocking message, it allocates a thread to execute its run method, and the PE immediately proceeds to receive the next message. When a PE receives a non-blocking message, it transfers the message to a dedicated thread that that executes successive messages' run methods to completion. This distinction between blocking and non-blocking messages yields a modest performance benefit by reducing reducing thread-switching overhead (See Figure 3). More importantly, however, it yields the semantic benefit of ensuring that non-blocking run methods are executed in FIFO order, a guarantee that can substantially simplify protocol design. (Since blocking messages' run methods are executed asynchronously in independent threads, they may effectively be executed out of order).

As a language construct, Messages provide a clean way for a class residing at one PE to communicate with instances of the same class at other PEs. Figure 1 shows a simple `RegisteredObject` class in which an object created at one PE is registered in a static table at all PEs. The message class is defined as a a static inner class, so its run method has direct access to class (static) variables, but the message class itself is not visible outside the class, and does not clutter up the class's specification.

3.2 Events

The `aleph.Event` class supports push-based communication. An event object is a kind of multicast channel. One PE can notify others when an event occurs by calling that `Event` object's `signal` method (with an optional argument). If a PE wants to be notified when an event has been signaled, it registers a `Listener` object with that event. Just as in the Abstract Window Toolkit (AWT), the listener is a dummy object that provides a void `actionPerformed(Object object)` method that is called (with the optional argument) when the event is signaled. If a PE loses interest in the event, it can unregister its listener.

Events provide a form of reliable anonymous multicast. The multicast is reliable because all PEs registered with an event will eventually be notified when the event is signaled. It is anonymous because a PE signaling an event need not know the identities of the other PEs listening to that event. We believe that anonymity is a precondition for scalability: registering or unregistering a listener should be a light-weight operation, analogous to joining or leaving an IP multicast group.

Events can be ordered or unordered. If an event is ordered, notifications are delivered to listeners in the same order. We use unordered events in barrier objects (many senders, many listeners), join objects (many senders, one listener). Ordered events are intended for push-based proxy or cache coherence protocols, in which PEs install incremental modifications to remote object proxies. Figure A simplified barrier using events appears in Figure 2.

```
public class Barrier implements Serializable {
  private int count;           // number of outstanding calls
  private Event event;         // used for communication
  /**
   * Construct a barrier, one thread per PE.
   **/
  public Barrier() {
    this(PE.numPEs());
  }
  /**
   * Wait for all threads to reach this barrier.
   **/
  public synchronized void waitFor() {
    event.setListener(new Listener() { // anonymous class
      public void actionPerformed(Object object){
        synchronized (Barrier.this) {
          count -= 1;
          Barrier.this.notifyAll();
        }
      }});
    event.signal();
    while (count > 0) {
      try { wait(); } catch (InterruptedException e) {};
    }
  }
}
```

Fig. 2. Illustrating use of aleph.Event

There are two kinds of signals: *normal*, and *flush*. When a PE registers a listener with an event object, it is notified of all signals back to the most recent flush. The distinction between normal and flush signals is intended to allow the application to inform the Event implementation when it is safe to discard information about past notifications. For example, a PE might multicast incremental changes to an object using normal signals, but then periodically multicast the object's complete state using a flush.

Our notion of ordered multicast can be contrasted to that used in systems employing virtual synchrony [3, 7, 23]. In those systems, PEs belong to a *process group* whose membership is common knowledge among the group members. Each time a PE enters or leaves the group, the members undertake a kind of global consensus protocol to ensure that all current participants agree on the group membership. By contrast, Aleph Events are intended to permit PEs to enter or leave the multicast group with a minimum of disruption.

3.3   Remote Threads and Functions

A thread running within one PE can invoke a thread within another PE, and optionally wait for that thread to finish. For example, in the classic "hello world" application, the remote thread that will execute at each PE is defined as:

```
static class HelloThread
                extends aleph.RemoteThread {
  public void run() {
    System.out.println("Hello World from "
                        + PE.thisPE());
  }
}
```

Remote threads extend the abstract class RemoteThread. Like regular Java threads, the class must provide a public void run() method to be called when the thread is started.

As usual for Java programs, the top-level class must include a method with signature

```
public static void main(String[] args)
```

to be called when program starts. The main method creates an instance of a remote thread object.

```
HelloThread thread = new HelloThread();
```

As with regular threads, a remote thread does not execute until it is explicitly started. The main method then creates a Join object for synchronization, enumerates all PEs, starts an instance of HelloThread at each PE[2], and waits until all remote threads have completed.

```
Join join = new Join();
for (Enumeration e = PE.allPEs();
     e.hasMoreElements();)
  thread.start((PE) e.nextElement(), join);
join.waitFor();
```

There is also a RemoteFunction class that allows remote threads to return values.

4   Toolkit Implementation

Programming in Java to standard APIs supports portability and interoperability among different operating systems. Even so, there is another important dimension to portability that remains a challenge: effectively and economically

---

[2] Because starting a RemoteThread actually starts a copy of the thread object, a single RemoteThread instance can be started more than once.

exploiting emerging hardware platforms for network switching, memory interconnection, and clustered computing. A sensible way to isolate applications from such shifts in hardware foundations is to identify the modules most likely to be affected by advances in technology, and to isolate each one behind a Java *interface*, a language construct that constrains method signatures (and implicitly constrains functionality). For each such module, the Aleph toolkit provides one or more *default* implementations. Users are encouraged to substitute their own customized implementations, especially "native" implementations that exploit specialized or exotic hardware. We now give a brief description of the principal packages.

- *Communication Manager* Transport-level communication within the Aleph toolkit is mediated by the *Communication Manager* interface. Aleph currently provides two Communication Manager implementations: one uses Java RMI (based on TCP stream sockets), and the other uses IP Datagrams. These packages are discussed further in the performance section below. We are about to acquire an ATM switch, and we are in the process of constructing a "native" implementation for that medium.
- *Directory Manager* The *Directory Manager* locates a shared object's proxies. Aleph currently provides two implementations of the directory manager interface: a conventional "home directory" scheme, in which each object has a home PE that keeps track its current location and status, and a novel "arrow" directory [13, 9] scheme, based on a simple path reversal algorithm, which has better scalability properties. We consider directory manager implementations a rich source of future research.
- *Event Manager* Aleph Event implementation is encapsulated behind the *Event Manager* interface. Techniques for reliable anonymous multicast remain an active area of research (for example, [10, 17]). Most techniques for *ordered* multicast originate from the Virtual Synchrony community (for example, [3, 7, 23]), but the global synchronization needed to track group membership changes would defeat our goal of achieving scalability through anonymity. Several members of our research group are working on novel techniques for event implementation. In the meantime, the current Aleph release provides a simple Event Manager implementation that orders each event's signals via a "home" PE for that signal.
- *Transaction Manager* Aleph also provides support for atomic transactions encompassing threads that run within a single PE. We are working on a distributed transaction manager, as well as an integrated user-level checkpointing scheme.

Aleph also provides some support for instrumentation, and a registry service for long-lived PEs.

5   Performance

In this section, we examine the performance of the basic Aleph communication primitives. We will see that we can achieve reasonable communication latencies

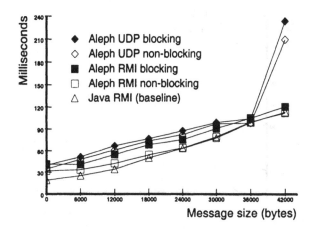

Fig. 3. Round-Trip Message Latency (Digital Unix)

on a local area network, and that different implementations of the communication and directory managers provide different levels of performance.

Each time shown is a duration measured in milliseconds by calls to `System.-currentTimeMillis()`, and each such duration is the average of one hundred successive tests. All programs were executed with the default just-in-time compiler. We ran tests on both Sun workstations running Solaris 5.6 and JDK1.1.7A, and Alpha Workstations running Digital Unix V 4.0 and JDK1.1.6. The workstations are linked by a complex mixture of 10MB and 100MB ethernets.

The first set of benchmarks measures round-trip times for simple messages, expressed as function of message length. The very first message-passing benchmark measures the latency of a null *remote method invocation* (RMI) from one host to another using the standard `java.rmi` package. This benchmark is not a test of the Aleph software. Instead, it is intended to establish a baseline for Java-based communication to which the Aleph implementation can be compared. This remote method takes an variably-sized object as an argument, and immediately returns its argument. The argument object includes an array of bytes whose size was varied from zero to 42000 in increments of 6000.

The remaining message-passing benchmarks tested round-trip times for Aleph messages. In each test, one PE sends a message to another. On delivery, that message's run method sends back a pre-allocated reply message. We measured the interval at the first PE between sending the first message and receiving the reply. Numbers shown are the average of 100 successive round trips. This interval encompasses the following steps: serializing, transmitting and deserializing the first message, executing its run method in a separate thread at the receiving PE, serializing, transmitting, and deserializing the reply message and executing its run method in a separate thread.

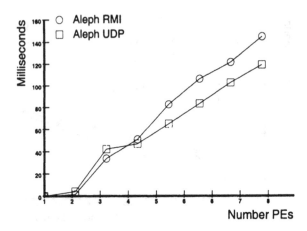

Fig. 4. Null remote thread creation (Solaris)

We tested two implementations of the Aleph `CommunicationManager` interface: one that uses Java RMI (TCP-based) and one that uses UDP datagram sockets. The results are shown in Figure 4 for two Digital Unix workstations. In the RMI-based communication manager, the thread that receives the message immediately passes a non-blocking message the message to a second thread, which then executes the message's run method. If the receiving thread were to execute the run method directly, then a deadlock could occur if the run method were to send a reply message back to the sender (a common occurrence). The RMI-based implementation incurs two costs over the raw RMI benchmark: executing the message's run method, and inter-thread communication. This cost difference is visible for small messages, but becomes insignificant when sending larger messages. The UDP-based implementation is slightly slower than the RMI-based implementation. It too incurs costs associated with executing the message's run method, and inter-thread communication. (Originally, the UDP-based implementation was faster, but the RMI-based implementation has been more thoroughly tuned).

The second benchmark measures how long it takes to create a null thread at a collection of PEs. This benchmark tests both point-to-point message-passing and event performance. The first PE creates a remote thread at each of the others, and, using a Join object, waits until they all finish. The Join object is implemented as an Aleph `Event` object, where the calling thread is the only listener. This interval encompasses the time needed to serialize the messages (sequentially) to transmit, deserialize, and run each message (in parallel), and to collect the responses via the Event object that implements the Join object. The results are reported Figure 4. To save space, we present only the Solaris results.

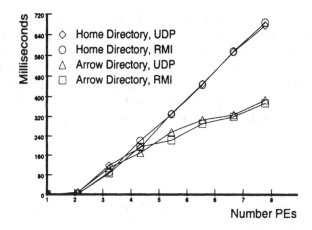

Fig. 5. Incrementing shared counter (Solaris)

The third benchmark measures the time needed to increment a shared counter. The results are reported in Figure 5. Here, the "arrow" directory management protocol consistently outperforms the standard "home" directory structure. An algorithmic analysis of this performance difference lies beyond the scope of this abstract, but is available elsewhere [9].

5.1 Status

Aleph has been tested on Digital Unix, SUN Solaris, Linux, Windows NT and Windows 95. Installing Aleph on a new platform typically requires changing a few lines in a single configuration file (usually just the pathname of the java interpreter). The latest version of the Aleph toolkit is available via

`http://www.cs.brown.edu/~mph/aleph.html`.

The benchmarks described above can be found in the `bench` subdirectory.

6 Related Work

Pioneering work on DSM systems includes Ivy [18], Munin [5], Treadmarks [16], Midway [6], and others. Early work on language support for DSM includes Linda [2] and Orca [4]. The early Aleph design was substantially influenced by experience using the Cid DSM system [20]. In Cid, as in CRL [15], an object is constrained to be a contiguous region of memory, a restriction not well-suited to languages such as C++ or Java where objects are typically implemented as non-contiguous list structures.

We are aware of two DSM projects based on Java: Java/DSM [26], and Mocha [22]. Java/DSM implements a parallel Java Virtual Machine (JVM) running on top of Treadmarks [16]. The Infospheres [8] project is also based on Java, but has less of an emphasis on shared objects. Mocha, like Aleph, provides the ability to run threads at different nodes, and to share objects among those threads, without modifications to the JVM. Mocha provides a substantially different API, with an emphasis on fault-tolerance and replication. The Jini system [25] provides Java-based support for distributed systems with a focus on "federating" distinct services. JavaParty [14] provides language support for remote objects and threads.

References

1. S. V. Adve and K. Gharachorloo. Shared Memory Consistency models: A Tutorial. *IEEE Computer*, 29(12):66–76, December 1996.
2. S. Ahuja, N. Carriero, and D. Gelernter. Linda and Friends. *IEEE Computer*, 19(8):26–34, August 1986.
3. Y. Amir, D. Dolev, S. Kramer, and D. Malki. Transis: A communication subsystem for high availability. In *Twenty-Second International Symposium on Fault-Tolerant Computing*, pages 76–84, July 1992.
4. H. E. Bal, M. F. Kaashoek, and A. S. Tanenbaum. Experience with Distributed Programming in Orca. In *Proc. of the 1990 Int'l Conf. on Computer Languages*, pages 79–89, March 1990.
5. J. K. Bennett, J. B. Carter, and W. Zwaenepoel. Munin: Distributed Shared Memory Based on Type-Specific Memory Coherence. In *Proc. of the Second ACM SIGPLAN Symp. on Principles and Practice of Parallel Programming (PPOPP'90)*, pages 168–177, March 1990.
6. B. N. Bershad, M. J. Zekauskas, and W. A. Sawdon. The Midway Distributed Shared Memory System. In *Proc. of the 38th IEEE Int'l Computer Conf. (COMPCON Spring'93)*, pages 528–537, February 1993.
7. K. P. Birman. The process group approach to reliable distributed computing. *Communications of the ACM*, 36(12):37–53, December 1993.
8. K. M. Chandy, A.dam Rifkin, P. Sivilotti, J. Mandelson, M. Richardson, W. Tanaka, and Luke Weisman. A world-wide distributed system using java and the internet. In *IEEE International Symposium on High Performance Distributed Computing (HPDC-5)*, August 1996.
9. M. Demmer and M.P. Herlihy. The arrow directory protocol. In *Proceedings of 12th International Symposium on Distributed Computing*, September 1998.
10. S. Floyd, V. Jacobson, C. Liu, S. McCanne, and L. Zhang. A reliable multicast framework for light-weight sessions and application level framing. *IEEE/ACM Transactions on Networking*, 5(6):784–803, December 1997.
11. Message Passing Interface Forum. Mpi: A message-passing interface standard. Technical Report CS-94-230, University of Tennessee, Knoxville, TN, April 1994.
12. A. Geist, A. Beguelin, J. J. Dongarra, W. Jiang, R. Manchek, and V. S. Sunderam. Pvm 3 user'sguide and reference manu. Technical Report ORNL/TM-12187, Oak Ridge National Laboratory, May 1993.
13. Maurice P. Herlihy and Michael P. Warres. A tale of two directories: Implementing distributed shared objects in java. www.cs.brown.edu/~mph/grande.ps, submitted for publication.
14. M. Jacob, M. Phillipsen, and M. Karrenback. Javaparty, a distributed companion to java. www.icsi.berkeley.edu/~phlipp/JavaParty.

15. K. L. Johnson, M. F. Kaashoek, and D. A. Wallach. CRL: High-Performance All-Software Distributed Shared Memory. In *Proc. of the 15th ACM Symp. on Operating Systems Principles (SOSP-15)*, pages 213–228, December 1995.

16. P. Keleher, S. Dwarkadas, A. L. Cox, and W. Zwaenepoel. TreadMarks: Distributed Shared Memory on Standard Workstations and Operating Systems. In *Proc. of the Winter 1994 USENIX Conference*, pages 115–131, January 1994.

17. B. N. Levine and J.J. Garcia-Luna-Aceves. A comparison of reliable multicast protocols. *Multimedia Systems Journal (ACM/Springer)*, 6(5), August 1998.

18. K. Li and P. Hudak. Memory Coherence in Shared Virtual Memory Systems. *ACM Trans. on Computer Systems*, 7(4):321–359, November 1989.

19. Sun MicroSystems. Java remote method invocation specification. `www.javasoft-.com/products/jdk/1.1/download-pdf-ps.html`, 1997.

20. R. S. Nikhil. Cid: A Parallel, "Shared Memory" C for Distributed-Memory Machines. In *Proc. of the 7th Int'l Workshop on Languages and Compilers for Parallel Computing*, August 1994.

21. A. Pope. *The CORBA reference guide: Understanding the Common Object Request Broker*. Addison-Wesley, 1997.

22. B. Topol, M. Ahamad, and J.T. Stasko. Robust state sharing for wide area distributed applications. Technical Report GIT-CC-97-25, Georia Institute of Technology, Atlanta, GA, September 1997.

23. R. van Renesse, K. P. Birman, R. Friedman, M. Hayden, and D. A. Karr. A framework for protocol composition in horus. In *Proc. of the 14th Annual ACM Symp. on Principles of Distributed Computing (PODC'95)*, pages 80–89, August 1995.

24. T. von Eicken, D.E. Culler, S.C. Goldstein, and K.E. Schauser. Active messages: a mechanism for integrated communication and computation. In *Proc. of the 19th Annual Int'l Symp. on Computer Architecture (ISCA'92)*, May 1992.

25. J. Waldo. Jini architecture overview. `www.javasoft.com/products/jini-/whitepapers/index.html`, 1998.

26. W. M. Yu and A. L. Cox. Java/DSM: a Platform for Heterogeneous Computing. In *ACM 1997 Workshop on Java for Science and Engineering Computation*, June 1997.

Combining Adaptive and Deterministic Routing: Evaluation of a Hybrid Router

Dianne R. Kumar and Walid A. Najjar

Department of Computer Science,
Colorado State University,
Ft. Collins, CO 80523 USA

Abstract. A novel routing scheme is proposed for virtual cut-through switching that attempts to combine the low routing delay of deterministic routing with the flexibility and low queuing delays of adaptive routing on k-ary n-cube networks. In this hybrid routing scheme a message is routed as soon as possible along a minimal path to its destination even though the routing choice may not be optimal. Results show that the disadvantages of making a non-optimal routing decision are offset by its speed. Two pipelined implementations of this hybrid routing mechanism are evaluated and compared to traditional deterministic and adaptive implementations. The experimental evaluations show that both hybrid implementations do indeed achieve their objectives under various types of traffic patterns.

1 Introduction

This paper reports on the implementation and evaluation of a hybrid routing scheme that combines the advantages of deterministic and adaptive routing.

In the deterministic, or dimension-order, routing algorithm a message is routed along decreasing dimensions with a dimension decrease occurring only when zero hops remain in all higher dimensions. Virtual channels (VCs) are included in the router to avoid deadlock [7]. Deterministic routing can suffer from congestion since only a single path between source and destination can be used.

In adaptive routing, messages are not restricted to a single path when traveling from source to destination. Moreover, the choice of path can be made dynamically in response to current network conditions. Such schemes are more flexible, can minimize unnecessary waiting, and can provide fault-tolerance. Several studies have demonstrated that adaptive routing can achieve a lower latency, for the same load, than deterministic routing when measured by a constant clock cycle for both routers [13, 15].

The delay experienced by a message, at each node, can be broken down into: *router* delay and *queuing* (or waiting) delay. The former is determined primarily by the complexity of the router. The latter is determined by the congestion at each node which in turn is determined by the degrees of freedom the routing algorithm allows a message. Note that the router delay is directly related to

A.Sivasubramaniam, M.Lauria (Eds.): CANPC'99, LNCS 1602, pp. 150–164, 1999.

the clock cycle time of the router. The main performance advantage of adaptive routing (besides its fault-tolerance) is that it reduces the queuing delay by providing multiple path options.

However, the router delay for deterministic routers, and consequently their corresponding clock cycles, can be significantly lower than adaptive routers [2, 5]. This difference in router delays is due to two main reasons: number of VCs and output (OP) channel selection. Two VCs are sufficient to avoid deadlock in dimension-order routing [7]; while adaptive routing (as described in [9,4]) requires a minimum of three VCs in k-ary n-cube networks. In dimension-order routing, the OP channel selection policy only depends on information contained in the message header itself. In adaptive routing the OP channel selection policy depends also on the state of the router (i.e. the occupancy of various VCs) causing increased router complexity and higher router delays.

The results reported in [2,5] show that the router delays for adaptive routers are about one and a half to more than twice as long as the dimension-order router for wormhole switching. The advantage of adaptive routing in reducing queuing delays is evaluated and reported in [10] for wormhole switching. A typical comparison of deterministic versus adaptive routing message latency (accounting for the differences in cycle times) is shown in Figure 1: at low traffic and for short to moderate message sizes, the latency of deterministic routing is smaller [10, 16]. However, the flexibility of adaptive routing provides smaller queuing delays and a much higher saturation point.

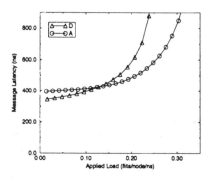

Fig. 1. Message latency of deterministic (D) and adaptive (A) routing on a 10-ary 3-cube network under random uniform traffic and with message length of 8 flits

In this paper we propose and evaluate a novel routing scheme for virtual cut-through switching that attempts to combine the low router delay of deterministic routing with the flexibility and low queuing delays of adaptive routing. The hybrid routing scheme is similar in concept to the hot potato algorithm and making the common case fast [3]: a message is routed as soon as possible although the choice may not be optimal, and this routing decision is fast. The results show that the disadvantages of making a non-optimal routing decision are offset by its speed. This hybrid routing mechanism relies on pipelined implementations where different paths and stages are used for different routing modes. The experimental evaluation of this router shows that it can achieve, under most conditions, the low latency of the deterministic approach as well as the high saturation point of the adaptive one.

The deterministic and adaptive routing algorithms and the routing delay model for virtual cut-through switching are described in Section 2. Section 3 describes the hybrid routing scheme. Results from the experimental evaluation comparing the hybrid router to the deterministic and adaptive ones under various traffic patterns for k-ary n-cube networks are reported in Section 4. Section 5 discusses related work and concluding remarks are given in Section 6.

While the work described in this paper relates to a k-ary n-cube, the concepts and router architecture can easily be extended to other topologies. These results are valid for networks designed for chip or multi-machine level implementations (NOWs).

2   Deterministic and Adaptive Routing

The interconnection network model considered in this study is a k-ary n-cube using virtual cut-through switching [14]: message advancement is similar to wormhole switching [17], except that the body of a message can continue to progress even while the message head is blocked, and the entire message can be buffered at a single node. Note that a header flit can progress to a next node only if the whole message can fit in the destination buffer. For simplicity all message lengths are equal.

2.1   Routing Models

In the *deterministic* routing scheme (dimension-order routing) [7], a message is routed along decreasing dimensions with a dimension decrease occurring only when zero hops remain in all higher dimensions. By assigning an order to the network dimensions, no cycle exists in the channel-dependency graph and the algorithm is deadlock-free.

The *adaptive routing* scheme considered in this work (Duato's or *-channels algorithm) is described in [9, 4]. In this algorithm, adaptive routing is obtained by using adaptive VCs along with dimension-order routing. A message is routed on any adaptive channel until it is blocked. Once blocked, a message is routed using dimension-order routing if possible. Note that a message may return to the adaptive channels in the following routing decisions if the adaptive channels are available. This algorithm has been proven to be deadlock-free as long as the message size is greater than the buffer size (i.e. size of the the VC) and as long as a message's header flit is allowed to advance to the next node only if the receiving queue at that node is empty. If the message size is less than the buffer size, deadlock is prevented by allowing a message to advance only as long as the whole message fits in the receiving queue at that node. This algorithm requires a minimum of three VCs per dimension per node for each physical unidirectional channel. Therefore, the number of VCs grows linearly with network size.

2.2   Switching Models

In this study, both the deterministic and adaptive routing schemes use one *unidirectional physical channel* (PC) per dimension per node. Figure 2 shows a schematic for each of the routers in 2D. In the deterministic routing case, both high and low VCs of each dimension are multiplexed onto one PC. In the adaptive routing case, the two deterministic and one adaptive VCs are multiplexed onto one PC. For both cases there is only one PC for the sink channel. Once this channel is assigned to a message, it is not released until the whole message has finished its transmission.

The deterministic router uses storage buffers associated with OP channels, while the adaptive router uses storage buffers associated with IP channels. When using OP buffers, the routing decision must be made before buffering the message which is ideal for deterministic routing since only one choice is available for an incoming message.

When using IP buffers, the routing decision must be made after buffering the message. It is suitable for adaptive routing since a message can usually be routed on several possible OP channels. The adaptive router implements a round-robin input message selection policy which checks for messages first among all adaptive buffers and then among all deterministic buffers.

OP channel selection is performed by giving priority to those channels in the dimension with the greatest number of hops remaining for the selected message. Each dimension with decreasing number of remaining hops is tried until a free channel is found or all channels have been tried. By using this OP channel selection policy, the greatest amount of adaptivity for a message is retained which reduces blocking.

2.3   Modeling Router Delay

In this section we describe a router delay model for the virtual cut-though deterministic and adaptive routers. The model is based on the ones described in [5, 2, 10]. These models account for both the logic complexity of the routers as well as the size of the crossbar as determined by the number of VCs that are multiplexed on one PC. These models were modified to account for the varying buffer space used in virtual cut-through switching.

The address decoding term (T_{AD}) includes the time for examining the packet header and creating new packet headers for all possible routes. The time required for selecting among all possible routes is included in the routing arbitration delay (T_{ARB}). The crossbar delay (T_{CB}) is the time necessary for data to go through the switch's crossbar and is usually implemented with a tree of gates. The flow control delay (T_{FC}) includes the time for flow control between routers so that buffers do not overflow. T_{SEL} is the time for selecting the appropriate header.

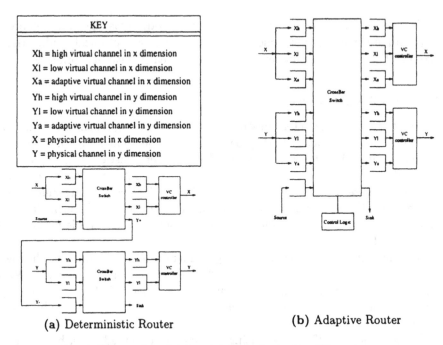

(a) Deterministic Router   (b) Adaptive Router

Fig. 2. Schematics of deterministic and adaptive 2D routers

Finally, the virtual channel controller delay (T_{VC}) includes the time required for multiplexing virtual channels onto PCs.

For all dimension-order routers simulated here, the number of degrees of freedom (F) equals one since there exists a single routing option for each message. The number of switch crossbar ports (P) is three because a deterministic router routes a message in either the same dimension on which the message came (on either the low or high channel) or routes it to the next dimension. For all of the adaptive routers, $F = P - 2(n-1)$ where n is the number of network dimensions. This relationship holds because adaptive routing can use the adaptive channels in all the dimensions while only two virtual channels per PC can be used in dimension-order (to avoid deadlock). Note that this relationship includes the delivery port.

Delay equations for the routers are derived using the above parameters. The constants in these equations were obtained in [5] using router designs along with gate-level timing estimates based on a 0.8 micron CMOS gate array process. Three main operations are used in all of the routers simulated here which contribute to the following three delays: T_r is the time to route a message, T_s is the time necessary to transfer a flit to the corresponding OP channel, and T_c is the time required to transfer a flit across a PC. The equations are:

$$T_r = T_{AD} + T_{ARB} + T_{SEL} = 4.7 + 1.2 log_2 F$$
$$T_s = T_{FC} + T_{CB} + T_{Latch} = 2.0 + 0.6 log_2 B + 0.6 log_2 P$$
$$T_c = 4.9 + T_{VC} = 6.14 + 0.6 log_2 C$$

Using the above equations, the delay values were calculated for each of the router algorithms simulated and are shown in Table 1. It is assumed that all three operations are overlapped through pipelining as described in [10], and therefore the clock period is determined by the longest delay: $T_{ccperiod} = Max(T_r, T_s, T_c)$

From the data in Table 1, we observe that increasing the buffer size in deterministic and adaptive routers, increases the overall router delay only when large buffer sizes are used. In deterministic routers, for small and moderate buffer sizes the clock cycle is dominated by the transfer time T_c while for larger ones it is dominated by the switching time T_s. In adaptive routers, the cycle time is dominated by T_r for small and moderate buffer sizes and dominated by T_s for large buffer sizes.

All of these added delays result in adaptive routers that are 15 to 16 % slower than deterministic routers. These results are similar to the results in [2] where 15% to 60% improvement is required for f-flat routers with similar number of VCs and under wormhole switching.

B	T_r	T_s	T_c	CC Period
8	4.70	4.75	6.74	6.74
16	4.70	5.35	6.74	6.74
24	4.70	5.70	6.74	6.74
32	4.70	5.95	6.74	6.74
48	4.70	6.30	6.74	6.74
64	4.70	6.55	6.74	6.74
96	4.70	6.90	6.74	6.90

a- Deterministic router
($C = 2$, $P = 3$, and $F = 1$ for all)

B	T_r	T_s	T_c	CC Period
8	7.80	5.79	7.09	7.80
16	7.80	6.39	7.09	7.80
24	7.80	6.74	7.09	7.80
32	7.80	6.99	7.09	7.80
48	7.80	7.34	7.09	7.80
64	7.80	7.59	7.09	7.80
96	7.80	7.94	7.09	7.94

b- Adaptive router
($C = 3$ and $P = 10$ and $F = 6$ for all)

Table 1. Deterministic and adaptive router delays (in $nsec$) for k-ary 3-cube networks

3 Hybrid Routing

This section describes the mechanism of the hybrid routing scheme along with two implementations: a Pipelined Hybrid Router (PHR) and a Super-Pipelined Hybrid Router (S-PHR).

3.1 Hybrid Router Model

The hybrid router consists of three logically independent and pipelined message paths: a Fast Deterministic Path (FDP), a Slow Deterministic Path (SDP), and an Adaptive Path (AP)[1]. The routing algorithm is shown in Figure 3 while the pipeline stages of the router are shown in Figure 4 and 5. Note that the longest stage in *all* paths determines the maximum cycle time of the hybrid router.

---

[1] Some physical stages are actually shared among these logically independent paths.

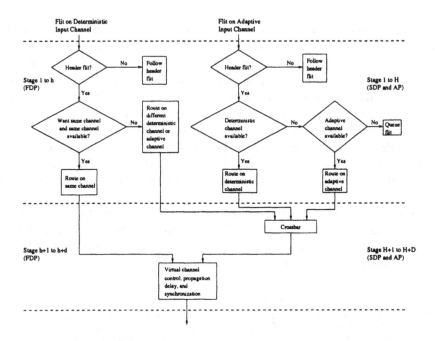

Fig. 3. Flow chart of hybrid routing algorithm

The FDP has the highest priority and is used for a message flit entering on a deterministic channel that is also able to leave on a deterministic channel of the same type (low/high) and dimension. Although the choice to route deterministically first may reduce adaptivity, the routing decision and switching logic along this fast path is simpler than the traditional deterministic and adaptive routing and requires the least number of stages: $h + d$ stages for a header flit and d stages for a data flit.

If a message cannot be routed along the FDP (i.e. if a deterministic channel of the same type is not available or a message is being switched to a different type or dimension), then the message is sent along the SDP which requires more logic and more stages than the FDP.

The AP is used to adaptively route a message and has the lowest priority. It is only used when both the FDP and SDP are unavailable. Both the SDP and AP take $H + D$ cycles for a header flit and D cycles for a data flit, where $(H + D) > (h + d)$. Although a header flit requires more cycles than a data flit, a data flit must always follow a header flit. Therefore, a data flit will block if the header flit has not yet advanced through a given stage.

This routing scheme is deadlock free: for any given message, the selection of paths is always a true subset of those that could be selected by the adaptive algorithm in [9]. Since the adaptive algorithm has been proven deadlock free, the hybrid is also deadlock free.

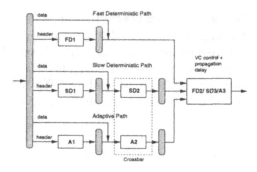

Fig. 4. Logic schematic of Pipelined Hybrid Router

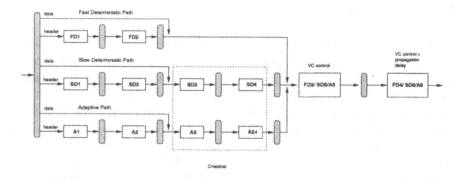

Fig. 5. Logic schematic of Super-Pipelined Hybrid Router

3.2 Pipelined Implementations

The *Pipelined Hybrid Router* (PHR) implementation is shown in Figure 4. It uses the flow chart in Figure 3 where $h = d = H = 1$ and $D = 2$ and corresponds to a 2/1 stage pipeline for the FDP and a 3/2 stage pipeline for the SDP and AP. Because the routing decision and switching logic of the FDP is simplest among all the paths, the T_r and T_s delays combine into one stage ($FD1$), while the T_c delay is kept in a separate stage ($FD2$). The SDP and AP are more complex and require separate stages for each of the T_r, T_s, and T_c delays, resulting in a 3/2 stage pipeline. Note that the crossbar is physically shared between both SDP and AP and all paths share the VC control logic.

The *Super-Pipelined Hybrid Router* (S-PHR) relies on deep pipelines to implement the hybrid router. Using deep pipelines can increase overall throughput at the cost of additional latch delays. Also the clock skew becomes more prominent: if the clock cycle becomes as small as the sum of the clock skew and latch overhead, further pipelining is no longer useful. An important factor to consider is an efficient use of the pipeline stages. Since the stages in all three paths are efficiently used in the PHR, the work in each stage of the PHR is divided into two stages in the S-PHR. Therefore, the 2/1 stage pipeline in the FDP of the

PHR becomes a 4/2 stage pipeline in the S-PHR, while the SDP and AP paths are modified from 3/2 stage pipelines to 6/4 stage pipelines. Once again, the crossbar is physically shared between both SDP and AP and all paths share the VC control logic. Figure 5 shows the new schematic for this super-pipeline. Note that the main difference between the PHR and S-PHR is the number of stages required for each path. The flow chart in Figure 3 is used in the S-PHR where $h = d = H = 2$ and $D = 4$.

3.3   Clock Cycle Times

The performance of the pipelined and super-pipelined implementations of the hybrid router is compared to the corresponding implementations of both the deterministic and adaptive routers.

Pipelined Router Implementation. Both the deterministic and adaptive routers are implemented as a 3/2 stage pipeline, where 3 stages are required for a header flit and 2 stages are required for a data flit. The cycle times for both are obtained using the equations in Section 2.3. Note that the deterministic router is not implemented using a 2/1 stage pipeline as in the hybrid router. This is because to accommodate both the routing and switching delays for the FDP into one stage would require the deterministic router's cycle time to be comparable to that of the adaptive router's. This greater cycle time would offset any advantage gained from having fewer number of cycles. Simulation results supporting this conclusion can be found in [1].

In the more complex hybrid router, the cycle time for its 3/2 stage pipeline path is much larger than that for the 3/2 stage pipeline in the deterministic router. Therefore all the necessary logic in the FDP of the hybrid router can fit into a 2/1 stage pipeline implementation without greatly increasing the cycle time of its 3/2 stage pipeline paths (SDP and AP paths). Since the cycle time is not greatly increased by adding the 2/1 stage pipeline path (FDP), the advantage of fewer number of cycles is retained. The cycle time of the pipelined hybrid router (PHR) is simply one gate delay larger than that of the adaptive router to account for the increased critical path length due to the inclusion of the 2/1 stage pipeline path (FDP).

Super-Pipelined Router Implementation. The super-pipelined implementation for the routers consists of dividing the work in each stage of its corresponding pipelined implementation into two. This results in a 6/4 stage super-pipeline for the adaptive router and a 4/2 stage super-pipeline for the FDP and a 6/4 stage super-pipeline for the SDP and AP of the hybrid router. The deterministic router's super-pipelined implementation is a special case and is discussed later.

The routing and switching delays for the *super-pipelined* implementation of all the routers is represented by T_R and T_S, respectively. These delays were calculated using their corresponding *pipelined* delays (T_r and T_s) in Equation 1. Note that the T_R and T_S delays are represented as T_{S-PR} in Equation 1, while their corresponding T_r and T_s delays are represented by T_{PR}. The setup time for the latch (L) is 0.8 ns and the delay for one gate (G) is 0.6 ns.

$$T_{S-PR} = \left\lceil \frac{(T_{PR} - L)}{2.0 * G} \right\rceil * G + L \qquad (1)$$

The T_R and T_S delays involve subtracting the latch setup delay to obtain the combinational logic delay which is then split in two in the super-pipelined router. The number of integer gate delays is then calculated and the latch setup time is added back.

Since the T_c delay (pipelined channel delay) consists of a set of gates as well as a wire, this case is considered separately. The two stages for the super-pipelined implementation of this delay consist of the VC controller delay ($T_V = 1.24 + 0.6log_2C$) in one stage and the propagation delay which is required for transferring a flit across the physical wire ($T_P = 4.9$) in the other stage.

The cycle time for the super-pipelined router (CC_{S-PR}) is then determined by the longest delay among all super-pipelined stages.

$$CC_{S-PR} = Max(T_R, T_S, T_V, T_P) \qquad (2)$$

As previously mentioned, the deterministic router's super-pipelined implementation is a special case. When the above equations are used for the deterministic router, T_P is found to be the bottleneck. Since the deterministic router's T_r delay of 4.7 ns is already smaller than the T_P delay of 4.9 ns, the super-pipelined routing delay (T_R) is the same as that of the pipelined routing delay (T_r). All other delays are calculated using the above equations which result in a 5/4 stage super-pipeline. The delays for this super-pipeline are found in Table 2a.

A further reduction in the number of stages in the deterministic router can be performed without greatly increasing the overall router cycle time. This is because T_V is quite small as seen in Table 2a and its delay can be combined with the two super-pipelined switching stages (T_{S1} and T_{S2}). This results in a 4/3 stage super-pipeline. These delays are shown in Table 2b. This 4/3 stage super-pipeline was used for all the deterministic router super-pipeline simulations.

B	T_R	T_{S1}	T_{S2}	T_V	T_P	CC Period
8	4.70	3.20	3.20	2.64	4.90	4.90
16	4.70	3.20	3.20	2.64	4.90	4.90
32	4.70	3.80	3.80	2.64	4.90	4.90
96	4.70	4.40	4.40	2.64	4.90	4.90

a - 5/4 stage super-pipeline

B	T_R	T_{S1}	T_{S2}	T_V	T_P	CC Period
8	4.70	3.00	3.00	-	4.90	4.90
16	4.70	4.40	4.40	-	4.90	4.90
32	4.70	4.40	4.40	-	4.90	4.90
96	4.70	5.00	5.00	-	4.90	5.00

b - 4/3 stage super-pipeline

Table 2. Super-pipelined deterministic router delays ($C = 2$, $P = 3$, $F = 1$) for k-ary 3-cube networks (in $nsec$) for two different super-pipeline implementations

The cycle times for the pipelined and super-pipelined implementations of the three routers are shown in Table 3.

	Deterministic		Adaptive		Hybrid	
B	PR	$S-PR$	PR	$S-PR$	PR	$S-PR$
8	6.74	4.90	7.80	4.90	8.40	5.00
16	6.74	4.90	7.80	4.90	8.40	5.00
32	6.74	4.90	7.80	4.90	8.40	5.00
96	6.90	5.00	7.94	4.90	8.54	5.00

Table 3. Clock cycle times for all three routers (in *nsec*) for *k*-ary 3-cube networks

4   Experimental Evaluation

Simulations of the deterministic, adaptive and hybrid routing implementations were performed using a discrete-time simulator on an 8-ary 3-cube network. The simulations use a stabilization threshold of a 0.005 difference between traffic 1000 clock cycles apart to determine steady state. Message sizes varied from 8 to 32 flits and buffer sizes used in the simulation are all equal to a single message length. The adaptive and hybrid routers use three VCs per dimension, while the deterministic router uses two. The simulator implements a back-pressure mechanism and varies traffic from 0.1 until saturation was reached in 0.1 increments. The following five traffic patterns were simulated: random uniform, complement, perfect shuffle, bit-reversal, and butterfly.

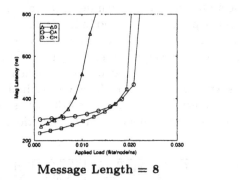
Message Length = 8

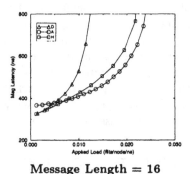
Message Length = 16

Fig. 6. Message latency of deterministic, adaptive and hybrid pipelined implementation routers in an 8-ary 3-cube under random uniform traffic

4.1   Performance of Hybrid Routing

Figure 6 shows the message latency versus applied load plots of the deterministic, adaptive and hybrid pipelined implementations under random uniform traffic and message lengths of 8 and 16 flits. Figure 7 shows similar plots as well as the accepted traffic versus applied load for complement traffic which has representative behavior of most traffic patterns simulated. An expanded version of this paper with complete results can be found in [1].

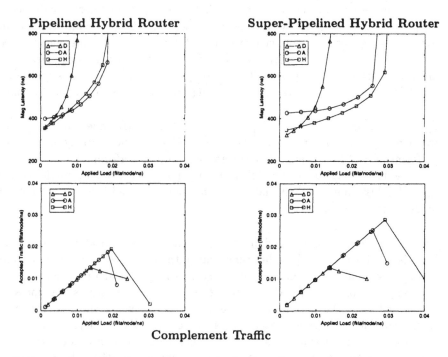

Pipelined Hybrid Router   **Super-Pipelined Hybrid Router**

Complement Traffic

Fig. 7. Comparison of pipelined and super-pipelined implementations of deterministic, adaptive and hybrid routers for 8-ary 3-cube (L=16)

Message Latency. Under random uniform traffic, for small messages (8 flits) the latency of the Pipelined Hybrid Router is not only lower than the pipelined adaptive one but is also lower than the pipelined deterministic one at low traffic. This is due to the fact that the Pipelined Hybrid Router has a 2/1 stage pipeline for header/data flits, while the deterministic router has a 3/2 stage pipeline. Even though the delay per stage in the deterministic router is shorter than the Pipelined Hybrid Router's, the greater number of stages dominates. For medium messages (16 flits) the latency of the Pipelined Hybrid Router is very close to that of the deterministic one at low traffic and follows the adaptive one at higher traffic. For larger messages (32 flits) the Pipelined Hybrid Router latency is less than the adaptive one at low traffic and greater than the adaptive one at high traffic. In general, the latency of the Pipelined Hybrid Router follows the deterministic one at low traffic and the adaptive one at high traffic.

Effects of Message Length. As message size increases under random uniform traffic, the performance advantage of the PHR decreases compared to the deterministic and adaptive pipelined routers. This is due to the fact that more messages, and therefore headers, are needed to achieve the same utilization with short message length and the PHR has a performance advantage for header flits, especially at low utilization. While the deterministic router has a 3-stage header flit pipeline with a low cycle time, the PHR has a 2-stage deterministic header flit pipeline with a higher cycle time. Since the number of pipeline stages dominates performance (and not the cycle time), the performance difference between the routers is greater for small message sizes than for large message sizes. This difference also exists at high traffic, although it's much smaller due to the fact that more message blocking occurs covering up differences in header flit time.

Effects of Traffic Patterns. The performance of the PHR under all non-random traffic patterns is similar to that for random uniform traffic. Once again, the PHR performs best at low traffic, while the adaptive router performs slightly better at high traffic. This is due to the higher priority given to the deterministic paths in the PHR: less choices are available as a message is routed through the network on deterministic channels.

Saturation Point. Under random uniform traffic, the saturation point of the PHR is, in all cases, much higher than that of the pipelined deterministic router and is very close to the adaptive one. One reason for the slight decrease in saturation point for the PHR with respect to the adaptive router, is that messages are routed onto the deterministic channels first, reducing the number of options available to a message later on. As traffic increases, this effect causes more blocking and slightly smaller saturation points. Under all non-random traffic the PHR's saturation point is once again much higher than that of the pipelined deterministic router and is very close to the adaptive one.

4.2   Effects of Super-Pipelining

The effects of super-pipelining on message latency are shown in Figure 7. Under all traffic patterns, the super-pipelined implementations for all routers achieve better overall performance gain than the pipelined implementations. This is due to the higher throughput that is achieved by deeper pipelines. Because of the higher throughput, all super-pipelined routers achieve higher saturation points than the pipelined implementations.

4.3   Effects of Path Priorities

The hybrid router's implementation for all the previous results includes first routing on the FDP, then on the SDP, and finally on the AP. This scenario is referred to as the SDP scenario. However, by routing the AP last, adaptivity that could be utilized at high loads may be lost. Therefore, simulations were performed to see if switching the priorities of the AP and SDP would improve performance near saturation. In this scenario, the FDP is still given highest priority. However, the AP is given the next highest priority, followed by the SDP. This scenario is called the AP scenario.

The simulated results between these two scenarios for all traffic patterns are so close that the resulting graphs will not be shown here. However, such close results demonstrate that although the AP scenario may allow more routing choices as load increases, the SDP scenario performs equally well because of the high priority and low cycle time of the FDP. Since the FDP has the highest priority, the benefit of retaining messages on deterministic channels allows the FDP path to be utilized more often and offsets any adaptivity loss.

5   Related Work

Some of the earliest work in understanding the effects of router complexity on cycle time involved deterministic routers [8, 6, 11]. The deterministic router complexity was then compared with adaptive router complexity for wormhole switching [2, 5, 10]. However, the comparison in [2, 5] does not account for the reduced queuing delay in adaptive routing. In [10] the reduction in queuing delay for wormhole switching is taken into account and the comparison is based on a constant total buffer area.

The Triplex routing algorithm is an example of a multi-class routing algorithm in which the dynamic selection of oblivious, minimal fully adaptive, and non-minimal fully adaptive routing is possible [12]. In the Cray T3E router, messages can be routed deterministically or adaptively by simply setting a bit in the header [18]. The router supports a shortcut for messages that continue traveling in the same dimension and uses direction-order routing for its deterministic routing algorithm. It also implements a routing function that bases the VC selection on the current VC and destination and implements a VC optimization scheme for VC balancing.

6   Conclusions

This paper reports on the empirical evaluation of a hybrid routing scheme which combines the low router delay of deterministic routing with the flexibility and low queuing delays of adaptive routing. This hybrid routing mechanism is realized using two different implementations (PHR and S-PHR) in which different paths and stages of the router are used for different routing modes. The scheme also relies on making the "common case fast" and is similar in concept to the hot potato algorithm.

The results from the simulation evaluation of this scheme show that both implementations of the hybrid router do achieve their objectives: a message latency comparable to that of the deterministic router at low traffic and a saturation point close to that of the adaptive router at high traffic. In addition, deeper pipelines achieve better overall performance gain than the pipelined implementations.

References

1. http://www.colostate.edu/ ~ najjar/papers/hybrid.pdf.
2. K. Aoyama and A. Chien. The cost of adaptivity and virtual lanes in wormhole router. *J. of VLSI Design*, 2(4), 1995.
3. P. Baran. On distributed communication networks. *IEEE Trans. on Commun. Systems*, CS-12:1–9, March 1964.
4. P. Berman, L. Gravano, G. Pifarre, and J. Sanz. Adaptive deadlock and livelock free routing with all minimal paths in torus networks. In *Proc. of the Symp. on Parallel Algorithms and Architectures*, pages 3–12, 1992.
5. A. Chien. A cost and speed model for *k*-ary *n*-cube wormhole routers. In *IEEE Proc. of Hot Interconnects*, Aug. 1993.
6. W. Dally and P. Song. Design of a self-timed VLSI multicomputer communicaton controller. In *Proc. of the Int. Conf. on Computer Design*, pages 230–40, 1987.
7. W. J. Dally. Virtual-channel flow control. *IEEE Trans. on Computers*, 3(2):194–205, March 1992.
8. W. J. Dally and C. L. Seitz. The torus routing chip. *J. Dist. Computing*, 1(3):187–196, 1986.
9. J. Duato. A new theory of deadlock-free adaptive routing in wormhole networks. *IEEE Trans. on Parallel and Distributed Systems*, 4(12):1320–1331, December 1993.
10. J. Duato and P. Lopez. Performance evaluation of adaptive routing algorithms for *k*-ary *n*-cubes. In *Parallel Computer Routing and Communication*, pages 45–59, 1994.
11. C. Flaig. VLSI mesh routing systems. Master's thesis, California Institute of Tehnology, May 1987.
12. M. Fulgham and L. Snyder. Integrated multi-class routing. In *Proceedings of the Workshop on Parallel Computer Routing and Communication*, 1997.
13. C. L. Glass and L. M. Ni. The turn model for adaptive routing. In *Int. Symp. on Computer Architecture*, pages 278–287, May 1992.
14. P. Kermani and L. Kleinrock. Virtual cut-through: a new computer communication switching technique. *Computer Networks*, 3:267 – 286, 1979.
15. Annette Lagman. *Modelling, Analysis and Evaluation of Adaptive Routing Strategies*. PhD thesis, Colorado State University, Computer Science Department, November 1994.
16. D. Miller and W. Najjar. Empirical evaluation of deterministic and adaptive routing with constant-area routers. In *Parallel Architecture and Compiler Techniques*, 1997.
17. L. M. Ni and P. K. McKinley. A survey of wormhole routing techniques in direct networks. *IEEE Computer*, pages 62–76, 1993.
18. S. Scott and G. Thorson. The Cray T3E networks: Adaptive routing in a high performance 3D torus. In *Proceedings of Hot Interconnects IV*, August 1996.

Deadlock-Free Routing in Irregular Networks with Dynamic Reconfiguration[1]

Rafael Casado[2], Francisco J. Quiles[2], José L. Sánchez[2], and José Duato[3]

[2] Dept. of Computer Science, Escuela Politécnica Superior de Albacete,
Universidad de Castilla-La Mancha, 02071- Albacete, Spain.
{ rcasado, paco, jsanchez }@info-ab.uclm.es. Univ.
[3] Dept. of Information Systems and Computer Architecture,
Universidad Politécnica de Valencia, P.O.B. 22012, 46071- Valencia, Spain.
jduato@gap.upv.es

Abstract. High-speed local area networks (LANs) support many distributed applications. These applications require some system availability guarantees. However, LANs may change their topology due to switches and hosts being turned on/off, link remapping, and component failures. In these cases, a distributed reconfiguration algorithm is executed. This algorithm analyzes the topology, computes the new routing tables, and downloads them to the corresponding switches. Unfortunately, in most cases user traffic is stopped during the reconfiguration process to avoid deadlock. Although network reconfigurations are not frequent, they may take hundreds of milliseconds to execute, thus degrading system availability significantly. In this paper, we propose a new deadlock-free distributed reconfiguration algorithm that is able to asynchronously update the routing tables without stopping user traffic. This dynamic reconfiguration algorithm is valid for any topology, including regular as well as irregular topologies.

1 Introduction

Current high-speed LANs (Autonet [1], Atomic [2], Myrinet [3], and ServerNet [4]) use techniques that have been successfully applied in interconnection networks for parallel computers such as point-to-point links between switches and pipelined switching techniques. These networks have also inherited some characteristics from conventional LANs, such as wiring flexibility and topology variability. The unique properties of high-speed LANs give rise to some problems related to topology configuration and message routing. In particular, high-speed LANs may change their topology due to switches and hosts being turned on/off, link remapping, and component failures. In these cases, in order to provide a high system availability, a

---

[1] This work was partly supported by the Spanish CICYT under Grant TIC97-0897-C04, and Caja Castilla-La Mancha.

A.Sivasubramaniam, M.Lauria (Eds.): CANPC'99, LNCS 1602, pp.165 -180, 1999.

reconfiguration algorithm must update the routing tables so that communication is possible between different components, as long as the network remains connected.

Reconfiguration mechanisms in current high-speed LANs are based on static reconfiguration techniques. Autonet [1] is the most representative example. In this technique, a distributed reconfiguration algorithm is triggered when a significant change in the topology occurs, spreading it to the whole network, and updating the routing tables in hosts and switches. This algorithm does not solve the problem of deadlocks during the reconfiguration process. Instead, the problem is avoided by stopping application traffic before starting the reconfiguration process. When the reconfiguration finishes, packet transmission is allowed again. As a consequence, performance degradation of the interconnection network is produced. In [5,6], Rodeheffer and Owicki analyzed the reconfiguration effect on average packet latency. Fig. 1 shows this effect:

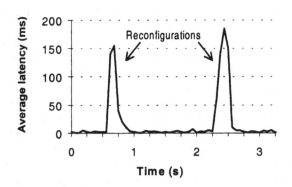

Fig. 1. Consequences of the static reconfiguration in Autonet. Under normal conditions, the network latency varies from 50 to 200 microseconds. Each reconfiguration needs from 150 to 300 milliseconds. These measures depend on several parameters: topology, load, etc.

Nowadays, many distributed multimedia applications such as real-time video compression and decompression, video-on-demand servers, distributed databases, etc., require computing power beyond that available in current uniprocessors. These applications require a very high network bandwidth, which can be provided by means of a high-speed LAN.

When multimedia applications are executed on a local area switch-based network, topology changes may affect their behavior. If static reconfiguration is used, the average latency increases dramatically during the reconfiguration. If we cannot stop the flow of information generated by the applications, then it will not be possible to guarantee the required QoS [7].

In our study, we tackle the reconfiguration of the interconnection network from a dynamic point of view: Performing network reconfiguration without stopping the transmission of user packets. The application of a dynamic reconfiguration technique will reduce the negative effects of the reconfiguration process, eliminating the spikes observed in Fig. 1. Dynamic reconfiguration provides a higher system availability [8] and is especially suitable for the distributed multimedia applications mentioned above, which require a guaranteed QoS. It would be noted that dynamic reconfiguration by itself does not provide QoS guarantees. However, The converse is true: If dynamic reconfiguration is not implemented, it will be impossible to guarantee QoS during the reconfiguration because message traffic will be stopped for tens or hundreds of milliseconds.

In this paper, we propose a new distributed deadlock-free reconfiguration algorithm suitable for generic topologies, including irregular ones. This algorithm is able to asynchronously update the routing tables without stopping user traffic. It has been developed for virtual cut-through (VCT) switching because it is easier to avoid deadlocks in VCT networks than in wormhole (WH) networks. This is not a serious constraint because VCT may replace WH in the near future to transmit messages in networks of workstations (NOW). Effectively, the distance between switches in a NOW is much longer than in a multicomputer. As a consequence, WH buffers must be very large in order to support channel pipelining [3]. On the other hand, in VCT, buffer capacity is determined by packet size, being independent of wire length. This switching technique requires a bounded packet size but it is not a significant restriction because current software messaging layers use a fixed packet size to increase performance by pipelining through the network interface card [9].

The most important problem that arises when using dynamic reconfiguration is the presence of deadlocks. We assume that switches operate asynchronously. Indeed, all the commercial switches operate in this way [3,4]. Thus, it is not possible to update the routing tables of several switches at once. For this reason, during a reconfiguration process, certain switches will route messages according to the old routing tables while other switches will already be using the new ones. More than one routing function may be simultaneously working in the network (one for each topology change).

Guaranteeing deadlock freedom when facing this situation can be complicated. To study the deadlocks generated by the interaction of several routing functions on an irregular topology we have implemented a tool that analyzes the properties of the interconnection network [10]. This tool allows the definition of network topologies and routing algorithms, and determines the existence of cyclic dependencies between channels. It also allows the analysis of the network behavior when switches/hosts are added to or removed from the network.

In Section 2, we present an informal description of the algorithm. Section 3 introduces different aspects related to the up*/down* routing algorithm. Section 4 presents our dynamic reconfiguration technique called Partial Progressive Reconfiguration. Finally, the last sections present our conclusions and future work.

2   Informal Description

This section describes the protocol for dynamic reconfiguration in an informal way. As indicated in the introduction, the key contribution of this protocol is its ability to update routing tables asynchronously without stopping message traffic while guaranteeing the absence of deadlock.

The first step in network reconfiguration is detecting the addition and removal (or failure) of network components (links, switches, and/or hosts). This issue has been addressed elsewhere [1,5,6] and is beyond the scope of this paper.

Once a change in the topology has been detected, it is necessary to update the routing tables at one or more switches and/or hosts. Our primary focus is on achieving a distributed update of the routing tables without stopping message traffic and without introducing deadlocks. As most commercial switches do not provide any support to synchronize that operation, routing tables must be updated asynchronously. Note that changes in the host routing tables cannot lead to deadlocks in the network, provided that the routing algorithm implemented by the switches is deadlock-free. However, switch routing table updates may lead to deadlock. Therefore, in this paper we will only focus on updating switch routing tables without introducing deadlock.

Several researchers proposed distributed deadlock-free routing algorithms for irregular interconnection networks [1,11-14], as well as general methodologies for the design of routing algorithms [12,13]. A straightforward way to avoid deadlock consists of removing cyclic dependencies between network resources (i.e., links and buffers) [15]. It may seem that when the topology changes, we only need to define a deadlock-free routing algorithm for the new topology, and update the routing tables. This would be true if all the routing tables could be updated synchronously and the switches purge pending messages traffic. As this is not possible, previously proposed solutions either may lead to deadlock or require stopping message traffic until all the routing tables have been updated. The reason is that the new routing algorithm may introduce some resource dependencies that did not exist in the old one. Of course, it will have to remove other dependencies to avoid cyclic dependencies and deadlock. The problem arises when routing tables are updated asynchronously because the new additional dependencies may arise before the old ones are removed, possibly leading to deadlock.

This problem cannot be solved by establishing an appropriate ordering to update the routing tables. Even for some very small networks, we found that there is no sequence of switch routing table updates that could guarantee deadlock freedom at all times. Note that every routing table update at a given switch must lead to a connected routing algorithm, i.e., the routing algorithm must be able to route messages destined for any host at any switch. Otherwise, some messages cannot be routed and would have to be discarded or would remain in the network.

The solution proposed in this paper consists of performing sequences of partial routing table updates, as opposed to completely updating a given routing table. Entries in each table are progressively removed and added step by step until the routing table corresponding to the new routing algorithm is reached. After each partial update, each switch must synchronize with some of its neighbors. The protocol proposed in this paper guarantees that the global routing algorithm remains connected and deadlock-free at any time.

The proposed protocol is very efficient. It interleaves short control messages between user messages. A single control message serves two purposes: carrying information about the required update in the routing table at the receiving switch, and guaranteeing that all the messages that have to be routed with the old routing table have already been forwarded from the sender switch. Therefore, a particular switch processes messages with the current routing table until it receives a control message requesting a partial table update. When this message is received, the routing table is immediately updated, and successive messages arriving through the same link are routed according to the updated routing table. The efficiency of the proposed protocol comes from the fact that table update delay is several orders of magnitude shorter than the time required to stop traffic in the entire network, download the new routing tables, and notify all the switches that the update is done. Moreover, dynamic reconfiguration only affects a (usually small) region of the network. Traffic in the regions of the network not requiring routing table updates is not affected at all by the reconfiguration process. However, with static reconfiguration, traffic is stopped in the whole network until all the routing tables have been updated.

In this paper we have focused on the up*/down* routing algorithm. Nevertheless, our reconfiguration technique can be applied to several adaptive routing algorithms that use up*/down* routing as escape channels [12,13]. Up*/down* routing algorithm defines a logical tree in the network. Messages are first routed toward the root of the tree until they find a common ancestor. Then messages are routed down the tree until they reach the destination switch. For this algorithm, we have found that it is easy to add switches without introducing cyclic dependencies between resources. Simply, we add them as leaves of the tree. Unfortunately, this may be inefficient in some cases because messages cannot be routed through leaf switches. Therefore, we may need to reconfigure the tree to make it more efficient. Moreover, if the new switch connects two subnetworks that were initially isolated, it will become a leaf belonging to two trees. This situation is depicted in Fig. 3. The leaf switch is node q. It should be noted that both subnetworks remain disconnected after adding the new switch because the up*/down* routing algorithm does not allow traffic through leaf switches. Additionally, now the network has more than a single root node. Similarly, when the root switch of a tree is removed, two or more root nodes may appear. Fig. 4 shows an example. Again, the up*/down* routing algorithm does not allow traffic between root nodes, which become logically isolated.

In order to allow traffic between all the switches, the tree has to be reconfigured. This can be done by changing the orientation of the links in the tree. As an example, Fig. 11 shows the network presented in Fig. 3 after changing the orientation of some links. As can be seen, there is a single root node after reconfiguring the tree. These link orientation changes must be performed step by step, possibly updating each routing table partially, and synchronizing with neighbor switches.

In order to simplify link orientation changes, we analyze the network in a hierarchical way. Several switches can be grouped together, forming a region. Fig. 5 shows how the switches in Fig. 3 can be grouped into several regions. Note that the use of regions considerably simplifies the network graph (see Fig. 7) while retaining the important properties, i.e., the existence of more than a single root node.

Finally, in order to establish the order and the consequences of link orientation changes, and guarantee the correctness of the proposed protocol, we propose some definitions (root node, break node, etc.). These definitions will considerably simplify link orientation changes through nontrivial results. For example, moving the position of the root switch in the network does not require any change in the routing tables, as long as it does not cross any break node. The following sections propose some definitions, and present the dynamic reconfiguration protocol formally.

3   Up*/Down* Routing Algorithm

Up*/down* routing is a partially adaptive deadlock-free routing algorithm suitable for irregular topologies. This algorithm is based on a cycle-free assignment of *direction* to the operational links in the network. This assignment is always possible, regardless of network topology [1]. Therefore, the network is configured as an acyclic directed graph. For each link, a direction is named *up* and the opposite one is named *down*.

To avoid deadlocks, legal routes never use a link in the *up* direction after having used one in the *down* direction. The other sequences (*up-up, up-down, and down-down*) are allowed. In other words, messages can cross zero or more links in the *up* direction, followed by zero or more links in the *down* direction. The name up*/down* derives from this fact (in some grammars, the asterisk indicates a list). In this way, cycles in the channel dependency graph [15] are avoided, thus preventing deadlock.

Fig. 2 shows an example where each link has been assigned a direction. Arrows indicate the *up* direction. In this paper, the graphs will only include switches as mentioned in Section 2.

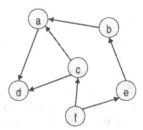

Fig. 2. Example of link assignment in an up*/down* routing algorithm. In order to avoid deadlocks, certain routes such as (*a→c→d)* and (*c→f→e)* are not allowed.

3.1   Properties of Correct and Incorrect Graphs in Up*/Down* Routing

A *root node* is a node in a directed graph that is not the source of any arc. The up*/down* routing algorithm requires the existence of a single root node in the graph. The reason is that there are no legal routes between two root nodes because each possible route would require *down* to *up* transitions. This restriction is required for *network connectivity*. In Fig. 2, the root node is node *d*.

A *break node* is a node that is the source of two or more arcs. In the up*/down* routing algorithm, these nodes prevent certain connections (input port - output port) from being used by the messages crossing it. These restrictions are necessary for deadlock freedom. There must exist one break node in every cycle of the original undirected graph of the network, but its position is unrestricted. We can see two break nodes labeled as *c* and *f* in Fig. 2.

In up*/down* routing, the associated directed graph will contain one and only one root node. Additionally, that graph will be acyclic. A directed graph that is acyclic and contains a single root node is called a *correct graph*. A correct graph may include several break nodes within its topology, as many as necessary to break all the cycles. Fig. 2 shows a correct graph.

Obviously, an *incorrect graph* is one that does not meet the restrictions imposed in the previous definition. This implies the absence of a root node, the existence of more than one root node, or the existence of cycles. If there is no root node, then the graph will contain one or more cycles and the up*/down* routing cannot guarantee deadlock freedom. If there are several root nodes, then the up*/down* routing cannot guarantee network connectivity. There is always at least one *false break node* between two root nodes. A false break node is a break node in which two links with the down end connected to it do not belong to the same cycle in the undirected graph of the network. A false break node splits the network into two unreachable regions. Obviously, a correct graph contains no false break nodes. Fig. 3 shows an example of incorrect graph with several root nodes.

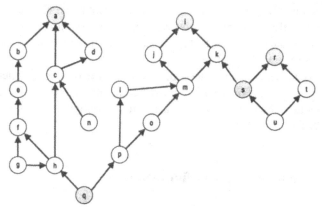

Fig. 3. Incorrect graph. Root nodes are labeled as *a*, *i*, and *r*, respectively. Break nodes are labeled as *c, g, h, m, p, u, q*, and *s*, respectively. The last two ones are false break nodes.

3.2   Handling Changes in Topology

For a given network topology, up*/down* routing is based on a link direction assignment that can be represented as a correct graph. When some switches are added to or removed from the network, its topology changes. Then, a correct graph may evolve into an incorrect graph. Next, we detail these situations.

Switch Activation

During the activation process we will avoid incorrect graph situations produced by either the absence of a root node or the presence of cycles in the graph. However, an incorrect graph may arise due to the appearance of several root nodes (it will be solved later).

When a new switch is added, a direction must be assigned to the links connecting to it. This assignment should not produce cycles in the directed graph. A simple approach consists of assigning a direction to those links in such a way that the down direction goes toward the new switch. By doing so, messages will be able to use the new links to route to/from the new switch, but not to cross it. The new switch will become a break node or a false break node if it is connected to the network through two or more links.

Switch Deactivation

When a switch detects that one of its neighbors has been deactivated, it starts a reconfiguration process similar to the activation process.

A switch deactivation cannot leave the directed graph without a root node, but it may produce the appearance of several new ones. The deactivation of several switches (including the root node), produces at least one new root node. Note that the directed graph is acyclic before switch deactivation. Fig. 4 shows an example of a correct graph that evolves into an incorrect graph after the deactivation of two switches, which produces several root nodes.

Switch deactivations imply that messages routed to removed components must be discarded. Also, messages requesting removed components must be discarded if they cannot use another route. In this case, a shorter reconfiguration time implies less discarded messages.

4   Partial Progressive Reconfiguration

Before changing the routing tables according to the new topology, it would be necessary to assign or modify the direction of several links to evolve from an incorrect graph into a correct graph.

We saw in the previous section that node activation/deactivation avoided incorrect graph situations produced by the absence of a root node. We also saw that the graph cannot contain cycles. However, the directed graph may contain several root nodes. In what follows, we will show how to correct incorrect graphs with several root nodes.

It should be noted that a static reconfiguration algorithm stops traffic and computes the direction assignment for every link in the network starting from scratch, i.e., it discards the previous configuration. On the other hand, a dynamic reconfiguration algorithm should not stop traffic. It progressively changes the orientation of the links, until it reaches a correct graph according to the new topology. Now we present a five-step dynamic reconfiguration algorithm:

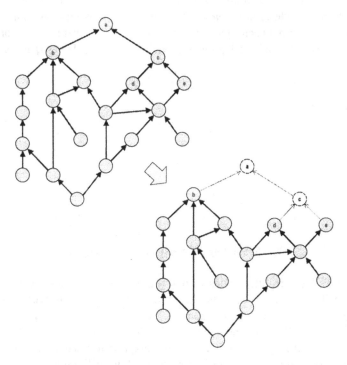

Fig. 4. Switch deactivation. After deactivation of switches *a* and *c*, the root node disappears. Then, three new root nodes, labeled as *b*, *d*, and *e*, appear.

4.1   Step 1: Generation of Correct Regions

When a directed graph contains several root nodes, it is not possible to route messages between root nodes. In this case, it is possible to split the directed graph into several correct subgraphs. A *correct region* is a subgraph of an incorrect graph that is correct. The reconfiguration process must determine the correct regions in the network. As the directed graph for the network contains no cycles, the network has as many correct regions as root nodes (one root node in each correct region). Fig. 5 shows the graph in Fig. 3, also indicating the correct regions.

4.2   Step 2: Obtaining the Virtual Inter-Region Graph

We call *frontier* nodes those switches that have at least one upward link crossing the limits of a region containing them. Certain switches are frontier nodes in every region in which they are included. We will only consider these switches. In Fig. 5, these switches are nodes *q* and *s*.

Between every pair of overlapping regions, the reconfiguration algorithm should select one frontier node as *router node*. A router between two regions is the only valid communication path between them. In the graph in Fig. 5 there is only one frontier node between each pair of overlapping regions. They are labeled as *q* and *s*.

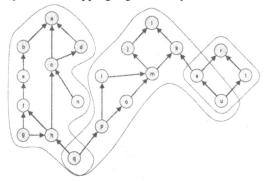

Fig. 5. Splitting the graph into correct regions.

If there are multiple frontier nodes in one region, only one must be elected as the router. Note that frontier nodes can choose the router by themselves. A distributed and independent election can be done if every frontier node applies the same algorithm. We select as router node the one with lower UID.

We define a *virtual inter-region graph* as the graph composed of all root nodes, all router nodes, and the paths interconnecting them. A virtual graph is an abstraction of the incorrect information in a graph in order to simplify the dynamic reconfiguration. We will manipulate the virtual graph until a correct graph is obtained. Fig. 6 shows the virtual graph corresponding to the example shown in Fig. 5.

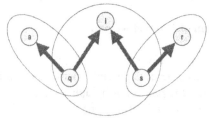

Fig. 6. Virtual inter-region graph. The orientation of each link in the virtual graph matches the orientation of the complete path it represents (composed of several links in the graph).

4.3   Step 3: Correcting the Virtual Graph

A virtual graph resulting from an incorrect graph is also incorrect. In particular, it has as many root nodes as the original graph. Therefore, it is necessary to modify the graph to make it correct by changing the orientation of some links. In order to achieve it, we identify a spanning tree of the virtual graph. The spanning tree is computed using a distributed algorithm proposed by Perlman [16]. In this algorithm, root and router nodes exchange tree-position packets. When the spanning tree computation finishes, the incorrect virtual graph has evolved into a correct one because only one *primary root node* remains in the virtual graph. The other ones are no longer root nodes, and will be referred to as *secondary root nodes*. The primary root node does not modify its position in the virtual inter-region graph. On the other hand, secondary root nodes reverse the orientation of the path to the router close to the primary root node. If a secondary root node can be attracted by several routers, it will go toward the router with the lower UID. Fig. 7 shows the virtual graph in Fig. 6 once it has been corrected.

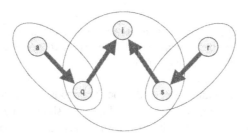

Fig. 7. Correct virtual graph. After computing the spanning tree of the virtual graph, it evolves into a correct graph completely connected according to the up*/down* routing algorithm.

4.4   Step 4: Correcting the Real Graph

Once the virtual inter-region graph has been corrected, path orientation changes must be propagated to physical links. Some conditions should be met when changing the orientation of the links in the network. Every change in link orientation should be carried out without disconnecting the routing algorithm. As a consequence, only the orientation of the links connected to root or break nodes can be changed. Otherwise, some nodes may be unreachable after changing a link orientation. Fig. 8 shows an orientation change in a link that is not connected to any of these nodes.

Taking into account the previous restriction, the real graph is corrected as follows. Each secondary root node begins its *movement*, exchanging its position with a neighboring node; this one exchanges its position with the following node, and so on. The movement of a root node requires the individual and sequential direction reversal of the corresponding links. From now on, we will use the expression "to move the root/break node" although in fact we are reversing link direction assignment.

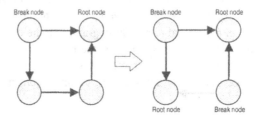

Fig. 8. Orientation change in a link not connected to root or break nodes. After the change in the lower link orientation, the network is split into two disconnected regions. There are two break nodes and two root nodes in the same cycle.

The movement of a secondary root node does not produce any change in the routing tables and therefore it does not cause deadlocks, as shown in Fig.9. In up*/down* routing, deadlocks are avoided by the restrictions imposed on the break node. Therefore, the position of the root node is irrelevant. For this reason, an orientation change in a link connected to a root node does not affect the routing tables. We can even perform the movement across several nodes in a single step.

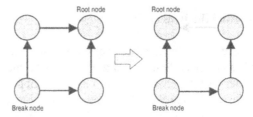

Fig. 9. Root node movement. The movement of the root node does not affect the routing tables.

There is a special situation when a root node reaches a break node. As shown in Fig. 10, a moving root node cannot move over a break node because a cycle arises and the root node disappears.

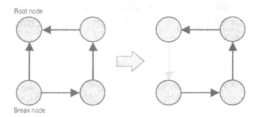

Fig. 10. Movement of a root node over a break node. A cycle appears in the directed graph after changing the orientation of the leftmost link. The resulting graph has no root node.

With this restriction, it is possible that there is no valid path between the secondary root node and the router node that must be reached. In Fig. 5, node *a* must reach node *q* but break nodes *c, g,* and *h* avoid it. The solution consists of previously moving as many break nodes as necessary, keeping them away from the path followed by the root node. In [17], it is shown how break node movements are performed without producing deadlocks. This movement has a high associated cost, requiring the synchronization of several nodes. For this reason, the path that minimizes the number of break node movements must be chosen. The secondary root node determines this path. Fig.11 shows the initial real graph once that it has been corrected.

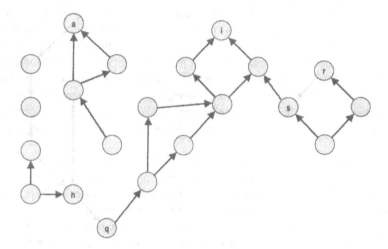

Fig. 11. Corrected real graph. Node *a* can be moved through several paths. The selected path only needs to move the break node labeled as *h*.

4.5   Step 5: Updating the Routing Tables

When a switch detects a change in the topology of the network, it triggers a reconfiguration process through a control message. This message is propagated to every node in the network by flooding. Each node will mark its routing table as invalid, although it will still use it.

The reconfiguration process defines the correct regions in the graph. Then, each node can generate its inter-region routing table. The process finishes if the reconfiguration process defines only one correct region in the graph. Otherwise, if several correct regions appear within the graph, then it is necessary to determine the inter-region routers and to correct the virtual graph. Then, each router node provides the topology of its region to the neighboring regions. At this time, it is possible to generate the complete routing table at each node, because it knows the whole topology.

When some components are removed from the network, routing tables must be updated so that messages are not routed toward nonexistent components. If a message blocks because it requested a nonexistent component before routing tables were updated, it may happen that the only possible action consists of discarding that message. Note that the updated routing function may not offer any path to some messages. In these cases, it could be necessary to send a notification message to the source node.

5 Conclusions

Several distributed applications demand high system availability. Additionally, multimedia applications require some quality of service (QoS) guarantees. In particular, audio and video streams must be delivered within some deadline, also minimizing jitter. When executed in a local environment, distributed multimedia applications require high-speed LANs with point-to-point links. Unfortunately, high-speed LANs may suffer frequent reconfigurations due to the activation and deactivation of switches and hosts, link remapping, and component failures. In these cases, a distributed reconfiguration algorithm analyzes the topology, computes the new routing tables, and asynchronously downloads them to the corresponding switches.

Current reconfiguration algorithms stop user traffic during routing table update to avoid deadlocks. As a consequence, these networks are not suitable to support multimedia applications because message latency may increase by three orders of magnitude, and consequently QoS may no longer be guaranteed.

In this paper, we have proposed a new distributed dynamic reconfiguration algorithm (DRA) that asynchronously updates routing tables without stopping user traffic. This algorithm is valid for any topology and guarantees the absence of deadlocks during the reconfiguration process [17]. After introducing some graph concepts, this paper analyzes the activation and deactivation of network components, showing how to build a network graph and update routing tables in such a way that no deadlock can arise. However, the routing algorithm may be disconnected, i.e., some parts of the network may be unreachable. Then, we propose a distributed protocol that produces a sequence of partial routing table updates, which are able to reconnect the routing algorithm. We show that the routing algorithm at every intermediate step is deadlock-free, and that the final routing algorithm correctly routes messages between every pair of nodes.

6 Future Work

In this paper, we have selected as primary root node the one with lower UID. However, more elaborated approaches to select the primary root node could be based on minimizing the cost associated with node movement, paying special attention to the number of break nodes to cross.

Also, we plan to formally state the dynamic reconfiguration protocol (DRP) to check reliability and deadlock-freedom.

We also plan to evaluate the performance of our algorithm, comparing it with conventional techniques such as the ones used in Autonet or Myrinet. Then, we will quantify the total reconfiguration time, determining whether the additional overhead introduced is cost-effective or not.

Finally, we plan to modify this simulator to support adaptive routing [18]. We expect that the influence of the reconfiguration process on network performance will decrease when using adaptive routing.

References

1. Schroeder M.D. et al.: Autonet: A high-speed, selfconfiguring local area network using point-to-point links. IEEE Journal on Selected Areas in Communications, vol. 9. n° 8. October 1991.
2. Felderman R. E., et al.: Atomic: A High Speed Local Communication Architecture. J. High Speed Networks, vol. 3, n° 1, pp. 1-29, 1994.
3. Boden N. et al.: Myrinet: A gigabit per second LAN. IEEE Micro. February 1995.
4. Horst R.W.: Tnet: A reliable system area network. IEEE Micro. February 1995.
5. Rodeheffer T. L., Schroeder M. D.: Automatic Reconfiguration in Autonet. SRC Research Report 77. September 18, 1991.
6. Owicki S. S., Karlin A. R.: Factors in the performance of AN1 Computer Network. SRC Research Report 88. June, 1992.
7. Knightly E. W., Zhang H.: D-BIND: An accurate traffic model for providing QoS guarantees to VBR traffic. IEEE Trans. on Networking, vol. 5, n° 2. April, 1995.
8. Pfister G. F.: In search of clusters. Prentice Hall, Englewood, NJ 1995.
9. Pakin S., Lauria M., Chien A.: High performance messaging on workstations: Illinois fast messages on Myrinet. Supercomputing 95. November 1995.
10. Casado R., Caminero M. B., Cuenca P., Quiles F. J., Garrido A., Duato J.: A tool for the analysis of reconfiguration and routing algorithms in irregular networks. Lecture Notes in Computer Science, vol. 1362. pp. 159-173. Proc. of the CANPC'98. USA. February 1998.
11. Qiao W., Ni L. M.: Adaptive routing in irregular networks using cut-through switches. In proceedings of the 1996 International Conference on Parallel Processing, August 1996.
12. Silla F., Malumbres M. P., Robles A., López P., Duato J.: Efficient Adaptive Routing in Networks of Workstations with Irregular Topology. Workshop on Communications and Architectural Support for Network-based Parallel Computing. February 1997.
13. Silla F. Duato J.: Improving the efficiency of adaptive routing in networks with irregular topology. International Conference on High Performance Computing. December 1997.
14. Abali B.: A Deadlock Avoidance Method for Computer Networks. Proc. of the CANPC'97. USA. February 1997.
15. Dally W.J., Seitz C.L.: Deadlock-free message routing in multiprocessor interconnection networks. IEEE Transactions on Computers, vol. C-36, n° 5. May 1987.
16. Perlman R.: An algorithm for distributed computation on a spanning tree in a extended LAN. Ninth Data Common Symp. Whistler Mountain. British Columbia. Sept.10-13. 1985. pp. 44-53.

17. Casado R., Quiles F.J., Sánchez J. L., and Duato J.: An Efficient Protocol for Dynamic Reconfiguration in Irregular Networks. Technical Report. TR-DI1-UCLM98.
18. http://raap.info-ab.uclm.es/public/techreports/techs.htm
19. Duato J.: A new theory of deadlock-free adaptive routing in wormhole networks. IEEE Trans. on Parallel and Distributed Systems, vol. 4, n° 12, pp. 1320-1331. December 1993.

Implementing Application-Specific Cache-Coherence Protocols in Configurable Hardware

David Brooks and Margaret Martonosi

Dept. of Electrical Engineering
Princeton University
{dbrooks,mrm}@ee.princeton.edu

Abstract. Streamlining communication is key to achieving good performance in shared-memory parallel programs. While full hardware support for cache coherence generally offers the best performance, not all parallel machines provide it. Instead, software layers using Shared Virtual Memory (SVM) can be built to enforce coherence at a higher level. In prior work, researchers have studied application-specific cache coherence protocols implemented either in SVM systems or as handlers run by programmable protocol processors. Since the protocols are specialized to the needs of a single application, they can be particularly helpful in reducing the long latencies and processing overhead that sometimes degrade performance in SVM systems. This paper studies implementing application-specific protocols in hardware, but not via an instruction-based protocol processor as is typical. Instead, we consider configurable implementations based on Field-Programmable Gate Arrays (FPGAs). This approach can be faster than software-based techniques and less expensive than some hardware-based techniques. We study one application, appbt, in detail, including a VHDL-level design of the configurable protocol design. We sketch out approaches for other applications as well. Implementing protocol operations in configurable hardware improves communication performance by roughly 11X for a 32-node system. While overall speedups are a more modest 12%, our method is promising because of its flexibility and because it offers a new way of harnessing configurable hardware at the network interface, where it already exists or could be easily added to current systems.

1 Introduction

Writing shared-memory parallel programs is thought to be easier than message-passing programs because of the simplified memory and communication model involved. Supporting fully cache-coherent shared-memory in hardware, however, can be expensive. Some systems instead opt to implement a shared-memory programming model using a software-based shared virtual memory (SVM) system [1].

Whether implemented in hardware or software, the key to good shared memory performance lies in the protocol implemented. To address this, prior research has considered implementing application-specific protocols. In such approaches, the cache coherence protocol is specialized to the communication needs of a particular program. Such protocols are possible in cases where the coherence mechanism (either hardware or software) can be changed or customized at program run-time. Past work

A.Sivasubramaniam, M.Lauria (Eds.): CANPC'99, LNCS 1602, pp.181 -195, 1999.

has evaluated such protocols running in SVM software on the main compute nodes themselves, or in handler code running on separate protocol co-processors.

Our work investigates a third option: implementing application specific protocols using a "configurable" hardware approach based on Field-Programmable Gate Arrays (FPGAs). These SRAM-based chips can be infinitely reprogrammed just by downloading a new stream of bits to rewrite configuration settings. Once configured, they behave like hardware, however, with a gate-based, rather than instruction-based, interface to their functionality. Since current network interface boards like Myrinet already contain FPGAs (for other purposes) it seems natural to evaluate their utility for application-specific protocols. Only small changes to existing network interface boards would be needed to make the proposed ideas feasible.

Studying shared memory approaches and prior research in application-specific protocols we note:

1) Flexible protocols can be conveniently implemented in configurable hardware, rather than in software. This facilitates overlapping computation and communication and can also accelerate the protocol handlers themselves.

2) Coherence protocols have characteristics amenable to FPGA computing: bit manipulation, hardware parallelism, and simple integer computations.

3) Existing tools designed to facilitate developing application specific protocols in software can be retargeted to automatically synthesize hardware implementations.

4) The network interface boards that interconnect compute nodes typically have several FPGAs on them anyway. Only minimal industry cooperation is needed to get more space for implementing protocols.

With these observations in mind, this paper explores the possibility of implementing an application-specific protocol processor in configurable hardware. A detailed study for one application, *appbt*, showed an 11x speedup in communication time compared to other implementations. Other applications show viability as well.

Sections 2 and 3 discuss previous research on application-specific coherence protocols and why we believe configurable hardware is a viable alternative. Section 4 gives an in-depth description of our proposed architecture. In Section 5, we outline the methodology for evaluating our architecture. Section 6 evaluates the feasibility of this new method with a detailed case study using *appbt*. Section 7 investigates additional parallel applications with general descriptions of possible implementations. Section 8 gives our conclusions.

2   Why Application-Specific Protocols?

Recently, application specific protocols have been recognized as a valid means of improving protocol performance. Several different strategies have been proposed for their implementation. One approach to implementing application-specific coherence protocols has been the development of *Tempest* by the Wisconsin Wind Tunnel Project [2]. *Tempest* provides a standard, system-independent parallel programming user/system interface that offers programmers access to a variety of different communication mechanisms, including active messages, bulk data transfer, virtual memory management, and fine-grain access control [3].

Tempest defines the architecture of a communication interface for shared-memory parallel programs; *Blizzard* is one implementation of that architecture [4]. *Blizzard* runs the coherence protocol code in software on each of the main compute nodes.

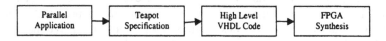

Fig. 1. Proposed Design Flow

Studies with *Blizzard* on applications with a wide variety of communication patterns have shown that application-specific coherence protocols can provide substantial speedups over even carefully-tuned implementations using a stock coherence protocol. This approach allows great flexibility in customizing the protocol to application characteristics: everything is done in software. Naturally a major disadvantage is that it slows down the host processor which is responsible for both computation and protocol processing. Another speed disadvantage is that the host processor is not physically located next to the network interface and an associated DMA engine.

These disadvantages have spurred interest in moving functionality from the main compute nodes down into the network interface. In some studies, such functionality is implemented as extra handler code run by a programmable network interface processor such as the LANai processor in a Myrinet network interface [5] [6] [7]. Other approaches have provided even more aggressive levels of hardware support, up to full hardware cache coherence [8] [9]. Our proposal, which implements protocol processing in configurable FPGA chips on the network interface, represents an intermediate position between full-hardware or full-software implementations.

3   Why Configurable Hardware?

Field Programmable Gate Arrays (FPGAs) allow the hardware functionality of a chip to be infinitely reprogrammed through a stream of configuration bits. Unlike an EPROM, an FPGA can be reprogrammed simply by downloading new configurations to its SRAM-based configuration memory bits. Because FPGAs are fabricated with the same manufacturing process as CMOS SRAMs, they can be low-cost commodity parts. The inexpensive hardware flexibility of FPGAs has led to their use in areas traditionally associated with custom hardware. This has been especially true for rapid prototyping and low-volume production. More recently researchers explored ways to use FPGAs to be reconfigured within applications.

There has recently been some research interest in coupling configurable logic with the network interface. McHenry et al. [10] have proposed an FPGA-based front-end processor that filters information to an ATM firewall host to ensure network security. Guillaud et al. [11] have proposed a communication interface board for PCs which incorporates a transputer, an FPGA, and a VRAM to implement reconfigurable high level communication services for distributed real-time data and multimedia communication. None of these approaches have considered configurable network interfaces with parallel computing applications in mind. Our research demonstrates the use of configurable hardware to implement application-specific coherence protocols within SVM systems.

Reconfigurable hardware has several unique features that are amenable to protocol processing. Since the protocol processing hardware is customized for each application, all of the available resources can be used for the particular application. In addition, configurable hardware inherently allows extensive fine-grain parallelism. Finally, FPGAs are well suited to the types of computation prevalent in protocol processing: integer-oriented address calculations, counter operations, and bit-manipulations.

One obstacle to the acceptance of an architecture like the RPP is that writing application-specific coherence protocols in software can already be a challenge; implementing hardware designs seems even tougher. Researchers at Wisconsin have developed a language called Teapot which aids programmers in writing and verifying coherency protocols [12]. We can circumvent the application-specific hardware hurdle by implementing a VHDL backend for Teapot. This would allow the automatic synthesis of FPGA-based hardware from a Teapot specification.

Figure 1 outlines a potential design flow for the design of an FPGA-based protocol processor. First, the sharing patterns of the parallel application must be analyzed and described in a language such as Teapot. The Teapot compiler would create high level VHDL code to be passed to commercial CAD tools for synthesis into the FPGA configuration bitstream.

4   Our Proposal: A Reconfigurable Protocol Processor

Figure 2 shows a diagram of the proposed system architecture. The reconfigurable protocol processor (RPP) is tightly coupled to both a DMA engine and the network interface (NI) CPU. It allows the protocol processor to closely interact with the DMA and the NI with FIFOs serving as buffers between parts. Another advantage to this architecture is that FPGAs are already available on some current network interface boards [5]. Thus, realistic implementations of similar architectures are feasible in the near-term.

The RPP system offers several performance benefits for application-specific protocols:

Background protocol processing: Software SVM relies on the microprocessor for protocol processing; it must stall main program execution and incur interrupt overhead in two cases: (i) whenever a message is prepared and sent to the NI and (ii) whenever an incoming message is received at the NI. With the RPP system, the hardware can send or receive a message or other protocol event, process the event, and transact with main memory, leaving the microprocessor to continue with program computation.

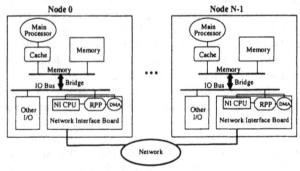

Fig. 2. Proposed System Architecture

Fast, Intelligent DMA: In our proposed architecture, the RPP is closely coupled to a DMA engine. There are two major reasons why this is beneficial. First, we achieve the benefits of fast, *intelligent* data transfer from the network interface directly to memory, or vice versa. Allowing the RPP, rather than the compute node, to control the DMA reduces the performance degradation when sending short, non-contiguous sections of memory, because it can easily be customized for strided accesses.

Specialized processing on both sending and receiving messages: In managing communication, the compute node is no longer limited to simple, general-purpose protocol commands such as "Send memory location 17 to node 2," but can issue brief, application-specific commands such as "Send update data pattern 8". The RPP interprets these and expands them into a complicated message. Extremely brief commands by the microprocessor can set the RPP at work doing complex processing. This improves communication/computation overlap and also reduces the software overhead of communication processing both at the sending and receiving ends.

5 Methodology

In order to evaluate the proposed reconfigurable protocol processor, we devised a simulation environment that allows us to realistically compare applications running on an RPP system to those running on a software SVM system. Several simulation models were developed to achieve this. First, VHDL designs and simulations were used to verify our design and to determine feasible clock speeds. Our second model simulates the performance of the system when a particular application runs with its RPP configured for that application. Finally we simulate the performance of the system when an application uses software-based coherence.

5.1 VHDL RPP Model

In the final system, a Teapot-VHDL translator would facilitate RPP design. Here, however, we hand-designed the RPP in order to get performance estimates for it. To simulate RPP performance for a given application, the RPP is first designed at a register-transfer level, and then state transition diagrams are constructed to determine how many cycles various protocol functions will take to execute. Finally, a full VHDL design determines the cycle time for the RPP. Section 6.3 elaborates on the VHDL design for the detailed *appbt* case study.

5.2 Multiprocessor Application Simulator

The high-level application simulator is based on MINT, a multiprocessor, event-driven simulator [13]. MINT simulators accept an application program as input and simulate the program's performance, using a user-defined back-end. MINT passes all read, write, and other relevant events to the back-end. Here, we simulate the operation of coherence protocols as they service memory requests and maintain coherency. In addition, user-generated events simulate other functionality, such as bulk-data transfers or protocol-specified active messages.

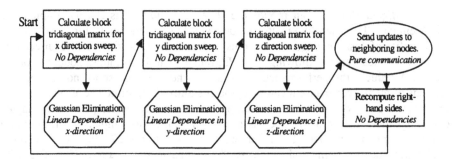

Fig. 3. Overall structure of an Appbt iteration, showing computation and communication. This structure describes all iterations after the first iteration.

5.3 System Timing

Protocol Timing: We consider three types of costs in simulating the message handlers for the SVM system: (i) a handler dispatch of 150 processor cycles to save the machine state and start an interrupt, (ii) the handler functions incur latency to start each transfer or receipt of data from the network interface, and take time to actually transfer data over the PCI bus. (iii) the processor takes a small amount of time to perform synchronization operations within message handlers – for instance, the clearing or setting of a counter. As a low estimate, we charged the message handler 1 cycle for each counter clear and 2 cycles for each counter increment.

Baseline Compute Node Timing: For our baseline system, we assume a microprocessor running the MIPS instruction set at 300 MHz. The processor has an on-chip write-through data cache with 32-byte lines and 1024 entries. Cache misses take 20 processor cycles to fill, using the memory bus. The baseline configuration utilizes 32 processors in a grid interconnect network.

We also assume a 33 MHz, 64-bit PCI bus serving as the I/O bus for each processing node [14]. This is consistent with the speeds of current Myrinet network interface boards. We assume that each PCI transaction is limited to at most 64 PCI cycles. Reads or writes to sequential addresses need no time between sending or receiving 64-bits of data. Between reads to non-consecutive addresses, a turn-around cycle is required between the cycle where the master drives the address on the bus and the cycle where the memory responds with data. Between writes to non-consecutive addresses, no turn-around cycle is needed because we utilize the PCI "Fast Back-to-Back Transactions" functionality [15].

Network Timing: Our network timing assumes a 2D mesh-connected network with wormhole routing. We assume 100ns per hop for the head of the message to establish a path, and 20ns per hop for subsequent 16-bit chunks. To limit simulation time, we simulate a contention-free network because previous work has shown that network contention is not a major bottleneck in these applications [16]. We also assume a device driver overhead of 40 processor cycles for each transmission or receipt of data from the microprocessor to the network interface or the RPP.

6 A Case Study: *Appbt*

To demonstrate our idea, we have performed a detailed design and evaluation for an RPP customized for the *appbt* program. *Appbt*, one of the NAS parallel benchmarks, is an iterative, three-dimensional, computational fluid dynamics application [17]. For each iteration, it performs a number of calculations to compute new values for each grid point. Some calculations rely on values for that grid point only, while other calculations also utilize values that are one or two grid points away. The "value" of each grid point consists of 90 different double precision floating point numbers that summarize the state of the fluid being studied. The Wisconsin Wind Tunnel (WWT) project has optimized *appbt* in order to measure the potential speedups from application-specific coherence protocols on a parallel shared memory system. We used their version of *appbt* as a starting point for our research.

Speedups from our reconfigurable protocol processor only affect the communications aspects of program execution time, because we are only focusing on improving the communication handlers. Thus, we next describe these communication patterns in detail.

6.1 Appbt Communication

Figure 3 shows a flowchart of communication in *appbt*. There are two major types of communication: during the Gaussian elimination phase and communication during the update phase.

Gaussian elimination: Gaussian elimination phases occur three times per iteration to transmit newly calculated values in the x, y, and z directions for both "forward elimination" and "back-substitution." Forward elimination transmits newly calculated values to dependent grid points on the right. Back substitution transmits values to the left. The RPP has separate communication handlers for each of these two types of communication.

Update Phase: The update phase of communication occurs shortly before the end of each iteration. Each node sends updates to all neighboring nodes. The updates are the entire face, two grid points deep, shared between a node and its neighbor.   Since these faces are not needed until the beginning of the next iteration, we hide some inter-node communication delay behind the remaining computation time. We have implemented separate communication handlers for each update axis (x, y, and z).

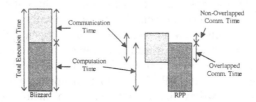

Fig. 4. Communication in Blizzard vs. RPP.

6.2 *Appbt* communication speedup methods

In this section we describe the enhancements that our reconfigurable protocol processor incorporates in order to improve communication time in *appbt*. In the original *Blizzard* systems, all protocol handling is performed by the compute node; protocol handling and compute time cannot be overlapped. As shown in Figure 4, the RPP decreases communication time in two main ways: (i) decreasing the overall amount of communication time, (ii) overlapping some communication with computation. Note the computation time stays constant with both systems. Only the communication time is decreased and overlapped with computation. In the following paragraphs we explore in detail the enhancements that the RPP uses to decrease the communication time.

Background message processing: In some cases, messages sent to a processor may not be needed immediately. For example, update messages are not needed until the beginning of the next iteration. In such cases, computation may continue before all the messages have arrived. With the software implementation, each message causes the processor to stop computation and handle an interrupt. With the RPP implementation, the processor never has to process an intermediate interrupt to service a message. Rather, the RPP deals directly with memory, placing the arriving updates in their appropriate memory locations. A counter, discussed below, notifies the processor when all updates have arrived.

Fast, Intelligent DMA: As previously discussed, the close association of the RPP with the DMA engine allows intelligent, application-specific DMA transfers, particularly smaller, non-contiguous transfers. In *appbt*, combining smaller messages into larger ones involves accessing multiple non-contiguous sections of memory. With the RPP, such non-contiguous memory accesses are simple. The RPP splits messages into their component parts, does some simple address calculations while waiting for the current DMA operation to complete, and feeds data and addresses to the DMA engine until the message is complete. Using the RPP also decreases message size (since the receiving RPP can also calculate some address and length information on its own).

Synchronization Squashing: Regardless of whether the update messages are sent as single grid points or entire faces, any given node will expect multiple messages from multiple processors before it can proceed with more computation. In software, synchronization for this is implemented with a software counter for the x, y, and z directions. The data received is unused until the counter indicates that all the data for that dimension has been received.

With the RPP much of this processing can be avoided. When the program begins, the microprocessor sends a message to the RPP telling it how many updates to expect from each dimension. Since the communication is totally static, this can be fixed through the entire execution. Whenever the RPP receives an update message, it sends the update data to memory. But instead of incrementing a software counter, the RPP simply increments its own version of the counter located on chip. When the counter reaches the critical value, the RPP knows that all updates for that dimension have been received, so it writes the counter value to main memory. Thus, many intermediate reads and writes to increment the counter are reduced to a single write when the data is ready.

Forward Elimination: In a software-based implementation, each data transmission during the forward elimination stage actually consists of 11 different messages, each 5 doubles long. With the RPP all the data may be sent as one message that the receiving RPP splits to place in the appropriate areas of memory. This is possible because the sending and receiving RPPs can perform address calculations and control the transfer of data from memory to the NI and vice-versa.

Update: During the end-of-iteration update messages, the *Blizzard* implementation forwards each grid point as separate message of 5 doubles. Again the RPP can be configured to accept a much longer message, break it into its component parts, and write the appropriate data to memory. In our implementation, the RPP sends the data in whole-face chunks, so that updating a neighboring processor takes two messages.

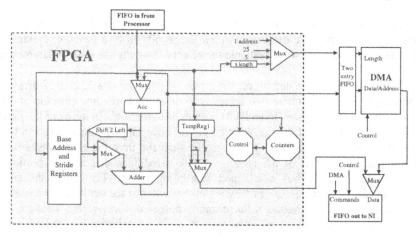

Fig. 5. Block diagram of Send datapath.

6.3 VHDL Design of RPP

To get accurate results with our simulator, a full VHDL implementation of the RPP was necessary in order to determine the speed of our design when tailored for *appbt*.

In order to meet pin and CLB[1] constraints, we made a decision to split the design into one FPGA for sending and one FPGA for receiving. However, with the denser FPGA technology available today, the entire design would easily fit onto one chip. Figure 5 shows a block diagram of the send datapath that we used for *appbt*. The control logic consists of the finite state machines for the five send handlers and five receive handlers. The simplest handlers consist of eight sequential state transitions, while the more complex handlers have a few more states with loops. The receive datapath is very similar and much of the logic could be shared. However, the control logic made the design too large to fit onto the largest FPGA available for our CAD tools. A 40-bit version (capable of 40-bit address calculations) was implemented in VHDL and synthesized using FPGA Express [18]. ViewSim was used for simulation [19]. Xilinx place and route tools were then used to generate bitstreams and determine cycle times [20]. See Table 1 for results.

---

[1] A configurable logic block (CLB) is the basic unit of which FPGAs are comprised. It can implement roughly 10 simple gates of logic and includes 2 flip-flops for state.

	Cycle Time	Clock Rate	Occupied CLBs	F&G Function Gens.
Send	61.4ns	16.3 Mhz	558	835
Receive	60.1ns	16.6 Mhz	496	757

Table 1. Cycle times from *xdelay* with 4013EHQ240-2

6.4 Simulation Results

In this section, we discuss the results of our simulations with the application *appbt*. In the first subsection we explore in detail the results from a baseline system. In the following subsections we investigate the effect of varying the system parameters.

Baseline System. The default problem size we consider is a 12x12x12 array with 60 iterations. For this datasize, we achieved a communication time speedup of 10.84 for the RPP system compared to an SVM system like *Blizzard*. In terms of the definitions introduced in Figure 4, this means that the non-overlapped communication time with the RPP system is nearly 11 times smaller than the time the SVM system spent on communication. Part of the reason for this speedup is that a large portion of the communication time was overlapped with computation. For *appbt*, the amount of overlap varies by processor. Processors in the center of the network have more update messages. Update messages have more potential for overlap because there is additional computation time available to hide communication delays while the program is in the "Re-compute right-hand sides" phase (see Figure 3). For the baseline system, 45.7% of the communication was overlapped on average. 52.6% of the total communication time for update messages were overlapped while 28.5% of the total communication time for Gaussian elimination messages were overlapped.

Because all of our speedup comes via improved communication, the fraction of overall execution time that *appbt* spends in communication is critical. With a software version, 11.6% of the overall time is spent in non-overlapped inter-node communication. The RPP's enhancements bring this number down to 1.2%. This reduction in communication time gives the RPP system a speedup of 1.12X over an SVM system for overall program execution time. In comparison, an ideal system that assumes all communication occurs instantaneously, would achieve a speedup of 1.13X over SVM.

While a total execution time improvement of 12% is not phenomenal, it is important to note that *appbt* is a full benchmark, not just a kernel with heavy communication. In this paper we focus on the communication aspects of the application–the portion of the application that the RPP succeeds in speeding up significantly–while keeping in perspective that the overall execution time is important as well.

RPP Speedups for varying number of processors. In our baseline system, we assume 32 processors, but smaller configurations are also common for low-end parallel processing systems for which the RPP might targeted. We compare the SVM and RPP protocol processing methods on a common *appbt* input set while varying the number of processors in the system.

Figure 6 shows the non-overlapped communication time in *appbt* for SVM and the RPP. From this figure we can see that for 32 processors there is a communication time speedup of 10.8. As we move down to 2 processors, the speedup increases to 13.5, a change of 25%. The fluctuations in the communication time are due to the way that each processor's subcube is partitioned. The size and shape vary as we change the number of processors, and this causes significant changes in the communication patterns. These increases in speedup correlate to the amount of communication that can be overlapped. For 32 processors, the overlap averages 45.7%. As we move down to 8, 4, and 2 processor networks the percentage of overlapped   communication   rises   into the 70s.

For the overall execution time speedup the amount of time that is spent in communication is critical, because this is the portion of the overall program execution that is reduced by protocol operations. As we increase the number of processors in the system, the amount of communication increases. For example at 2 processors SVM spends 1.5% of its total execution time in communication, but at 32 processors this number rises to 11.6%. Thus, as we move to systems with more processors, the RPP system achieves greater overall execution time speedups. For 2 processors, the execution time speedup was just under 1.02X, but at 32 processors this increases to 1.12X.

RPP Speedups for varying microprocessor speeds. Our baseline system, which assumed 300MHz, is about the clock rate of many current-generation microprocessors. It is interesting to explore the speedup that the RPP would obtain on faster or slower microprocessors.

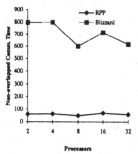
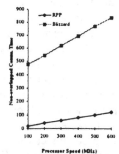

Fig. 6. Non-overlapped communication time for RPP and Blizzard when varying the number of processors and the processor speed (avg num. Kcycles per iteration).

Figure 6 shows *appbt*'s non-overlapped communication time for the SVM and RPP systems while varying the speed of the host processors. As we increase the speed of the microprocessors, the amount of non-overlapped communication time increases for both the RPP and SVM system. Since we have assumed the RPP cycle time to remain constant while a software approach benefits from clock rate improvements, the RPP is slower relative to the SVM system at high clock speeds. We would expect, however, that future generations of FPGAs would allow the RPP to increase in performance with the microprocessor. Furthermore, limitations of the 33MHz PCI bus become a factor at the high clock speeds. For these reasons our communication speedup varies considerably – from 25.2 for 100MHz processors to 6.9 for 600MHz processors.

The overall execution time speedup vs. SVM increases as we move to higher clock rates. For example, from 100MHz to 600MHz the speedup increases from 1.09 to 1.15. This is because the faster processors decrease the amount of time spent on computation. Hence, communication plays a larger role in the overall program execution time at higher clock speeds and this benefits the total execution time speedup. For SVM's 100MHz system, the fraction of time in communication was 9.4%. This increases to 14.8% for the 600MHz system. For the RPP, these numbers drop to 0.4% and 2.4% respectively.

7   Other Applications

The main focus of our discussion so far has been on the parallel application, *appbt*. The RPP techniques that were successful in improving *appbt*'s execution time are also applicable to a wide range of applications. Without going to the same level of detail, this section discusses possible RPP implementations for other applications.

7.1   EM3D

EM3D is another parallel benchmark application that models the propagation of electromagnetic waves through objects in three dimensions [21]. The program contains a set of E nodes, which represent electric fields, and H nodes, which represent magnetic fields. E and H nodes are arranged in a bipartite graph with directed edges linking E and H nodes that depend on each other. During each iteration, E nodes are updated based on the weighted values of neighboring H nodes and vice-versa. A common parallel implementation divides regions of E and H nodes up into computing node segments. Communication between processors occurs when E and H nodes are connected by a "remote edge", meaning that the neighboring E and H nodes are on different processors.

During the first iteration, the communication pattern has not been established so a general purpose protocol must be used. After the first iteration of *EM3D*, the sharing pattern between processors has been set and will stay the same for all subsequent iterations. That is, when an E or H node is updated, there is a known list of compute nodes that need to be sent a message with the updated data. At this point, application-specific update protocols can take over to enhance communication efficiency. The application-specific protocol for *EM3D* updates all remote nodes at the end of each half-iteration [4]. This approach made sense there because the processor is busy calculating new values of the current nodes, so it has no free CPU time available for protocol processing. In addition, leaving all of the updates to the end of the half-iteration allows one large message to be sent to each processor that needs update data. With an RPP most protocol processing could be entirely overlapped with computation. After each node has been calculated, the RPP sends that update message to the dependent processing node. The closely-coupled DMA engine allows efficient transfer of these small messages. Groups of messages are packaged and sent to a specific processor as in *appbt*. Furthermore, the RPP performs all protocol synchronization support which includes deciding when all incoming dependent nodes have been received. This type of synchronization is very efficient in FPGAs with bit manipulations.

Chandra, et al. have provided an in-depth analysis of communication and computation time for shared-memory and message-passing versions of *EM3D* [22]. The analysis notes that a *Blizzard* implementation running application-specific protocols allows the shared-memory version to perform equivalently with the message-passing version. Using this conclusion we roughly estimate the amount of speedup that the RPP could achieve. For the main loop there would be 26.5M cycles of computation and 40M cycles of communication. Thus approximately 26.5M cycles of communication would be overlapped with computation. The remaining 13.5M cycles of communication would likely be reduced by RPP enhancements. However, as a low-estimate to potential speedup we assume that these non-overlapped communication cycles remain the same. This results in a total execution time improvement of about 51% for the RPP over *Blizzard*. The increased amount of time spent in communication explains why *EM3D* promises more improvement on the RPP than *appbt*.

7.2 Unstructured

Unstructured is based on a computational fluid dynamics application that uses an unstructured mesh to model a physical structure [23]. Nodes make up the structure of the mesh and are connected by edges, when in pairs, and by faces, when in groups of three or four. A common parallel implementation groups related nodes together and then partitions edges onto various processors. Computation involves iterative loops over nodes, edges, and faces, and thus edges and faces that span processors will require shared data to maintain coherency. Like *EM3D*, the communication dependency pattern is fixed after the first iteration.

Because of the extensive amount of time spent in communication, *unstructured* is well-suited to an RPP implementation. The RPPs could track inter-node dependency synchronization for each node in the system. The RPP would count when incoming dependencies have cleared and when all messages have been sent out for a particular node. The RPP would also send update messages in the background. After each node is ready to be sent out, the processor would send a single message to the RPP, which would then send dependent data to the correct processors. Additional background processing would be possible as the RPP could send update messages for nodes in the edge-loop while the processor does computation in the face-loop.

8 Conclusion

This paper presents a new architecture for implementing application-specific cache coherency protocols.   This study (i) identifies a new, easily-adopted use of configurable hardware in mainstreams systems, and (ii) provides benchmark evaluations characterizing both communication behavior and whole program performance. We feel that our RPP architecture hits a performance/cost sweet spot between software and custom hardware approaches. With little additional hardware expense and design time, an RPP-style architecture could be implemented on many of today's high-speed network cards. Our approach speeds up communication time in the *appbt* application by a factor of 11X. For completeness, we have also considered whole-program performance, rather than just the individual protocol handlers; our whole-program performance improvements of 12% are also significant. In exploring other applications, we have identified several that show the potential for even more sizable performance improvements.

References

1. K. Li and P. Hudak. Memory Coherence in Shared Virtual Memory Systems. *ACM Transactions on Computer Systems* (Nov. 1989), vol. 7, no. 4, p. 321-359.
2. Steven K. Reinhardt, James R. Larus, and David A. Wood. Tempest and Typhoon: User-Level Shared Memory. *Proc. 21st Annual Int. Symposium on Computer Architecture*, April 1994.
3. M. Hill, et al. Tempest: A Substrate for Portable Parallel Programs. *COMP/CON Spring 95.*
4. Babak Falsafi, Alvin R. Lebeck, et al. Application-Specific Protocols for User-Level Shared Memory. *Supercomputing '94*, November 1994.
5. Nanette J. Boden, et al. Myrinet – A Gigabit-per-Second Local-Area Network. *IEEE-Micro*, Vol. 15, No. 1, pp. 29-36, Feburary 1995.
6. Angelos Bilas. Improving the Performance of Shared Virtual Memory on System Area Networks. Technical Report #TR-586-98, Princeton Computer Science Dept., August, 1998.
7. C. Liao, et al. Monitoring Shared Virtual Memory on a Myrinet-based PC Cluster. *12th ACM International Conference on Supercomputing (ICS)*. July, 1998.
8. Robert W. Pfile. Typhoon-Zero Implementation: The Vortex Module.   University of Wisconsin-Madison, August 31, 1995.
9. Mark Heinrich, et al. The Performance Impact of Flexibility in the Stanford FLASH Multiprocessor. *Proc. 6th Int. Conference on Architectural Support for Programming Languages and Operating Systems*. San Jose, CA, October 1994.
10. J.T. McHenry, et al. An FPGA-based coprocessor for ATM firewalls. *Proc. 5th Annual IEEE Symposium on Field-Programmable Custom Computing Machines*, April 1997.
11. J.-F. Guillaud, et al. A PC/ATM interface accelerator using reconfigurable technology. *Proc. of the SPIE*, vol. 2608, pp. 134-45. 1995.
12. Chandra, et al. Teapot: Language Support for Writing Memory Coherency Protocols. *SIGPLAN Conference on Programming Language Design and Implementation (PLDI)*, May 1996.
13. Jack E. Veenstra and Robert J. Fowler. MINT Tutorial and User Manual. Technical Report 452, Computer Science Department, The University of Rochester, June 1993 (Revised August 1994).
14. "PCI Local Bus Specification," PCI Special Interest Group, Hillsboro, Oregon, April 1993.
15. "Techniques for Increasing PCI Performance", Intel Co.,Sep. 1997.

16. W. Fang, et al.. Contention and Queueing in an Experimental Multicomputer: Analytical and Simulation-based Results. TR-508-96, Princeton Computer Science Department, Jan. 1996.
17. Bailey, et al.The NAS Parallel Benchmarks. TR RNR-91-002, Ames Research Center, Jan. 1991.
18. FPGA Express Version 2.0, Synopsys Co.
19. Workview Office Version 7.3, Viewlogic Co.
20. XACTstep Foundation Series F1.3 Software, Xilinx Co.
21. D. E. Culler, et al. Parallel Programming in Split-C. *Supercomputing 93*, Nov. 1993.
22. Chandra, et al. Where is Time Spent in Message-Passing and Shared-Memory Programs? *6th Int. Conf. on Architectural Support for Prog. Languages and Operating Systems*, Oct.1994.
23. S. Mukherjee, et al. Efficient Support for Irregular Applications on Distributed-Memory Machines. *5th Symposium on Principles and Practices of Parallel Programming*, July 1995.

Supporting Shared Memory and Message Passing on Clusters of PCs with a SMiLE

Wolfgang Karl, Markus Leberecht, and Martin Schulz

Lehrstuhl für Rechnertechnik und Rechnerorganisation, LRR–TUM
Institut für Informatik, Technische Universität München
{karlw,leberech,schulzm}@in.tum.de
http://wwwbode.in.tum.de/Par/arch/smile/

Abstract. With the rise of fast interconnection technologies and new concepts to utilize them without operating system interaction (like VIA [4]), compute clusters are becoming increasingly commonplace. Most of the interconnection networks focus only on message passing as their prime programming model neglecting the large code basis for shared memory. However, by utilizing the Scalable Coherent Interface (SCI) [19] with its ability to transparently perform remote memory operations, it is possible to support both efficient message passing and transparent shared memory on one single platform. This introduces a previously unknown flexibility into the cluster architecture.

1 Introduction

Networks of workstations (NOWs) have become widely adopted and increasingly popular as platforms for parallel processing. For example, the use of parallel programming libraries like PVM [7] supports parallel applications within such an every-day computing infrastructure consisting of powerful desktops and workstations connected by a standard LAN. However, the demand for low-latency and high bandwidth, especially for communication intensive applications, led to the development of new communication architectures with user-level communication [3, 2, 17]. The Virtual Interface Architecture (VIA) specification [4], jointly worked out by Compaq, Intel, and Microsoft, is the most significant development for low-overhead message-passing communication within a compute cluster. The common approach is to remove the operating system from the critical path of sending and receiving messages. Mapping parts of the network interface into the user's address space such that messages can be handled at user-level avoids expensive system calls as well as buffering in the network layer.

The VIA approach is well suited for system area networks (SAN) which allow direct access to the network interface. In addition, new interconnection technologies like the Scalable Coherent Interface (SCI, IEEE Std. 1596-1992) [19] or the DEC Memory Channel [8] facilitate communication via distributed shared memory (DSM) as individual load and store operations are turned into remote memory accesses.

A.Sivasubramaniam, M.Lauria (Eds.): CANPC'99, LNCS 1602, pp. 196–210, 1999.

The SMiLE (Shared Memory in a LAN-like Environment) project at LRR-TUM investigates in high-performance cluster computing with SCI as the interconnection technology. SCI-based parallel systems with NUMA characteristics (Non-Uniform Memory Access) consisting of PCs as compute nodes and SCI as network fabric serve as platforms for the software developments studying how to map parallel programming systems efficiently onto SCI hardware.

In this paper, we first demonstrate how SCI's hardware supported DSM can be utilized for fast, reliable, and low-overhead message-passing communication. We present three efficient implementations of message-passing communication libraries for SMiLE cluster platforms: Active Messages [22,15], socket communication over SCI [23], and a package with basic communication mechanism, the Common Messaging Layer. These libraries are communication substrates intended to be used as basis for MPI or PVM implementations over SCI [10].

While user-level communication architectures like the ones mentioned above can efficiently be utilized for message-oriented parallel programming, there is also the need to support the shared memory programming model as this is also widely used and accepted.

Shared memory offers, compared to the message passing paradigm, an easier way to parallel programming. This is achieved by providing a single global address space allowing for a similar programming style to that on sequential machines. This ease comes at the cost of higher implementation complexity. Due to this, shared memory programming can mostly be found on tightly coupled machines, like SMPs. The only way to utilize shared memory on standard cluster architectures is through pure software DSM systems [1, 20] which lack efficiency and/or transparency.

SCI with its remote memory capabilities through a hardware DSM abstraction closes this gap by bringing shared memory programming models onto loosely coupled architectures like clusters of PCs. This allows to exploit clusters using this easier way of programming as well as for the large already existing code basis of applications written for shared memory machines. However, in order to be able to support transparent shared memory on top of SCI, techniques used by SW-DSM systems have to be merged with the remote memory capabilities.

In summary, with SMiLE both widely accepted parallel programming paradigms – message passing and shared memory – are provided for SCI-based parallel systems. This offers a previously unknown flexibility in terms of parallel and distributed cluster programming support as demonstrated within this paper.

The reminder is organized in the following manner. Section 2 gives a brief introduction into SCI and describes our experimental platform. The implementation of the message passing layers are then discussed in Section 3 followed in Section 4 by a description for a global virtual memory layer for SCI clusters. Section 5 discusses some related projects, while Section 6 provides a brief outlook into the future and closes with some concluding remarks.

2   Bringing it together with the help of SCI

The SCI standard [19] specifies the hardware interconnect and protocols allowing to connect up to 64 K SCI nodes (processors, workstations, PCs, bus bridges, switches) in a high-speed network. A 64-Bit global address space across SCI nodes is defined as well as a set of read-, write-, and synchronization transactions enabling SCI-based systems to provide hardware-supported DSM with low-latency remote memory accesses. In addition to communication via DSM, SCI also facilitates fast message-passing. SCI nodes are interconnected via point-to-point links in ring-like arrangements or are attached to switches. The logical layer of the SCI specification defines packet-switched communication protocols. An SCI split transaction requires a request packet to be sent from one SCI node to another node with a response packet in reply to it. This enables every SCI node to overlap several transactions and allows for latencies of accesses to remote memory to be hidden. Optionally, the SCI standard defines a directory-based cache coherence protocol.

For the software developments a SCI-based PC cluster is being used. This platform consists of four high-end PCs and SCI hardware. Each PC is equipped with a Pentium-II processor running at 233 MHz, 128 MB of main-memory, a 33 MHz 32b PCI bus, and the 440FX chipset. Additionally, a PCI-SCI adapter card (Rev. B, LC-1) from Dolphin Interconnect Solutions [6] is plugged in the PC's PCI bus such that the four PCs are connected up into an SCI ring. No cache coherence mechanism is being implemented as it is not prossible to snoop the PC's I/O bus for all processor-memory operations. Therefore, SCI address spaces are non-cacheable by default to ensure consistency. The running SCI clusters described above delivers a raw communication performance of about $2.6\mu s$ latency and 44 MB/s bandwidth.

Each SCI node can create shared memory segments in physical address space and export them into the SCI network. Pages comprising exported segments are pinned down in memory. A process may further map DSM segments into its I/O and from there into its virtual address space. Once the settings are established, internode communication can be performed at user-level. Figure 1 demonstrates the levels of memory mappings.

3   Message passing on top of SCI

3.1   Concept and design

The support for *asynchronous, point-to-point message passing*, is the basic building block for all three messaging layers described further below.[1] Since our primary goal is to achieve high communication performance over the SCI cluster interconnect, this basic messaging mechanism must therefore be made as efficient as possible.

---

[1] We use the term message passing to denote data transfers in general, including those taking place over stream sockets.

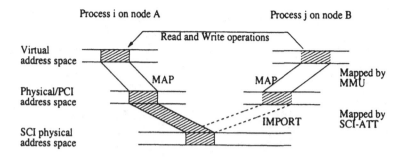

Fig. 1. Memory mappings in SCI-based systems

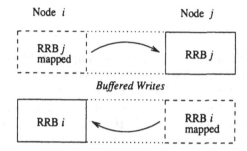

Fig. 2. Communication areas between nodes in SCI DSM

As a result, a number of design guidelines pertaining to performance have been put forth for the library implementations. Communication is performed at user level whenever possible and profitable in order to avoid context switches and operating system overhead. Furthermore, each layer's design aims to reduce copy operations to the minimum required by the API semantics or the network transfer. Buffered remote write operations over DSM should be applied, simultaneously inefficient remote reads avoided as far as possible. If available, the most profitable SCI communication mechanism available for a given message size (programmed I/O or DMA-based transfers) should also be chosen.

3.2 Implementation

The messaging mechanism over SCI DSM is based on a shared data structure called the *receive ring buffer (RRB)* in the sequel. The RRB is a ring structure where the sending node writes messages into and the receiver searches for and copies out messages. The RRB physically resides in the local memory of the receiving node, made up of pages locked in memory, and is exported and mapped into the address space of the sending process. This is depicted for bidirectional communication between nodes in Figure 2.

An RRB and an associated address mapping are set up for each sender and receiver pair.

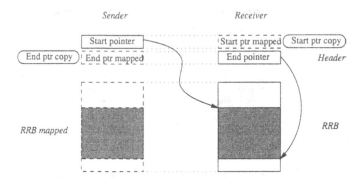

Fig. 3. Use of RRB

All the three communication platforms comprise a *library* that is linked to the application program, and a *daemon process* that assists the library in setting up these communication areas (besides other tasks).

Simple flow control is achieved by maintaining a *start pointer* and an *end pointer* in order to delimit the RRB area that contains valid data (sent messages). Choosing the physical locations of the pointers appropriately, i .e. putting the start pointer at the receiver's end and vice versa, allows them to be updated with buffered writes, while additional local copies allow to avoid inefficient remote read operations when they need to be checked before data transfers.

In most cases, the libraries rely on the memcpy() function for as efficient copy operations as possible.

While all the libraries share this common communication mechanism over SCI DSM, the details of the RRB and its use vary. In particular, the RRB size and the number and granularity of the RRB entries is different. For example, both AM and the CML have fixed-sized slots for messages (or fragments thereof), while the SSLib can transfer a variable amount of data, according to the stream socket semantics.

This communication style implies that there are two copy operations involved in each data transfer: one copy into the RRB out of the sending process' data structure, and one copy out of the RRB into the data structure of the receiving process. Additional copy operations are avoided as far as possible.

3.3   Message passing APIs

Active Messages 2.0. Active Messages (AM) can be regarded as lightweight asynchronous remote procedure calls (RPCs), each of which is a request/reply pair [5]. A request AM becomes active on the receiving end in that it invokes a user-level, non-blocking message handler to service the request and to send back a reply AM, which in turn is handled by the reply handler on the requesting node. AM typically are short, supporting a fixed set of primitive data types.

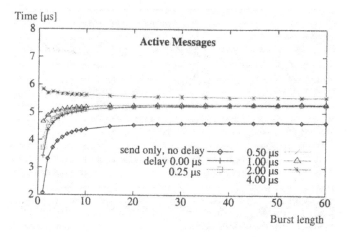

Fig. 4. LogP model curves for the Active Messages layer timing bursts of shortest messages (0 bytes of data).

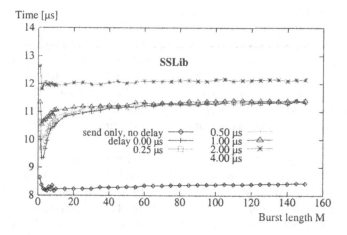

Fig. 5. LogP model curves for the SCI Socket layer timing bursts of shortest messages (1 byte of data).

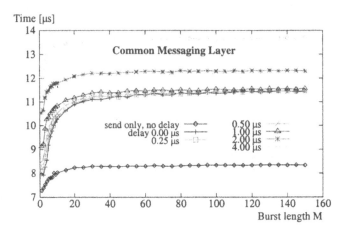

Fig. 6. LogP model curves for the Common Messaging Layer (CML) timing bursts of shortest messages (1 byte of data).

Our SCI AM layer implements AM Specification 2.0 [15] which defines *communication endpoints*. These provide basic multi-user support and protection mechanisms, thus incurring higher message processing overhead, e.g. for invoking the message handler via a handler table in the endpoint. Bulk data transfers are supported as well. More details of the SCI AM library are given in [9].

Connection setup with the AM layer is performed during startup through the AM daemon which removes itself completely from the communication path after it has been established. Polling is used for the reception of messages as opposed to remote interrupts. While these do exist on the current SCI hardware, their incorporation into the operating system proves to be too heavyweight. Device driver recognition of a remote interrupt, posting a signal, and the combined signal-delivery times to the application prove to be too high to utilize any of the short latencies offered by the hardware and are thus not used in the experiments. A comparable system environment in [11] showed SCI-generated interrupts to exhibit latencies of about twenty times of those achieved with polling.

SCI Socket Library. The SSLib offers the Berkeley Sockets API, the de facto standard for network programming on Unix platforms [14]. The SSLib conforms to all the semantics of the standard sockets API as closely as possible. Both TCP and UDP semantics are implemented at user level for communication *within* the SCI cluster. Currently, there is no router functionality to the TCP/IP world.

SSLib currently runs on Solaris, Linux and Reliant Unix platforms using Dolphin SBus-SCI and PCI-SCI adapter cards. Details can be found in [23].

In contrast to the Active Messages, SCI socket connections are established on demand by contacting the *SCI socket daemon (SSD)*. The SSDs of a distributed system establish SCI DSM communication areas amongst each other. Initiating a socket communication exists of again establishing pinned shared memory regions across the participating nodes and handing them over to the application. Furthermore, queuing of requests in accordance with the BSD socket semantics is also performed. The actual data transfers are performed analogously to the transfers in the AM layer. Again, polling is used for receiver notification for the same reasons cited above.

Common Messaging Layer (CML) for PVM and MPI. The CML API provides functions for sending and receiving point-to-point messages from and to user memory. Messages can be received by blocking or non-blocking functions as required by the higher level libraries.

Also included are means of message identification in the form of *tag* and *communicator* values, thus allowing higher communication layers to retrieve selected messages from the network. Furthermore, to prevent possible deadlock situations, the CML provides a mechanism to clean up the message receive buffer while waiting for a certain message.

The CML also contains support for connecting and disconnecting nodes and for packing and unpacking data – both required for PVM. A further feature is optional thread safety for MPI. It runs on multiple platforms (Solaris, Linux, and Windows NT) in order to make MPI and PVM implementations portable. More details of the CML are available in [10].

Due to hardware limitations to the number of SCI shared memory segments, the CML removes potentially blocking messages from the RRB into a so-called *unexpected-message queue (UMQ)*, increasing the number of potential copy operations. Furthermore, the RRB as well as the UMQ have to be checked on initiation of a receive operation.

3.4   Experiments and results

Short Message Performance. Short message performance was assessed using the *LogP* model described in [5]. The numbers for all three layers are shown in Table 1 and were derived from the graphs given in Figures 4, 5, and 6, respectively, while the roundtrip times (RTT) were measured seperately. They clearly reflect the implementation differences. Active Messages, being the layer with the leanest functionality, exhibits the lowest overall times. Since TCP/IP semantics only permit 1-byte messages as the smallest packet size, the overheads of the socket library grow: packet header plus payload have to be sent, necessitating a memory barrier otherwise unneeded. Intermediate copying also increases the receive overhead. The similar functionality of the Common Messaging Layer is finally reflected in its comparable performance figures.

Long Message Performance. The bandwidth tests for the three libraries unveil no surprises. With growing message lengths, the maximum throughput is about 35 Mbytes/s for AM and CML, and 37 Mbytes/s for SSLib which can use very large RRB sizes.

msg. layer	RTT	L	o_s	o_r	g
AM 2.0	14.0	2.7	4.3	0	5.0
SSLib	25.4	2.6	8.4	1.7	11.3
CML	26.6	3.0	8.3	2.0	11.5

Table 1. Round-trip time RTT and the LogP model parameters latency L, send and receive overheads o_s and o_r, and message gap g for all three messaging layers. All times in μs.

4   True shared memory

4.1   Concept and design

Unfortunately, SCI alone can not provide a global virtual memory abstraction as it is required by shared memory programming models. Both its hardware and software components only target the utilization of large, contiguous, and permanently pinned memory segments. To overcome these limitations and to reach a fully transparent implementation of a global virtual address space, the SCI remote memory capabilities have to be merged with mechanisms well known from traditional software DSM systems. The memory is distributed with the granularity of pages and these distributed pages are then combined into a global virtual address space. In contrast to pure software mechanisms though, no page has to migrated or replicated avoiding traditional software DSM problems like false sharing. All remote pages are simply mapped using SCI's HW-DSM and then accessed directly. The result is a fully transparent global virtual address space which we call SCI Virtual Memory or SCI-VM [18].

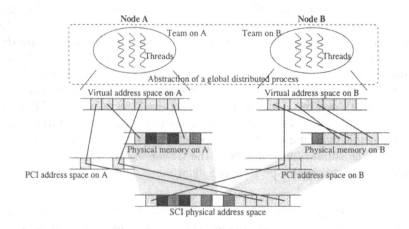

Fig. 7. Principle design of the SCI Virtual Memory

This concept is further illustrated in Figure 7 for a two node system. In order to build a global virtual memory abstraction, a global process abstraction also has to be built with team processes as placeholders for the global process on each node. These processes run on top of the global address space which is created by mapping the appropriate pages from either the local physical memory in the traditional way or from remote memory using SCI HW-DSM.

The mapping of the individual pages in done in a two–step process. First, the page has to be located in the SCI physical address space from where it can be mapped in the PCI address space using the address translation tables (ATT) of the SCI adapter cards. From there, the page can be mapped with the help of the processor's page tables into the virtual address space. Problematic is the different mapping granularity in these two steps; while the latter mapping can be done at page granularity, the SCI mappings can only be done at the basis of 512 KByte or 128 pages segment. To overcome this difference, the SCI-VM layer has to manage the mappings of several pages from one single SCI segment. The mappings of the SCI segments themselves will be managed with an on-demand, dynamic scheme very similar to paging mechanisms in operating systems.

4.2 Implementation challenges and problems

The design discussed above presents several interesting implementation challenges. The most severe one is related to the integration of the SCI Virtual Memory presented above into the underlying operating system and its virtual memory management. The SCI-VM has to be able to perform mappings at page granularity to construct the global virtual address space discussed above and to replace or enhance the operating system's page fault handler to introduce the SCI-VM functionality. In addition it needs control over the locking and unlocking of individual pages. While the latter issue is implementable using the kernel level functions of Windows NT, the other two are not supported and/or documented. The only way around this solution is to bypass the operating system and to manipulate the appropriate hardware resources directly, i.e. the page tables to perform mappings of single remote pages and the IDT (Interrupt Descriptor Table) to intercept the page fault handler. Experiments have shown that this is possible without interfering with Windows NT stability if appropriate clean-up routines are provided which allow to hide the manipulations from the VMM after program termination.

In addition, the integration of the SCI-VM concept into the currently existing software infrastructure also imposes problems as it is mainly intended to provide support for sharing large, pinned segments of contiguous memory. To solve this problem, the hardware has to be addressed directly through a specialized device driver which allows fast and direct mappings of small remote memory segments.

Third, it is normally not possible to cache remotely mapped memory due to the incoherent nature of the PCI bus. However, caching is necessary to overcome the problem of the large latencies involved when reading transparently from remote memory (around $6\mu s$ per access). The only solution here is to apply a relaxed consistency model that allows to enable caching while coping with the possible cache inconsistency. We currently use the standard POSIX consistency model that relies on synchronization points. At these points the memory is made consistent by flushing the caches.

4.3   First experiments and results

The current implementation of the SCI-VM is a prototype developed for Windows NT based on Dolphin's driver infrastructure. However, only the setup functionality and the physical access layer of this software are utilized by the SCI-VM. The actual control of the SCI hardware is directly implemented within the SCI-VM as described in the preceding section. The implementation also relies on an especially developed VMM driver that realizes the functionality to bypass the operating system. It allows the SCI-VM to access the page directories, to manipulate the cache settings, and to access kernel level VMM functions of Windows NT.

On top of this SCI-VM an SPMD programming model has been implemented that allows the parallel execution of programs across the cluster in a synchronous manner. Especially resource allocations have to be done synchronously by all nodes and synchronization is mainly done using global barriers. This results in a simple yet efficiently usable programming model that forms the basis for all following experiments.

We conducted the experiments using two artificial benchmark codes: a sum over a linear array and a standard matrix multiplication. Both are implemented without any source code level optimizations for locality or load balancing. They both operate on a working set of 512 KByte held in the global virtual address space which results in the sum program in an array of roughly 131000 values and in the matrix multiplication program in three matrices with 418x418 values each. The physical memory for this address space is distributed across the nodes in a round robin fashion at page granularity (4 KBytes) completely transparent for the application.

For both codes we measured the speedup on four nodes compared to sequential execution on local memory. In addition, we also measured the sequential execution on global memory distributed across all nodes to investigate the overhead caused by using the physically distributed memory provided by the SCI-VM. The results of all experiments can be seen in Table 2.

In both cases, a significant speedup of around 2.6 is achieved without applying any kind of locality optimization only relying on the transparency of the SCI-VM and its relaxed consistency model. Despite these similar numbers for both codes, however, the overhead numbers are radically different. The sum code is only able to utilize the cache for spatial locality as it traverses the global array only once. The overhead is therefore rather high, in contrast to the matrix multiplication which is able to utilize both spatial and temporal data locality. In the parallel case, however, all nodes operate on the same data causing memory conflicts on the SCI networks and cache invalidations on remote nodes. This reduces the efficiency in a way that the low overhead can not totally be transformed into speedups. In the sum code, on the other hand, each node works on distinct data sets (a subpart of the array) which eliminates the problems seen in the matmult code.

	Sum	MatMult
Sequential / local memory	53.59 ms	2822.42 ms
Parallel / global memory	20.65 ms	1057.70 ms
Speed-up	2.60	2.67
Sequential / global memory	98.42 ms	2881.07 ms
SCI-VM overhead	83.65 %	2.08 %

Table 2. SCI-VM speed-up and overhead numbers for 4 nodes.

5 Related work

Communication architectures with user-level communication are already mentioned in Section 1. [11] studies how to map parallel programming models efficiently onto an SCI-based workstation cluster which consists of eight Ultra-SPARCS interconnected by Dolphin's SBus-SCI adapters. For low-latency communication via Active Messages they use a similar approach as mentioned in this paper .

Work on shared memory models for clusters of PCs is mostly done with the help of pure software DSM systems like TreadMarks [1], Brazos [20], Millipede [12], and the SVMlib [16]. Only very little work has been done on direct utilization of HW-DSM for global memory abstractions in clusters. Examples for this kind of work, which are also based on SCI, are the utilization of HW-DSM for the implementation of Split-C [11] and SciOS [13], a system designed for swapping into remote memory regions while providing System-V style shared memory.

This work is in principle also applicable to any other non-cache-coherent NUMA architecture. One widely known commercial representative of this type of machine is Cray/SGI's T3D/E [24]. Also on this machines efficient low–level message passing, e.g. in the form of Fast Messages [17], and shared memory programming in the form of a restricted put and get functionality is available. However, no global virtual memory system like the SCI-VM presented above is provided. Other well known work for NUMA systems in academia can be found at Princeton University in the Shrimp project [3] and at the University of Rochester in the Cashmere project [21].

6 Conclusions and future work

In this paper we have shown that a cluster of PCs connected with the help of the SCI interconnection technology can efficiently support both major programming models for parallel systems, message passing and shared memory. The message passing capabilities have been demonstrated using three different libraries. With their VIA style implementation on top of SCI, they offer low latency messaging while still allowing for high bandwidth. To also support transparent shared memory, a programming model that is traditionally known from tightly coupled systems like SMPs, SW-DSM techniques have to be merged with the remote memory capabilities to create a global virtual memory. This forms the basis for efficient, low-overhead execution of shared memory codes.

The work in the SMiLE project will be continued for both programming models by developing higher level programming models and more detailed evaluations using real-world application. In the area of message passing, we will focus on the efficient implementation of PVM on top of the CML presented above and its evaluation using irregular communication intensive problems. The work on Shared Memory will continue the efforts towards a full SCI-VM implementation including a fully transparent shared memory programming model with an API compliant to the POSIX standards for multithreading. Additionally, the concepts will also be evaluated using several large applications.

To summarize, the SMiLE project extends the architecture of clusters of PCs to transparent shared memory while still enabling highly efficient message passing with low latencies and high bandwidth. This increased flexibility broadens the numbers of codes that can directly be used on this architecture and with that also the group of potential users. Furthermore, the choice of a programming model for newly developed code will no longer be forced by the architecture, but rather be decided by the preference of the programmer. All of this will make the architecture of clusters even more attractive and will raise their importance as a low cost alternative for parallel computing.

Acknowledgments

This work is supported by the European Commission in the Fourth Framework Programme under ESPRIT HPCN Project EP23174 (Standard Software Infrastructure for SCI based parallel systems – SISCI). Driver software is kindly provided in source by Dolphin ICS (Windows NT) and the University of Paderborn (Linux).

References

1. C. Amza, A. Cox, S. Dwarkadas, P. Keleher, H. Lu, R. Rajamony, W. Yu, and W. Zwaenepoel. TreadMarks: Shared Memory Computing on Networks of Workstations. *IEEE Computer*, Feb. 1995.
2. A. Basu, V. Buch, W. Vogels, and T. von Eicken. U-Net: A User-Level Network Interface for Parallel and Distributed Computing. In *Proc. of the 15th ACM Symposium on Operating Systems Principles*, Copper Mountain, Colorado, Dec. 1995. ACM Press.

3. M. A. Blumrich, K. Li, R. Alpert, C. Dubnicki, E. W. Felten, and J. Sandberg. Virtual Memory Mapped Network Interface for the SHRIMP Multicomputer. In *Proceedings of the 21st ISCA*, volume 22 of *CAN*, pages 142–153, Chicago, Illinois, Apr. 1994. ACM.

4. Compaq Computer Corp. and Intel Corporation and Microsoft Corporation. *Virtual Interface Architecture Specification*, Dec. 1997. Available with NDA via www.viarch.org.

5. D. Culler, L. T. Liu, R. P. Martin, and C. O. Yoshikawa. Assessing Fast Network Interfaces. *IEEE MICRO*, 16(1):35–43, Feb. 1996.

6. Dolphin Interconnect Solutions, AS. *PCI-SCI Cluster Adapter Specification*, May 1996. Version 1.2.

7. A. Geist, A. Beguelin, J. Dongarra, W. Jiang, R. Manchek, and V. Sunderam. *PVM: Parallel Virtual Machine A Users' Guide and Tutorial for Networked Parallel Computing*. MIT Press, Cambridge, Massachusetts, 1994.

8. R. B. Gillett. Memory Channel Network for PCI. *IEEE Micro*, 16(1):12–18, Feb. 1996.

9. H. Hellwagner, W. Karl, and M. Leberecht. Fast Communication Mechanisms–Coupling Hardware Distributed Shared Memory and User-Level Messaging. In *Proceedings of PDPTA'97*, Las Vegas, Nevada, June 30–July 3 1997.

10. B. G. Herland, M. Eberl, and H. Hellwagner. A Common Messaging Layer for MPI and PVM over SCI. In *High-Performance Computing and Networking (Proc. HPCN Europe)*, number 1401 in LNCS, pages 576–587, Amsterdam, The Netherlands, Apr. 1998.

11. M. Ibel, K. Schauser, C. Scheiman, and M. Weis. High-Performance Cluster Computing Using SCI. In *Hot Interconnects V*, Aug. 1997.

12. A. Itzkovitz, A. Schuster, and L. Shalev. Millipede: a User-Level NT-Based Distributed Shared Memory System with Thread Migration and Dynamic Run-Time Optimization of Memory References. In *Proceedings of the 1st USENIX Windows NT Workshop*, Aug. 1997.

13. P. Koch, E. Cecchet, and X. de Pina. Global Management of Coherent Shared Memory on an SCI Cluster. In *Proceedings of SCI-Europe '98, a conference stream of EMMSEC '98*, pages 51–57, Sept. 1998.

14. S. J. Leffler, M. K. McKusick, M. J. Karels, and J. S. Quarterman. *The Design and Implementation of the 4.3BSD UNIX Operating System*. Addison-Wesley, 1989.

15. A. Mainwaring and D. Culler. Active Messages Applications Programming Interface and Communication Subsystem Organization. Technical report, Computer Science Division, University of California at Berkeley, Nov. 1995.

16. S. Paas, M. Dormanns, T. Bemmerl, K. Scholtyssik, and S. Lankes. Computing on a Cluster of PCs: Project Overview and Early Experiences. In W. Rehm, editor, *Tagungsband zum 1. Workshop Cluster Computing*, number CSR-97-05 in Chemnitzer Informatik–Berichte, pages 217–229, Nov. 1997.

17. S. Pakin, V. Karamcheti, and A. Chien. Fast Messages (FM): Efficient, Portable Communication for Workstation Clusters and Massively-Parallel Processors. *IEEE Concurrency*, 1997.

18. M. Schulz and H. Hellwagner. Global Virtual Memory based on SCI-DSM. In *Proceedings of SCI-Europe '98, a conference stream of EMMSEC '98*, pages 59–67, Sept. 1998.

19. I. C. Society. *IEEE Std 1596-1992: IEEE Standard for Scalable Coherent Interface*. The Institute of Electrical and Electronics Engineers, Inc., 345 East 47th Street, New York, NY 10017, USA, August 1993.

20. E. Speight and J. Bennett. Brazos: A Third Generation DSM System. In *Proceedings of the 1st USENIX Windows NT Workshop*, Aug. 1997.

21. R. Stets, S. Dwarkadas, N. Hardavellas, G. Hunt, L. Kontothanassis, S. Parthasarathy, and M. Scott. CASHMERE-2L: Software Coherent Shared Memory on a Clustered Remote-Write Network. In *Proceedings of SOSP'97*, Oct. 1997.

22. T. von Eicken, D. E. Culler, S. C. Goldstein, and K. E. Schauser. Active Messages: a Mechanism for Integrated Communication and Computation. In *Proceedings of the 19th ISCA*, volume 20 of *CAN*, pages 256–266, Gold Cost, Australia, May 1992. ACM Press.

23. J. Weidendorfer. Entwurf und Implementierung einer Socket-Bibliothek für ein SCI-Netzwerk. Master's thesis, Technische Universität München, 1997.

24. WWW:. CRAY T3E Series
http://www.cray.com/products/systems/crayt3e/, Nov. 1998.

Low Latency Message-Passing for Reflective Memory Networks

Matt Jacunski, Vijay Moorthy, Peter P. Ware, Manoj Pillai,
and Dhabaleswar K. Panda, and P. Sadayappan

Department of Computer and Information Science
The Ohio State University, Columbus, OH 43210
Phone: (614) 292-0053, Fax: (614) 292-2911
{jacunski,moorthy,ware,pillai,panda,saday}@cis.ohio-state.edu
http://www.nowlab.cis.ohio-state.edu/

Abstract. In this paper we present an efficient design for message passing over a reflective memory network[1]. First, we consider the attributes of reflective memory communication networks and the requirements to efficiently build message-passing functionality on these networks. We then introduce the Bill-Board Protocol, a lock-free protocol which provides low-latency send, receive, and multicast functionality to higher-level applications over reflective memory networks. The communication protocol and an implementation on SCRAMNet is described in detail. Lastly, the performance of this protocol is demonstrated.

1 Introduction

Clusters of Workstations are becoming increasingly popular as a platform for parallel and distributed computing. For parallel computing, clusters offer a cost effective alternative to conventional parallel computers[1, 3, 13]. For distributed computing they offer good scalability and high availability. Since they use commodity processors and networks, the performance of clusters of workstations is often comparable to that of massively parallel processors (MPP's) but at a much lower cost.

Unlike conventional parallel processors which use customized interconnection networks for communication [6], workstation clusters use commodity networking technologies. In recent years many new high performance networking technologies have emerged such as ATM [2], Fast Ethernet [11] and FiberChannel [14]. These networks provide high bandwidth but have high latency due to network routing and high software overhead. For high performance in parallel processing, however, low latency is very critical. As a result considerable effort has been put into developing low latency networking technologies such as Myrinet [4] and messaging software such as Illinois Fast Messages [12] and U-Net [15].

Reflective memory networks provide a limited amount of non-coherent shared memory across a cluster of workstations. Each workstation is equipped with a

---

[1] This research is supported by NSF-SBIR Grant DMI-9761318.

A.Sivasubramaniam, M.Lauria (Eds.): CANPC'99, LNCS 1602, pp. 211–224, 1999.
© Springer-Verlag Berlin Heidelberg 1999

network interface card (NIC) which possesses a memory bank. Memory on the NICs is not physically shared but each update to a location on any one of the NICs is transmitted to the other NICs on the network. This causes the memory at each NIC in each workstation to be a reflection of the memory of the other NICs. However, reflective memory networks provide non-coherent shared memory. That is, if multiple nodes make updates to the same shared location, different nodes may see the updates in a different order.

Examples of reflective memory networks include Encore's Reflective Memory Network (later DEC Memory Channel), SCRAMNet, and VMIC (VME Microsystem International Corporation) Fiber-Optic Reflective Memory product.

Shared memory and message passing are two programming models available for parallel programming. Each of these models may be implemented on distributed memory systems. We aim to use reflective memory to provide low latency message passing for small message sizes and use the mirrored aspect for improved multicast messages. These reflective memory networks have advantages over conventional interconnects :

- **Low latency:** Since communication is effected by writing to a location in memory, protocol overhead is done away with. Consequently, latency for sending messages is very low. This is particularly advantageous for shorter messages.
- **Multicast Capability:** The very nature of reflective memory networks lends itself to multicast communication, since a write by one process becomes visible to many other nodes. It has been shown that the performance of other collective operations can be improved by improving multicast performance. Some conventional networks do provide some multicast ability. ATM provides multicast, but it comes with the overhead of establishing a multicast connection. Ethernet provides broadcast, but does not have the flexibility to specify a group of receivers. In reflective memory networks, it is possible to do multicast at a cost just a little higher than that for sending a message to one receiver.

This paper is organized as follows. Section 2 describes the motivation and design goals for developing low latency message passing for reflective memory networks. Section 3 describes the BBP architecture and our initial implementation on SCRAMNet, Section 4 presents the performance of BBP on the SCRAMNet network, and Section 5 presents our conclusions.

2   Motivation and design goals

The importance of low communication latencies and small-message bandwidth has been demonstrated in [15]. Additionally, for parallel computing, the latency of the multicast operation typically has an impact on application performance.

DEC's Universal Message Passing (UMP) library implementation on MEMORY CHANNEL [10] provides good message passing performance over reflective memory. Their implementation uses a combination of lock-free and lock-controlled buffers for point-to-point messages and only lock-controlled buffers for multicast functionality. The cost of acquiring and releasing an uncontested spin-lock takes approximately 130 and 120 microseconds, respectively [10]. This is a significant cost which would be eliminated if the reliance on spin-locks could be eliminated.

Here, we present a framework for implementing efficient message passing functionality on reflective memory networks. We describe the Billboard Protocol (BBP), and its implementation on SCRAMNet, a reflective memory network. There were several underlying design goals:

- *Provide efficient user-level message passing primitives that provide typical send/receive functionality to application programs.* Much of the overhead in messaging software is copying messages from user space to kernel space and in between layers of the messaging software. The most efficient way of sending messages is to eliminate this copying.
- *Allow for multiple processes on a single machine.* A single workstation may have multiple processes running which need to communicate through the network. The protocol should permit more than one process per node to share the same NIC.
- *Provide feasibility for adding write protection.* Messages are sent on the network by writing to network memory. When there are multiple participating processes, the protocol should implement write protection.
- *Provide in-order delivery between any two processes.* Messages from a process A to process B must be delivered in the same order in which they are sent.
- *Minimize accesses to the NIC over the I/O bus.* The processor in the workstation has to go through the I/O bus to read network memory. Since the network memory can receive updates over the network, and not just the host processor, it cannot be cached. Also I/O buses are slower than system buses so it takes the processor more time to access network memory than the main memory. The I/O bus is normally shared with other devices. Hence it can be a bottleneck, and accesses over the I/O bus must be minimized.
- *Implementation of the protocol should not require any locks.* In shared memory systems, there is substantial overhead involved in waiting for, acquiring and releasing locks. For low latency operation, the protocol should be lock-free.
- *Design memory access and use protocol such that applications may benefit from the inherent broadcast/multicast capability of the network.*

3   Design and implementation of Bill-Board Protocol (BBP)

In this section we present the design and implementation of the BBP. The general design goal of the BBP was to provide low-latency *send, receive,* and *multicast* primitives for reflective memory networks. Throughout the design process, the higher level requirements of MPICH [7] implementation and use of the library as a platform for TreadMarks [9], such as pairwise in-order delivery, were considered.

Although reflective memory hardware may provide a variety of features, the only functionality assumed by the BBP is the ability to map a portion of a process' virtual address space to the reflective memory area.

3.1 Reflective memory organization

The BBP divides the reflective memory into two distinct partitions: the message data partition and the control partition. The message data partition contains only the actual payload of messages while the control partition contains all other information pertaining to messages. Each of these partitions is further divided into NUM_PROC separate areas, one for each process as described below.

Each process is associated with two areas: a message data area and a control area. A key aspect of the reflective memory organization for this protocol is that only a single process is permitted to write to any particular memory location, allowing lock-free operation.

The message data area is managed and written to by only the associated process. A portion of this area is allocated for each message sent (we'll refer to this as a message buffer). Other processes will read message data from this area when appropriate.

Also associated with each process is a portion of the control partition, a control area. A process' control area contains message descriptor blocks, outgoing message (MSG) flag blocks, and incoming acknowledge (ACK) flag blocks.

There's an array of NUM_BUF message descriptors which are written only by the associated process (NUM_BUF is the maximum number of available message buffers). Each message is associated with a message descriptor by buffer number. A message descriptor contains all information required by a destination process to receive the message. The current implementation's message descriptor includes fields for message length, message data location, message type, and a sequence number.

There are NUM_PROC arrays of MSG flags and NUM_PROC arrays of ACK flags, each associated with a single destination process. Each of these flag arrays contains NUM_BUF bits, one for each message buffer this process may send. The ACK flags are used to acknowledge a message and are written to by only one destination process.

Figure 1 illustrates the layout of reflective memory for the protocol.

3.2 Communication protocol

Use of reflective memory for message passing with the BBP involves allocation and initialization of a structure which provides storage of (a) logical address of this process, (b) pointers to message and control partitions and areas, and (c) communication state. After initialization, messages may be sent and received using the functions provided by the API listed in Figure 2.

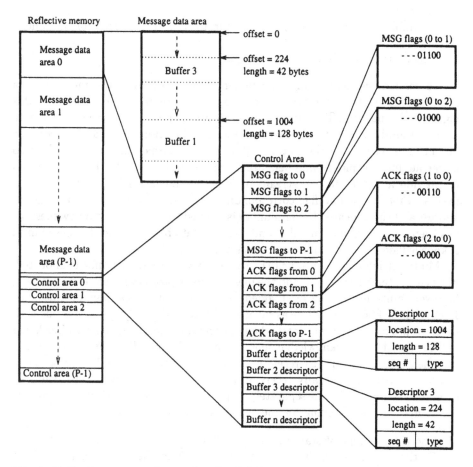

Fig. 1. Reflective memory layout for the Bill-Board Protocol for P processes and n buffers for each process. Process 0 has allocated 2 message buffers of length 128 and 42 bytes each. Both of these buffers are associated with outstanding (unacknowledged) messages. Note that a message is unacknowledged when the MSG flag and ACK flag are in different states: buffer 1 is unacknowledged by process 1 and buffer 3 is unacknowledged by both processes 1 and 2.

These are the communication components of sending a message or a multi-cast:

- Allocate a message buffer (which may require reclaiming previously used message data areas).
- Copy message data from process memory to message data area on reflective memory.
- Assemble and copy message descriptor to appropriate location in control area.
- Toggle state of appropriate MSG flags.

To send a message, a message buffer is allocated from the message data area. This allocation reserves a contiguous block of reflective memory and a logical buffer number. The message contents are then copied to the message data area at the allocated location. Message length, location, type, and a sequence number are written to the message descriptor corresponding to the allocated buffer number. Sequence numbers are generated independently by each process to provide an order to the stream of messages being sent by any particular process. Finally, the MSG flag corresponding to both the appropriate destination address and the allocated buffer number is toggled to indicate that a new message has been sent. The buffer number and message data block will not be reused until acknowledgement by the receiver is confirmed.

Multicast is handled in much the same way as a send. A buffer is allocated, message contents are copied, and the message descriptor is written. For multicast, however, multiple MSG flags are toggled, one for each of the specified destinations. Each of these MSG flags will be associated with the same message buffer but with different processes. For multicast, the buffer number and message data block will not be reused until acknowledgement is confirmed from all destinations.

There are two steps to receiving a message: checking for the presence of a new message and actually receiving the message. These two steps could be combined but are available separately to provide additional flexibility. These are the components of checking for the availability of new messages:

- Check for change of state in pertinent MSG flags.
- Of the MSG flags which have changed state, find the one with the earliest sequence number.

These are the components to then receive a message:

- Copy the message data from reflective memory to the specified location.
- Toggle the state of the appropriate ACK flag to acknowledge receipt.

To determine if a new message is available to be received from a specified source, the MSG flag array affiliated with this process is read from the source's control area. Each MSG flag which has changed state indicates a message from source destined for this process. Based on the sequence numbers read from the message descriptors associated with these toggled flags, the message sent earliest by source is selected as the next to be received. To actually receive this message, the specified number of bytes is copied from the source message data area to the specified receive buffer (the offset within the source message data area is found in the message descriptor). Finally, the appropriate ACK flag is toggled to indicate to the source that this process has received the message.

Logical buffer numbers and message data memory are limited resources. When either all buffers are allocated or message data memory is exhausted, previously used message buffers must be reclaimed. A message buffer may be reclaimed when all destinations have acknowledged receipt of the message. If the message buffer was allocated to send to a single destination, only a single ACK flag must be checked. However, if the message buffer was allocated for a multicast, state of a set of ACK flags must be verified to insure that all destinations have copied the message to a local receive buffer before reclaiming.

In the current implementation, the function which reclaims buffers is called when an attempt to allocate a buffer fails (either because replicated memory is exhausted or all buffers are already allocated). At this point the sender will spin until any previously sent message is acknowledged. A sender's outstanding unicast messages may have been sent to any other node so acknowledgement by any of these receivers will free up a buffer.

3.3 Implementation

We have initially implemented the BBP on Systran's SCRAMNet reflective memory product [5] with 2MB of memory on each card.

Initialization Proper operation relies on each process initializing BBP communication with a unique logical address and the same total number of processes. A fixed size control area of 4096 bytes is allocated to each process. The remaining memory is divided into equally sized message data areas, one for each process. Defining NUM_PROCS as the maximum number of processes, NUM_BUFS as the maximum number of logical message buffers for each process, and DESC_LEN as the length of a message descriptor in bytes, the memory bytes required for each control area, $M_{control}$, is

$$M_{control} = 2 \left(\frac{\text{NUM\_PROCS} \times \text{NUM\_BUFS}}{8} \right)$$
$$+ (\text{NUM\_BUFS} \times \text{DESC\_LEN})$$

When initializing for a 64 process system with a maximum of 64 buffers and a message descriptor length of 8 bytes, 1536 bytes (of the available 4096 bytes) of control area are used and the size of the message data area allocated to each process is 28,672 bytes. Pointers to each message data area as well as any flag arrays of interest are calculated and stored in the BBP structure. There is additional state information used to reduce the required traffic over the I/O bus which is also initialized. This state information includes space to buffer portions of reflective memory, message descriptor buffers, structures used to maintain the

---

bbp_init(int num_procs, int rank)

Allocates and initializes memory for the BBP state structure for process with logical address (rank) of (num_procs). This function returns a pointer to a bbp struct which is passed with all other function calls.

bbp_Send(struct bbp *this_proc, char *buf, int len, int dest,
short msg_type)

Sends len bytes located at buf to process with logical address dest based on current bbp state.

bbp_Mcast(struct bbp *this_proc, char *buf, int len, long *dests,
short msg_type)

Sends len bytes located at buf to processes indicated by *dests* based on current bbp state. dests is an array of NUM_PROC bits indicating which logical addresses should be sent.

bbp_MsgAvail(struct bbp *this_proc, int source)

Returns a valid logical address from which a message is available or (-1) if no message is available. If a valid source is supplied, only that source is checked. If (-1) is supplied, multiple sources may be checked in a fair manner.

bbp_Recv(struct bbp *this_proc, char *buf, int max_len, int source,
short msg_type)

Copies the next message (up to max_len bytes) sent by source into buffer beginning at buf.

Fig. 2. Bill-Board Protocol API.

allocation of message buffers, and space to hold a list of new messages which have been detected but not yet received. Use of this state information to improve efficiency is discussed in detail below.

Flags When a message is sent, one or more MSG flags are toggled. If the flag bit is 0, it is set to 1 and vice versa. At the receiver, instead of taking action when a flag that is set, action is taken when a flag changes state. To detect changes in state, a copy of a flag array's last state is stored as the basis for comparison. When changes in state are detected, action is taken for each flag with state change and the new array is stored for future use.

All outgoing flags are set to 0 at initialization. Because all flags are initially in the same state, 0, a message is unacknowledged while corresponding MSG and ACK flags are in different states.

PCI memory access optimizations Because of the high cost of accessing reflective memory over the PCI bus compared to cached main memory, our implementation attempts to reduce PCI accesses where possible. Four implementation details which reduce either the frequency or length of reflective memory accesses are discussed below.

- Keep cached copy of outgoing MSG and ACK flags. This avoids a read each time a new flag is written. Because only a single process writes any particular array of flags, that process may keep a cached copy of the state of these flags and use the cached copy to perform change of state logic instead of repeatedly reading the flag arrays over the I/O bus.
- Create a message list in sequential order when new message(s) are detected. To ensure in-order delivery, the descriptors of all new messages must be accessed to read sequence numbers. To avoid repeated reads of the same descriptors over the I/O bus, all new descriptors are read and inserted into a list ordered by sequence number. If 5 new messages are detected, 5 descriptors are read and inserted into the list. The next 4 calls to check message availability from this source return immediately without accessing the I/O bus.
- Shorten the length of the message descriptor. This is especially significant for keeping short-message latencies low. We have shortened the length of the message data location by encoding the offset as a number of multi-byte blocks rather than in bytes.
- Reduce the number of logical message buffers. The potential for this optimization will vary, depending on application requirements. To provide in-order delivery, all MSG flags must be checked so the earliest message sent may be received next. Therefore, the time required to read these flags increases as the number of buffers increases. Reducing the number of buffers per process reduces the time required to read the flags but also reduces the number of concurrent outstanding messages possible.

3.4   Realization of design goals

Our implementation of the BBP meets the stated design goals:

- We have provided efficient user-level message passing primitives including send, receive, and multicast.
- Multiple processes on a single machine may access the same NIC. In fact, there is no distinction made between processes on the same node and those on other nodes. The only identifier used is the logical process address assigned at initialization time.
- Addition of write protection is feasible with minor modification to the control area layout. Currently the control area consists of outgoing MSG flags, incoming ACK flags, and outgoing descriptors. If this layout was adjusted to include outgoing ACK flags (instead of incoming), the associated process would be the only writer to both the message data area and the control area.

- In-order delivery between any two processes is accomplished through the use of sequence numbers and the protocol requirement that all newly detected messages be considered when selecting the next to be received.
- The implementation details described above seek to minimize the costliest component of communication over the reflective memory systems being considered, data copy over the I/O bus.
- The implementation of the protocol does not require locks for either point-to-point operations or for multicast.
- The protocol makes use of the inherent multicast capability of reflective memory networks by allowing a single copy of message data to be read by multiple receivers.

4   Performance of BBP on SCRAMNet

This section describes SCRAMNet, a reflective memory network, and the performance of the BBP implementation on SCRAMNet.

4.1   Description and characterization of SCRAMNet network

SCRAMNet [5] is one type of reflective memory network, providing a limited amount of non-coherent shared memory across a cluster.

Physically, SCRAMNet is arranged as a ring of up to 256 nodes using fiber-optic or coaxial cable.

A fiber optic bypass switch ensures continuity in the ring when not all nodes are powered on. For systems larger than 256 nodes, a hierarchy of rings is used to accommodate more nodes. The data transfer latency over the ring is 250-800 nanoseconds per hop, depending on the mode of transmission being used and packet size. Fixed 4-byte transmission packets provide a throughput of 6.5 MBytes/second. Variable length packets (4 bytes to 1 KByte) can be used to attain the maximum throughput of 16.7 MBytes/second with higher latency.

SCRAMNet uses *Register Insertion* for Media Access Control on the ring. At each node, there is a switch which multiplexes incoming messages from the incoming link on the network and the NIC to the outgoing link. If a message arrives on the network, while the node is in the process of injecting a message into the network, then the network message is queued. A message is generated whenever a host writes to a location in SCRAMNet memory. Multiple writes are put in a FIFO queue on the NIC and sent out one by one. Each message traverses the entire ring once and then is removed from the network by the source node.

Communication is done on SCRAMNet by writing and reading to SCRAMNet memory. On average it takes 0.54 μs to write one word to SCRAMNet memory and 1.02 μs to read one word from SCRAMNet memory.

4.2   Performance experiments and results

We have implemented the BBP for SCRAMNet on a cluster of dual 300MHz Pentium II SMP boxes running *Linux* version 2.0.30. We have measured the amount of time spent in the various tasks involved in communicating over the network using the BBP. Figures 3 and 4 show these results. Results have been shown for two message lengths: 4 bytes and 128 bytes. One-way message latency is 7.8 μ - seconds for 4-byte messages on a 2-node ring.

Figure 3 shows the cost of sending a message using the BBP. The bulk of the time is spent in copying the message from user space to SCRAMNet memory. This component of the cost grows linearly with the message length. By avoiding unnecessary copying, the cost of sending has been kept down by keeping this component to a minimum. The software overhead of sending a message is the time spent in buffer allocation, writing the descriptor and notifying the destination process(es) of the message by toggling MSG flags. We show results for both 1 destination and 8 destinations. For the 128-byte case, there is only a 3.25 microsecond increase in the time required to complete the send to 8 destinations compared with the time required for a single destination. The dominating component, message copy, is independent of the number of destinations.

Figure 4 shows the cost of receiving a message using the BBP. Again, we see that bulk of the cost is involved in copying the message from SCRAMNet memory to user memory and since this is done without any intermediate copying, the receive overhead has been minimized. The receive components other than message copy include the time required to (a) read incoming message flags, (b) read the message descriptor, and (c) acknowledge the message once copied.

The results discussed above for the send and receive components are in line with measurements of one-way message latencies. The send portion is pipelined while the receive portion is not. As 32-bit words are written to the SCRAMNet NIC, they are transfered to the network. This overlaps the PCI-bus writes with network transmission. The protocol, however, does not begin a receive until the entire message has been written into the destination NIC's reflective memory and the MSG flag is set.

The above results describe the performance of the BBP on an unloaded network (no other messages on the network). Figure 5 shows the performance of BBP with increased network load. The latencies measured are for point to point communication between two processes. Load is generated on the network by communication between other processes on other nodes. As can be seen from the figure, there is degradation of performance with increased network load. Little degradation of performance was observed when multiple processes sent concurrent messages with length of 4 bytes.

5   Conclusions

Reflective memory has two principle advantages: low latency and inherent multicast. We've taken advantage of these characteristics to develop the Bill-Board Protocol that provides point to point, in-order message delivery and an efficient multicast delivery. In particular, the multicast latency (on SCRAMNet) is only slightly longer than that of a point to point message which takes 7.8 μ-seconds.

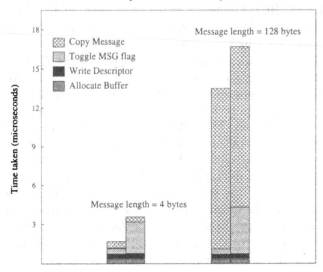

Fig. 3. Components of the Send operation in the BBP for 4-byte and 128-byte messages sent to 1 destination using `bbp_Send` and 8 destinations using `bbp_Mcast`.

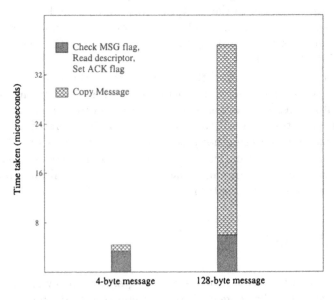

Fig. 4. Components of the Receive operation in the BBP for 4-byte and 128-byte messages.

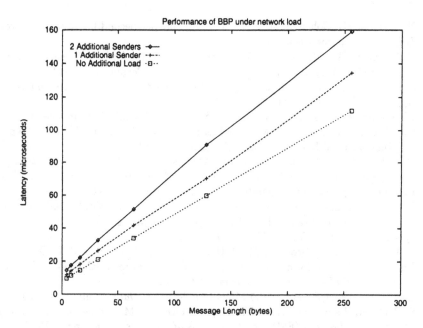

Fig. 5. Performance of BBP for 4-byte point-to-point messages with additional network load. Additional network load created by adding 1 or 2 additional senders of concurrent point-to-point messages with size=768 bytes. These measurements perform ed with a ring of 4 nodes.

Our protocol also avoids the principle problem associated with reflective memory systems: the relative high cost of accessing NIC memory over the PCI bus compared to accessing system memory. By allowing only a single process to write to each region of NIC memory we avoid the high cost associated with a locking protocol built on top of NIC memory. We've minimized the number of writes to the reflective memory thereby insuring the best possible performance.

Future work includes adding user level protection mechanisms to the protocol and possibly additional collective communication primitives such as barrier.

Additional Information: Additional papers and results related to this project can be obtained from the Web page of *Network-Based Computing* group at OSU (http://nowlab.cis.ohio-state.edu).

References

1. T. Anderson, D. Culler, and Dave Patterson. A Case for Networks of Workstations (NOW). *IEEE Micro*, pages 54–64, Feb 1995.
2. ATM Forum. *ATM User-Network Interface Specification, Version 3.1*, September 1994.
3. Donald J. Becker et al. Beowulf: A Parallel Workstation for Scientific Computation. In *International Conference on Parallel Processing*, 1995.

4. N. J. Boden, D. Cohen, et al. Myrinet: A Gigabit-per-Second Local Area Network. *IEEE Micro*, pages 29–35, Feb 1995.

5. T. Bohman. Shared-Memory Computing Architectures for Real-Time Simulation-Simplicity and Elegance. Technical report, Systran Corporation, 1994.

6. J. Duato, S. Yalamanchili, and L. Ni. *Interconnection Networks: An Engineering Approach*. The IEEE Computer Society Press, 1997.

7. W. Gropp, E. Lusk, N. Doss, and A. Skjellum. A High-Performance, Portable Implementation of the MPI, Message Passing Interface Standard. Technical report, Argonne National Laboratory and Mississippi State University.

8. C. Holt, J. P. Singh, and J. Hennessy. Application and Architectural Bottlenecks in Large Scale Distributed Shared Memory Machines. In *Proceedings of the International Symposium on Computer Architecture*, pages 134–145, May 1996.

9. P. Keleher, A. L. Cox, S. Dwarkadas, and W. Zwaenepoel. TreadMarks: Distributed Shared Memory on Standard Workstations and Operating Systems. In *Proceedings of the 1994 Winter Usenix Conference*, Jan. 1994.

10. J. V. Lawton, J. J. Brosnan, M. P. Doyle, S. D. O Riordain, and T. G. Reddin. Building a High-Performance Message-passing System for MEMORY CHANNEL Clusters. *DIGITAL Technical Journal*, Oct 1996.

11. Lee Melatti. Fast Ethernet: 100 Mbit/s Made Easy. *Data Communications*.

12. S. Pakin, M. Lauria, and A. Chien. High Performance Messaging on Workstations: Illinois Fast Messages (FM). In *Proceedings of the Supercomputing*, 1995.

13. G. F. Pfister. *In Search of Clusters*. Prentice Hall, 1995.

14. M. W. Sachs and A. Varma. Fibre Channel. *IEEE Communications*, pages 40–49, Aug 1996.

15. T. von Eicken, A. Basu, V. Buch, and W. Vogels. U-Net: A User-level Network Interface for Parallel and Distributed Computing. In *ACM Symposium on Operating Systems Principles*, 1995.

Author Index

Springer
and the
environment

At Springer we firmly believe that an
international science publisher has a
special obligation to the environment,
and our corporate policies consistently
reflect this conviction.
We also expect our business partners –
paper mills, printers, packaging
manufacturers, etc. – to commit
themselves to using materials and
production processes that do not harm
the environment. The paper in this
book is made from low- or no-chlorine
pulp and is acid free, in conformance
with international standards for paper
permanency.

 Springer

Lecture Notes in Computer Science

For information about Vols. 1–1513
please contact your bookseller or Springer-Verlag